EVENING IN RISHIKESH

A Climber's Journey Home

Longs Peak Trading Company Press

www.eveninginrishikesh.com

Thomas Quay Williams

Cover photo: Layton Kor pausing after his last big climb: the Salathe Wall by Galen Rowell. "In the early afternoon, I photographed Layton coming over the top. He stayed there-body below edge, head above-with a look of serenity I have never seen." Galen Rowell from *Beyond the Vertical*. Mountain Light Photography Inc. (Galen and Barbara Rowell).

ISBN 9780996247337

First Edition
ISBN: 0996247335

THANKS

This book is dedicated to Layton Kor (1938-2013), the father of Colorado rock climbing, and to the hermit in number thirteen, whose words inspired me to write it. I also dedicate this book to my great pal Larry Moffett, who succumbed to cancer in 2007. This project began as an independent study for my English Professor, Reg Saner, at the University of Colorado, Boulder, in 1991. Since then, I have put it down and picked it up many times, and it has gone through innumerable versions and revisions. I have tried to keep the end product true to the era it represents.

I would like to thank my parents for, if not their understanding, then at least their support and tolerance during my extended childhood. Special thanks go to my wonderful yoga teacher, Patricia Hansen, who was a driving force in my Indian experience; to author, educator, and climber Chip Lee, who actually took my writing seriously and gave many invaluable suggestions; and to remarkable Everest legend Ed Webster, for his warm encouragement. Jeff Long also generously offered some advice. Thanks are also in order for Rob Bignell, Patricia Hansen, Sonja Greenway, and Andrea Duffy, but foremost Chip Lee and Izzy the cat for their editing assistance.

PHOTOGRAPHY CREDITS

B ecause of prohibitive costs of publishing them in this first edition, all relevant photos are viewable online at www.eveninginrishikesh.com. Thanks to Mountain Light Photography Inc. (Galen and Barbara Rowell) for allowing me to reproduce the iconic photo Galen took of Layton Kor pausing after his last big climb the Salalthe Wall. I would like to thank Dudley Chelton for his friendship and allowing me to reproduce many of his inspiring black and white photos from the book *CLIMB!* that struck terror in my youth. Thanks to Glenn Randall Photography for the great photos of Jim Collins in action on *Genesis*. Special hanks go out to the generosity of Huntley Ingalls, a true climber in deed and spirit, who allowed me full access to his photos from the golden age of climbing with Kor, some previously unpublished. Thanks to Steve "Crusher" Bartlett and Dan Hare for allowing me to use their wonderful photos and to Roger "Strappo" Hughes for digging out the late Steve Dieckhoff's great shots of Derek Hersey. All uncredited photos are from the author's collection.

BOOK ONE

The Call to Adventure

"Let's reinvent the gods,
all the myths of the ages"
Jim Morrison-An American Prayer

THE 1960S UPHEAVEAL LAYTON KOR

"A FREE MASON"

*I*t was the stuff of legends and dreams. The premier climbers of the world—John Harlin, Dougal Haston, Chris Bonnington and Layton Kor attempting the north face of the Eiger by a new "direct" route in the winter of 1966. The tale jumped out of my book, calling my eleven-year-old's world to adventure. With sweaty hands, I gasped turning each page.

Growing up, I'd sit for hours in my bedroom mesmerized by gripping black and white photos and stories of the book CLIMB!, the definitive history of Colorado climbing. All the climbers were brave, but the standout Layton Kor was beyond belief. While reading of his exploits, usually written by terrified partners, the cold void tugged at my heels as if I was actually tied into the rope with the great pioneer as Kor swarmed up one first ascent after another, pounding his pitons—nail-like spikes—into submission with his mini-sledge hammer.

In 1965, Layton Kor arrived in Leysin, Switzerland and was quickly swept up in John Harlin's plan for a new route on the north face of the Eiger. For Kor's first climb in the Alps, it was merely one of the largest and *most notoriously dangerous mountain faces on the continent, and in winter no less. But Kor was no ordinary climber; tall, lanky Kor was a larger-than-life legend, the God Thor in knickerbockers. Colorado climbing has often been described as "before Kor, during and after." Terror and triumph swirled around the unstoppable Boulder bricklayer with his nervous energy. "A standard-setter in any generation," his contemporaries, like Royal Robbins, agreed. From crumbling desert towers to gigantic Yosemite granite walls, Kor had done the first ascent of every daunting wall or spire of any reputation, leaving innumerable features named after him: Kor crack, the Kor roof, the Kor traverse, ad naseum. His legendary energy drove him up one dangerous route after another in record time with mad, explosive joy. Kor spent the remainder of his time searching for climbing partners, traumatizing them with actual-brink-of-disaster exploits or invoking his dark sense of humor. "Don't fall now, or we'll both go," he would call down ominously, or "Oh no, the rope is cutting over an edge!"*

John Harlin, nicknamed the "Blonde God," was an American directing the International School of Modern Mountaineering who had already climbed the standard 1938 route on the Eiger and, as a result, experienced "beauty in everything he saw." Joined by the seasoned Scottish climber, Dougal Haston, the three-man team found themselves organizing masses of gear Harlin had procured from his sponsors: the London-based newspaper, "The Daily Telegraph," and the Mammut Rope Company at the hotel below the face in the village of Kleine Scheidegg. The famous British mountaineer, Chris Bonnington, joined the team as a photographer for the Telegraph, agreeing to stay in only a supporting role.

February 1966 experienced unusually unsettled weather, as Harlin's team set out only to find a party of well-organized Germans with the same intentions of pursuing a new route up the face. There was no time to lose in making an attempt on the Direct Route. A competition ensued, between the teams exaggerated by the press to make international headlines. The Eiger's deadly north face, or Nordwand, has had a long history of nationalistic competition. The efforts of the daring early Norwand climbers became political propaganda, culminating in Adolf Hitler awarding Olympic gold medals to the eventual first ascensionists in 1938—all German-Austrian nationals naturally. With both teams simultaneously attempting the Nordwand, a pre-war drama was being revived and the race was on!

Kor led a pitch called the Central Pillar that proved to be key to the success of the climb. Hard aid-climbing—utilizing rope ladders attached to pitons—through the steep rock bands, Kor succeeded without resorting to drilling the frowned upon bolts, using his specialized skills learned from a lifetime of climbing. Then his unfamiliarity with snow and ice climbing begged for Chris Bonnington to take over. Bonnington was not intending to lead and found himself facing a steeper ice pitch than he had ever tried before. Now they were higher than the Germans but, eschewing the media hyped competitive atmosphere, the two teams decided to join forces and push for the top.

Then it happened. A reporter witnessed the blur of a red object whizzing through the lens of his telescope stationed on the deck of the Kleine Scheidegg Hotel. Layton Kor and Chris Bonnington, who had descended for supplies, became concerned and mounted a ski reconnaissance to the base of the great wall to investigate. There they found the body of John Harlin. Kor and Bonnington were beside themselves with grief. It was the beginning of the end of Kor's climbing career.

Kor's drive for extreme routes slowly came to an end after his attempt on the bloodthirsty Swiss Eiger. Kor said he never imagined that someone so strong like Harlin could die, and he began to question his own life's direction. By 1968, the great Kor had disappeared from climbing completely. A new devotion to religion as a Jehovah's Witness replaced his vertical wanderlust. Chuck Pratt called him "the greatest rock climber of a generation," and Kor's absence only made his myth grow. For us young climbers, the legend of Kor stood like a shining beacon.

THE GENESIS OF IT ALL

I was completely stuck, paralyzed high on the *Bastille Crack*, while standing on exhausting little footholds. It was 1979, I was only twelve years old being guided up the *Bastille Crack* in Eldorado Canyon, Colorado. The Bastille is an especially steep and gloomy rock face—in other words, terrifying. My calf muscles began the dreaded "sewing machine" twitch: adrenaline pulsing through an unlucky climber's lower legs making them quiver up and down uncontrollably. It's nature's way of pushing you off a cliff.

Worst of all, I could not get the accident out of my mind. I had heard a yell and turned to see a man lying flat on his back on the dirt road writhing like a snake. He had fallen trying to lead the *Bastille Crack* and was howling in agony. "Severe spinal injury suspected," the Ranger diagnosed into his crackling walkie-talkie. The horrific incident shook me to the bone. I knew rock climbing was a dangerous game but I never thought I would witness that scene so soon. It could be me next.

On the *Bastille Crack's* second pitch I had gone up the wrong way. I followed a skinny finger-sized crack until it petered out. I had painted myself into a corner. I was hanging on desperately and getting more exhausted by the minute. The rope led sideways around the corner, setting me up for a huge swing, and eventually to my unsympathetic companions. I could feel their indignation for being kept waiting from the chill of air flushing through the crack. It was that awful moment every explorer or adventurer must face the heartless world devoid of warmth and kindness. That moment before one jumps out of the trenches to face the torrent of enemy machine gun fire. The road was just below, but I was a million miles from happiness and flowers, trembling under the infinite cold universe. The Bastille's oppressive shadows accentuated my friendless condition, a state of being easier to ignore in the bustle of the daily world below. I was merely a tiresome client to our guide, Bert, who belayed me because my parents paid. To Red, my new climbing partner, I existed only for ridicule. The way they viewed me, my demise would not infringe much upon their time. It was Kor's fault I was there at all.

My fascination with climbing began at age seven, the moment I saw the "Diamond," a perfectly chiseled vertical cliff on the east face of 14,259 ft. Longs Peak in northern Colorado. Arriving on a family summer vacation in 1973, my eyes rose to meet the sheer, stupendous one-thousand-foot precipice rising above the enshrining clouds. I became alive at that moment.

Ranch hands at the Swiss Inn where we stayed that summer spoke in low, reverent tones of the legendary Layton Kor, who had dared to climb the Diamond several times, usually by new routes even in winter. A deep longing stirred within me as I imagined myself as a young man clinging courageously like Kor to the vertical wall. From then on, climbing the Diamond became the most important thing in my world.

At age ten, while attending Cheley summer camp in Estes Park, I hiked Longs Peak, following the great mountain's only weakness, a gap called the Keyhole, which allows a scramble through the imposing cliffs without needing a rope. To us young greenhorns, the day was full of excitement. Starting well before dawn, we reached timberline to catch the sight of golden light expanding across the huge east face while the rest of Colorado was still in bed. After tiptoeing past the Narrows and up the sunny Home Stretch, the summit awaited, filling me with a kaleidoscope of emotions. In the thin air, I could feel the hulking Diamond below facing the eastern plains. My knees wobbled, and I knew that someday I had to climb it.

"Great things happen when youth and mountains meet," claimed F.W. Cheley's founding slogan. For one month every summer, I was allowed to trade Denver's hot flats for cool meadows and snowy peaks. Cheley Camp was a mountaineer's breeding ground, where Everest pioneer Tom Hornbein, Glen Porzak, and others caught the bug. Alpine myths of old lingered in the rustic wood buildings, in the smell of the dust, in the colors of the wild mountain flowers spilling down from the great ranges. Cheley is a church of nature with the great cathedral of Longs Peak watching overhead. There was even a mythical cowboy named Trigger Bill, whose wise quips were on display in the buildings. Wooden signs hosted sayings such as, "If it is to be, it is up to me." I bought the whole corny *Sound of Music* fairy tale, lock, stock, and barrel. But while the camp's hiking programs were rigorous, there was no technical rock climbing allowed at Cheley in the 1970s. If I was to scale the skyscraper-vertical and experts-only Diamond, I would have to learn the ropes on my own. Dying needlessly was not part of my plan, so I set out to become an expert technical rock climber.

"Time for you to die!" shouted up my neighbor, Scott Parker, as an afternoon breeze stirred across brown Denver rooftops. I was eleven years old when I stood on a Denver rooftop to set up my first rappel – that is, using a mountaineer's technique to lower down steep terrain. It was an odd proclamation considering it was *his* chimney I was about to rappel off.

Suburbanite children gathered below like the macabre "Eiger Birds" who flocked to Switzerland during the *Nordwand*'s most murderous period of the 1930s. In other words, they were hoping to witness my death.

By the time I stood on the Parker's roof, and it had to be off the Parker's chimney because their parents weren't home, and mine were getting suspicious about the rope and climbing books lying about, I had saved up weeks of lawn-mowing money to buy carabiners, a kind of aluminum snap link, a brake-bar, nylon webbing to fashion a primitive harness called a "Swiss seat," and a braided hemp rope the length of a two-story chimney.

I pulled the loop of stiff, slippery braided rope around the brake-bar, out through an oval carabiner, and down to my sweating brake hand. Looking down, I trembled. I had mastered the concept of friction, the system of holding much more weight on the rope than bare hands can, playing with it while watching *The Brady Bunch*. But this was real, and even after hours absorbing *Basic Rock Craft*, something could go wrong. It was a possibility the kids were hoping for below.

Excitement and terror shot through my chest and I gazed towards Longs Peak's distant pyramid shape rising above the plains one last time. Something or someone, perhaps Layton Kor, was pushing me toward the edge of the roof to begin my destiny. The trembling became convulsions as I looked down at the hard ground waiting below. I stalled for time, pretending to adjust the equipment.

"Are you going to go or what?" yelled a voice from the depths.

"Shut up!" I snapped back, wishing I had some privacy. A climber doesn't play to the crowds—the sentiment that separates a true mountaineer from a circus performer. Then I took a breath and stepped into space. At first, I swung wildly while my homemade harness cut cruelly into my sides, but it worked. I could do it. Though it was a struggle to breathe, a magnificent new world unfolded before my eyes as wondrous and improbable as the first landing on the moon. The joy of hiking beautiful peaks had increased tenfold with the intensity of technical climbing. Everything stopped; my emotions soared. All awareness merged into the pure present.

"Let go of the rope!" yelled Scott, in a last appeal for carnage.

Instead, I descended calmly to the ground. The mob of neighborhood kids dispersed back to their T.V.s, muttering their disappointment. In the time it took to rappel down a brick chimney, my old life vanished. I saw the suburbanites as an army of the dead. I had crossed the Rubicon and was a climber. My heart rejected mainstream fads, wasting hours gaping at the T.V. and doing what I was told. From that moment onward, I was devoted to the odd world of rock climbing.

Standing alone, I looked up past the chimney at clouds bathed in an eerie light and saw a revelation of my life to come: breathtaking rock walls, shining glaciers, crumbling desert towers painted in a thousand colors of gold, exotic lands filled with wild tribesmen, my footprints left on the sands of ancient worlds. It fits that each climbing adventure is a transformation of consciousness. A boon bestowed proportional to voluntary suffering like the trials faced on the "Hero's Journey" laid out by author Joseph Campbell. Those clouds promised that if I stayed true, climbing would take me to the palace of the gods to taste their elixir. My faith was unshakable. The sun and moon would be mine, and climbing is the way.

A few weeks after successfully rappelling from the Parker's chimney, I found myself stranded, on my own brick chimney, unable to go up or down. I had been experimenting with "prusik" loops, made by wrapping a thin cord around the main rope to grip it. When loaded, a prussik loop can hold your body weight, but can be loosened to slide up or down the rope. I had stupidly bought yachting cord that was too soft for the vertical world. Climbing manuals don't warn against this, and the spongy marina cord fused into place high on the chimney. I was stuck. After an hour of yelling for help, my father finally heard and came around with the ladder, shaking his head.

"Why do you do this mountain climbing foolishness?" he asked.

Such questions have provoked infamous responses such as: "Because it is there," by Everest pioneer George Mallory. As the years have passed, I have come to know mountain climbing to be not a kind of escapism or self-indulgence, but rather a brush with a higher reality earned through penance and hardship. It wasn't the typical instant gratification with no effort expended. Even in my youthful escapades, I was seeking something great and noble through climbing. I knew I was on the right track, reading the Reinhold Messner books a relative sent me each year for Christmas, in which Messner describes his altered, hallucinatory mental states while soloing Mount Everest leading to Messner's fascinating claim, "The white loneliness overcomes the black loneliness."

Messner writes in his book *The Big Walls*:

Self-fulfillment and Self-healing by Climbing

How many of us suffer in one form or another from the fact that our energies and skills are not being properly utilized? More than three-quarters of all the people in the West, say the statisticians. I don't know. I only know that under-realization of the bodily and emotional resources promotes a cancer of the soul, an unlived life. There are many ways one can safeguard oneself against this. Climbing big walls, for example, is one.

Messner made me realize that mountaineering is about striving for pure mental, physical, and emotional health through extreme challenges, but that philosophy is hard to put into words. So, as my father helped me down from the chimney in my first climbing rescue, disapproving all the way, there was nothing for me to say. I couldn't explain why I wanted to climb; it was a call to adventure and, therefore, a call to life itself.

"You'll end up like the long-haired ne'er-do-wells living in Boulder," scolded my dad. To him, Boulder, Colorado, was home to dirty weirdos and all that was wrong with America. If there was a protest or suspicious activity, it was the work of those filthy hippies thirty miles away. However, *my* Bible, the Colorado climbing history book *CLIMB!*, put it clearly: Boulder was hallowed ground. All the climbing gods—Pat Ament, Jim Erickson and Roger Briggs, and earlier the mysterious Layton Kor—made it their home and basecamp. Apparently, Layton loved Boulder so much that, as a boy, he told his parents, "If you move from here, you are going without me!"

In the world of mountain climbing, the style in which you choose your suffering is paramount. The era of direct aid climbing had passed. Gone were Kor's pitons, replaced by less damaging nuts, hexes, and high-tech camming devices; his aid climbing ladders gave way to chalked holds, sticky rubber shoes and wild gymnastic moves. To be at the top of the game, beginning in the mid-1970s, required a mastery of "free climbing," which meant a whole set of self-imposed rules based on style, where the climber is still roped but not allowed to hoist himself on the equipment using direct aid.

As I shamefully climbed down the rescue ladder to the full Himalayan storm of my father's lecture, I felt far from my great hero Layton Kor. My dad claimed that climbing was not only dangerous, but that it had no purpose. It was even against American values. Well, that was the whole point. Nothing could be more contrary to the American Dream than to suffer and work incredibly hard at something that yielded no monetary gain. Or more fun. When Dad talked about Boulder that way, the place took on the allure of forbidden fruit. I salivated for escape to the land of lefty-loonies. I was even willing to take public transportation to get there—quite a sacrifice for an American. That ladder on the chimney would, I vowed, be my last rescue.

"If I had some real climbing lessons you wouldn't have to pull me off the chimney," I argued slyly. "Will you sign the permission form?"

"Sign that waiver so you can have permission to go out and kill yourself?" My father shook his head. "No, thank you, buster!"

"Mom said she would."

Simultaneous to discovering climbing, my family was falling apart. This was the bright side to my parents' impending divorce. When they weren't noticing, I could play one off the other. Mom would never let me take rock climbing lessons either, but in the upheaval, Dad didn't know what was what. He sputtered and signed his name.

"Don't say I didn't warn you!" he said.

"Thanks. I'll be careful."

"You'll be sorry you took up that climbing nonsense. Why waste a Sunday afternoon swinging on a rock when a Bronco game is on? Randy Gradishar is on top of his rushing game, and best of all, he's white."

To prepare for my lessons, I climbed on everything I could find in the south Denver suburbs, the wall at the local 7-11 store, apartment buildings and, best of all, the brick walls at my new private middle school, Kent Denver Country Day. When it came to Colorado's blue-blood aristocracy, those students were the real thing—their family names were etched across Denver's skyscrapers or on sprawling car dealerships. I saw many students' parents daily on television putting a folksy touch on their mega-enterprises. They were from the finest, most accomplished families in Colorado—you know, assholes.

The reality was that the majority of these future world-and corporate-leaders lied, cheated, stole, and were already showing a fondness for cocaine and amphetamines in only the seventh and eighth grades. The school was a breeding ground for future executives whose crowning glory would be craftily adding mysterious charges to a customer's bill someday, fueling insider-trading schemes, creating legal "double speak," buying elections and generally gouging the public.

While the campus grounds were studded with beautiful lakes, and the curriculum promoted works of Hemingway, J.R.R. Tolkien, and Orwell, the real saving grace for me attending that upper-class stud farm were the stylish brick walls with protruding edges.

One day I was traversing across a brick wall pretending I was high over Boulder when a voice behind me said, "That looks like fun. Let me try."

"Okay, but don't let the teachers see."

The voice belonged to another lanky but broader-shouldered student named Red Olafson.

My new friend and I merrily traversed the wall like two bugs in the sun, and before long, Red wanted to go rock climbing for real. We nearly looked like twins, dark-haired and tall, and I thought I had found the perfect partner. Even then I knew that in climbing, a good partner meant everything. The Lone Ranger depended on Tonto less than Reinhold Messner did on Peter Habler, or Layton Kor on Bob Culp or Huntley Ingalls. And Red was a whole year older, so I felt honored.

"I bet I can climb better than you," said Red abruptly.

Climb better? I was dumbfounded. A heavy shadow suddenly darkened the ridiculous, light-hearted activity of fumbling across a brick wall. I hadn't yet thought about climbing *better* than someone. Weren't monkeys the best climbers? It was absorbing, humbling, thrilling, just to be climbing.

"I'll bet you can't," I countered. There began our rivalry.

After rappelling off my chimney a couple of times, Red signed up with me for climbing lessons at a school in Boulder. In the meantime, we would hang around Denver's Forrest Mountain shop, a quirky climbing store with an ice axe head for a doorknob, in a dusty, downstairs red-brick warehouse on the edge of downtown. To us, the shop was more magical than Willy Wonka's chocolate factory. There, we bought all the equipment our allowances would allow, including the *de rigueur* climbing shoes called E.B.'s.

One day, we saw an ad for a climbing-film night at the neighboring Forney Museum, home to a stunning collection of old cars, motorcycles and trains inside another historic red-brick building. The first movie, *Outside the Arena*, featured Kevin Donald and Roger Briggs climbing the Diamond. The second film, called *Free Climb on Half Dome* starred Jim Erickson and Art Higbee. Erickson, was trying to "free" the Northwest face of Half Dome with Higbee. Erickson was an especially ethical climber, even in the 1970's, who called unfair behavior like resting on the equipment, etc. "tainting" and even rejected the use of gymnast chalk: the drying white powder that made rock holds much easier to grip. Erickson later expanded this ethic to not attempting the same routes repeatedly. Even with the silly script and cheesy, overdramatic 1970s soundtrack, it made, in our minds, for the best climbing film of all time.

One evening soon after, I was invited to dinner at the Olafsons. Like many of the other students' families, Red's parents were extremely wealthy. They *owned* basketball teams and airlines. I had never imagined knowing such people before. At my mother's prodding, I wore my best Ralph Lauren Polo shirt to impress the horsey set, and I fit right in—or so I imagined. As we sat on an expansive covered porch overlooking their private tennis courts, Red's dad started telling stories.

"On my drive through the South to Harvard, I used to make nigger chasers," Mr. Olafson said. "Do you know what a nigger chaser is? It's a firecracker the size of a baseball bat that you light and throw into a crowd of porch monkeys. Whoo, you should have seen them boys run." He grinned like a Cheshire cat.

Mr. Olafson openly stated his life philosophy, which can be summarized as the strong have the right—no duty—to crush the weak. That meant controlling or eliminating the lower classes and especially those "God-damned unions." As he stormed on, I felt it was obvious he was no armchair racist but one who wanted to write history. Unfortunately, his views didn't seem out of place in Cherry Hills, nor at my new school.

The public school option for my neighborhood was to be bussed across town to Cole Junior High, a grim school on Colfax, or "Cold Facts" Avenue, where prostitutes, drug dealers and gangs roamed. It was hard to say which was worse but maybe I should have chosen Colfax, as the rich kids had a viciousness that haunts me to this day. A female student kept telling me that I reminded her of a guy who had committed suicide by hanging himself in a tree nearby. She kept bringing it up as though it were a suggestion for me to do the same, similar to the evil maid Mrs. Danvers in Alfred Hitchcock's *Rebecca* who tries to lure the heroine to jump to her death. It was then that I glimpsed the depth of ruthlessness the white oligarchy possesses that has ruled empire after empire for thousands of years.

English class introduced us to many great books though. I identified with Holden in J.D. Salinger's *The Catcher in the Rye*, a kid suffering through a similar private school, railing against the "phonies" around him, and fighting for his sanity as he failed out. I couldn't believe the school let us read the book; it was like giving away the prep school's plot. Then there was the subversive literature of Mark Twain. In *Huckleberry Finn*, the slave Jim says to Huck when they are almost to freedom: "...de old true Huck; de only white genlman dat ever kep' his promise to ole Jim." In that one

sentence Twain delivers the most damming and truthful indict-
ment of the white race and my world possible.

No less eye-opening was George Orwell's *Animal Farm.* I was
deeply moved by a sentence from his biography on the back cover:

"Orwell hated cant and cruelty, liars and lying especially
amoung the privileged."

Dining at the Olafsons, I realized that the dark characters of Orwell's novels weren't a fantasy conjured from the far
reaches of the author's mind. Indeed, sitting across from me
puffing on a big, fat cigar was *Animal Farms'* swaggering tyran-
nical pig, Napoleon incarnate, starting his every sentence with
"God-dammed..."

About a week later, the school lacrosse coach shouted at me.
He put his ugly red face inches from mine to make it clear who
was boss. As he spit fire through the screen of my helmet, it was a
turning point. If I could take my spankings, I could have joined
the well-connected, good-old-boys club; the doorway to an easy
life. While I considered this, a tall, lanky figure appeared like a
guiding light in my mind. It was Layton Kor reaching out like a
specter to pull me out of the quicksand trap of sterile conformity.
Layton Kor wouldn't put up with this crap. Kor was free and wild as a
Western outlaw roaming the mountains and valleys. He certainly
wasn't a phony—anything but—and wouldn't go for the quintessential campus fashion of pink polo shirts with the collar turned
up and Vuarnet sunglasses. Clearly, the school was a stud farm of
future tyrants; its sole purpose to mold us into Mr. Olafsons and
land a cushy job in Corporate America.

I sought Longs Peak's purple-hued pyramid shape on the western horizon and wondered: *Where is Kor? Where is the Colorado legend?* The lacrosse coach wasn't finished, but I was with everything
"preppy." I laid down my lacrosse stick and walked away.

The long-awaited day of climbing lessons arrived and Boulder was love at first sight. Victorian era buildings and a sandstone campus that sparkled against a majestic backdrop of green forested foothills and Flatiron shaped rocks that rose proudly into the air.

The Bob Culp Climbing School was housed in the Boulder Mountaineer whose walls were covered with stacks of mysterious ropes, pitons, shiny carabiners and other mysterious devices. Red and I stared open-mouthed at the colorful holy relics and at the staff who comprised the who's-who of the Boulder scene.

A guy named Bert was selected as our guide for a "multi-pitch" route which means leap frogging the climbers to cover a cliff higher than the length of the rope. The distance of the "pitch" is determined by the leader climbing out the length of the rope or, more commonly, finding a good stopping place on a nice ledge where his partner can comfortably join him. Each teammate climbs one at a time with someone belaying, or securing the rope in case of a fall. In traditional climbing, the leader puts in anchors for protection inside cracks as he climbs; the protection is then removed by the climber who follows—who has a safer time with a rope overhead.

The grades that determine a climber's worth originate from the Yosemite Decimal System. First-class is safe walking; second-class is trail hiking; third means there are obstacles and things are getting rough; but fourth-class is real scrambling where beginners or the insecure may wish for a rope. For those excited about modern rock climbing, fifth-class free climbing is certainly the one of interest. This is where it becomes a decimal system and represented by grades of how 5.0 to 5.6 are generally reasonable for beginners, 5.7 to 5.9 cover the intermediate realm and 5.10 and 5.11 are very respectable. In the seventies, 5.12 was about as close to god-hood as a climber could come.

The plan was to do the *Bastille Crack,* 5.7+, in Eldorado Canyon. As we walked into the State Park, the bright colors of the sandstone and lichen sculpted into jagged, twisting arêtes at a diagonal slant of sedimentary layering were more terrifying and beautiful than anything I could have ever imagined. Bert pointed out the routes of legend: the climbs on which our future would be played.

"That's the *Naked Edge*," he said respectfully, pointing to an eye-catching knife blade of serrated rock shooting to the top of the canyon and dominating the skyline.

The *"Edge"* boasted three pitches of 5.11 and one of 5.10, making it an ultimate free climb. Kor, naturally, had done the first ascent using pitons with direct aid, and Jim Erickson was the first to free climb it. The elegant, searing arête sent waves of terror and joy through me. *What would even one 5.11 move be like?* I wondered. I knew that someday, up there, I would find out.

The melancholy Bastille cliff face stood defiantly in ever-present shadow like the legendary north faces of the Alps. Named for the notorious French prison fortress, its cheerless walls held special trepidations for me: though it stood right above the road. The *Bastille Crack* was the only weakness of a reasonable grade through the dark and absolutely vertical wilderness.

Nervously, I watched Bert lead the first and most difficult pitch, which required both hand jamming and lie-backing techniques after stepping across from a large flake to the deep crack. Red followed without hesitation and was soon safely up, so it was my turn to face the crack splitting the steep wall. Only a few feet up my confidence began to slip along with my feet. I couldn't understand why. Perhaps it was because I was developing a serious medical condition termed "goonishness:" already the tallest kid in every class since kindergarten, I faced yet another unwanted growth-spurt that year. My feet swelled to size thirteen, earning me the nickname "flipper," and I stumbled around like a drunken giraffe, not sure what to make of this mean joke of a lanky body. I was tall like Kor but, apparently, that's where the similarities ended. Layton was agile, strong, fearless and, most importantly, obsessed. Damn it, this was *my* sport. *I* could recite all the stories about Layton Kor,

Pat Ament, Henry Barber and Jim Erickson by heart. Why couldn't I swarm up the rocks? What was wrong with me?

My breath grew raspy, my feet slipped completely out of the crack and the rope crunched tightly around my waist.

"I told you I could climb better," Red yelled down, squealing with delight. As I hung there, I could hardly breathe. I clawed up the rest of the crack, finishing only thanks to strong pulls on the rope from above.

"Man, did you take a lot of falls," Red greeted me grinning. "I didn't take any."

Bert was visibly disgusted and made no pretense about preferring Red's company. They both turned away from my cloud of shame and defeat. It was only the first pitch!

On the second pitch, Bert led a wide crack with pigeons flying out, warbling indignantly at the invasion. It was terrifying to look up, so I stared into the crack's cool depths, trying to forget the knots in my stomach. When it was my turn to follow, everything went to hell. First, I dropped Bert's favorite hexcentric nut, an eight-sided metal protection to wedge in constrictions, down the crack when I dismantled the belay. Above, I climbed straight up a thin crack to unclip a fixed piton, a spike that had been driven too hard by the pioneers to remove, but the crack petered out onto a blank wall. Bert and Red were out of sight; clearly annoyed, they shouted down commands, but to me it sounded like pigeons squawking. I was screwing up everything. Why did the wall have to be so steep and intimidating?

So there I was, high on the Bastille, when suddenly, the local guide, Kevin Donald, star of the film *Outside the Arena*, appeared, storming up the crack below me. Donald's wholesome John Denver-esque blond hair and muscular physique had been recently featured in a *Life* magazine article about the bizarre sub-culture of Colorado rock climbing. His good looks also won him a role in a '70s Grape Nuts commercial exemplifying the healthy outdoorsman.

"What the fuck you doing, kid?" Donald shouted. "The route goes over there."

I was dumb-struck and only bumbled more in front of the media star.

"Fucking hold him Bert," Donald shouted up into space. Before I knew what was happening, Donald pushed me off into a wild swing high on the Bastille.

I yelled, spun, and swung frantically, scratching the wall, but finally came to a stop at a line of good holds that I could continue up. I guess it was the only way I could have gotten back on route, but it was mad to do a big swing across the Bastille on my first climb. At the ledge, Bert was furious that I had lost his equipment. I hung my head in fake remorse. All I could think about beneath my sad, puppy-dog expression was how cool Kevin Donald sounded, skillfully working the forbidden word "fuck" into every sentence.

After an eternity, we wriggled up some melancholy chimneys and emerged into the sun on top. From our airy, sun-drenched perch atop the Bastille, we stared open-mouthed as *The Naked Edge* and its even steeper neighbor, *The Diving Board*, shot upward across the canyon into the blue May sky.

"There's something you won't find in your *CLIMB!* book," Bert said pointing at a section of Redgarden Wall. "That face across the canyon has just been free climbed by Jim Collins at 5.12+." My book *CLIMB!* was a couple of years old, and climbing wasn't standing still, but 5.12+? For me 5.8 was unfathomable. "It's called *Genesis*," Bert continued, "and the best climbers have been trying to free climb it for years. Now it's the hardest climb in the world."

I gasped at the beautiful, tilting headwall, the hardest international test piece ever climbed, in our own backyard. If I were to be a standard setter, like Kor, this was the climb to aspire to.

"Cool. Someday I want to free climb it." I said with conviction. I noticed Bert fighting back a smile.

"I know *I* will, but I doubt *you* ever could," said Red plainly.

We descended behind the Bastille back down to a grassy picnic spot by the river, where Red's mother had been watching with lunch ready for the conquerors of the mighty *Bastille Crack*.

"Oh Red, you did so well," she gushed. "It must be the Swiss blood in you. We have a climbing star in the family!"

Sitting by Eldorado's rushing creek, the newly dubbed "star" enjoyed recapping my poor climbing performance far more than he did the idyllic picnicking. He was boiling over to point out that performance equals human worth. According to that logic, my self-worth was pretty nonexistent.

I was no good at other sports, but that didn't bother me. I didn't want to play dodge ball; tennis was boring; basketball sucked. Those sports were for children. This was climbing! As Hemingway put it, "There are only three real sports: bull-fighting, car racing, and mountain climbing. All the others are mere games."

"If you had yelled 'falling' every time you did, your voice would be hoarse," snorted Red. "*You* climb *Genesis*? What a joke! That's the hardest climb in the world. You couldn't climb a 5.12 in a hundred years."

As we sat there, the thrilling day's climb was replaced by a lust for revenge. With my parents' divorce, everything that was secure in my world had been shattered. I felt a hurt and anger beyond all I knew with this nemesis spurring me on to the ultimate modern climber's goal beyond the Diamond and *Naked Edge*: free climbing *Genesis*. I looked up at the legendary climb and made myself a sincere promise: I would show Red. I *will* free climb *Genesis* some-day! That route had turned back the best in Boulder and the world. It was now my quest, my Holy Grail—to someday climb it free and give the finger to Red.

"I will climb *Genesis* someday," I said stubbornly. "You'll see. Someday I will."

Red laughed into the wind.

A WALK INTO BLACKNESS

There seemed no way for me to beat Red. I tried to work out and train, but my spindly, long arms showed no improvement. I even gave up eating my favorite cereal, Count Chocula, the one with the Vampire on the box that turned the milk chocolate-colored in seconds. I ambitiously substituted Grape Nuts, inspired by Kevin Donald's endorsement, even though they tasted like bits of moistened plywood.

The physical challenges of rock climbing were a major barrier in their own right, but it was the doubts and fears of my mind that interfered most. My brain churned with horror while also being completely entranced by the world of climbing. Like Layton Kor once said, "One can be defeated psychologically as well as physically."

One hot summer day, I persuaded a parent to hire Jim Collins, of *Genesis* fame, to guide me. I thought it was time to tackle the famous *Redgarden Route,* a 5.7, that wound the whole way up Eldorado's enormous Redgarden Wall for an astonishing eight hundred vertical feet.

I decided to train hard for the climb, as any budding rock athlete would. Inspired by the soundtrack to *Rocky*, which was inescapable in the 1970s, I jogged up to my local park in my blue sweat pants with white stripes down the sides, and spent hours doing all the pull-ups I could muster at the chin up bar. Unfortunately, I had picked the day before the climb to start. The next day, the day of the climb, I was too sore to move.

Reading about the route in *CLIMB!* was also a mistake. The first pitch was nicknamed the "Birdwalk" after Larry Birdman, who did the first ascent, and the black and white picture taken by Dudley Chelton in *CLIMB!* made it look absolutely terrifying. Restless with anticipation, I could hardly sleep the night before.

When I got off the bus in Boulder the next morning, I found Jim Collins couldn't make it to guide at the last minute. Instead his lesser-known, but also very talented partner and roommate, John Horne, met me.

"Do you ever get nervous climbing?" I asked John on the drive to Eldorado with a warble in my voice. The thought of the strenuous *Birdwalk* along with the imposing upper route was too much. I churned with dread imagining terrifyingly slippery rock, long pitches taking me higher than I'd ever been, and the sweltering heat making my feet swell painfully in my already excruciatingly tight E.B.s.

"Sometimes I get nervous, I guess, but not too much," he said plainly. "Why do you ask?"

"No reason," I replied quickly.

Of course I did have a reason. By the time John had finished leading *Birdwalk*, I was shaking in my E.B.s. I put my foot up on the first hold and started to cry. The route was just too big, too hot, too hard, and I was too sore. The pain of Red's superiority came gushing out. Eldorado was a twisted and cruel place.

John pulled tight on the rope, but I wasn't going anywhere. He was annoyed at my sobbing, having to rappel off and clean his own gear, but he still got his full-day guiding fee. What could John complain about? I had given up the chocolaty joys of Count Chocula only to experience complete paralysis.

I went home having not even raised both feet off the ground. I couldn't stop crying, and the shame of my tears only made me cry more. It was an utterly devastating experience; I was the weakest person alive. If Red heard I had chickened out on the *Birdwalk* without even trying, he would be over the moon. One thing was crystal clear: I would never, ever, be good enough for *Genesis*.

At home, my mother felt sorry for me and took us out to dinner at Shakey's Pizzeria, but I didn't stop sobbing there either. My height made me look older than twelve, so crying in public was an uncomfortable sight for the patrons. They gasped and shook their heads in disgust, quickly looking away. I cried at the salad bar. I cried when the pizza came. It was never going to end. My whole world, it seemed, was accelerating into a downward spiral of cowardice and defeat.

The in-house clown at Shakey's came over to comfort me. With the obligatory red nose, make up and wig, he blew up a balloon in my honor, but it was no use. Finally, the clown, quite out of character for his profession, looked me sternly in the eyes and said: "Shut up kid."

I noticed a leathery, lined, hardened face, maybe an ex-con's, beneath the clown's makeup that told a life of woe, possibly crime and homicide. It was the real, hardscrabble world rightfully slapping the cheek of my narcissistic soap opera. I shut up.

While trying to get stronger, I obviously had to do something about my apprehensions, or I was going to fall to pieces every time I went climbing. I religiously watched a show called *Kung Fu* about a Shaolin monk with seemingly mystic powers wandering the American West. The abilities of the monk, Kwai Chang Caine, convinced me to take an elective at my middle school on Eastern philosophy, meditation, and Tai chi. The teacher, an old beatnik, required we read *The Inner Game of Tennis*, a sport-psychology treatise based on Taoist and yoga philosophy. The book began with a dedication to the Guru Maharaji, who didn't seem like he played much tennis. Author Timothy Gallwey introduced the concept of *Self 1* being the painfully self-aware, fearful ego-consciousness that is constantly interfering with *Self 2*, which is described as one's natural mind, subconscious, or even one's true self. He gave the example of the two states of mind in the paradox of Lao-tzu, the enigmatic founder of Taoism, who was astounded to see a drunken man fall off a high roof and land unhurt. If the man had been sober, he surely would have tensed with fear and have been injured or killed.

The parable of the drunken man fascinated me. While climbing, how could I let go of fear, doubts, and even anger, without letting go of the holds? I came to believe that the traditions of the East somehow could unlock these mysterious powers that could pacify the mind without being drunk and teach me what it took to do the hardest climb in the world.

On my thirteenth birthday I had a breakthrough. My father, who was starting to accept my interest in climbing a little, kindly drove me to meet Jim Erickson, star of *Free Climb on Half Dome*, in Eldorado Canyon and paid for a guided climb. We arrived in Eldorado on a golden spring morning, and there he was: Jim Erickson, looking just like his photos in *CLIMB!* though in color. It was the happiest of days.

1980 was still the Wild West days of guiding; we scrambled unroped up the approach ramp to *Ruper*, a solid 5.8 wide crack, with no helmets and certainly no chalk. Trusting a newly thirteen-year-old kid to hip belay him, Collins started up in tennis shoes with the rope nonchalantly tied around his waist.

Erickson was a fantastic coach, and I couldn't believe the visionary for the film *Free Climb on Half Dome* was teaching *me* how to jam my hands and feet in the wide crack crux. I somehow blasted through it and arrived next to my guide, panting but elated in not falling in front of the superstar. The third pitch was easier, but the airy traverse across the rainbow-colored wall was higher than I had ever been before. Still, despite my heart in my throat, I did the whole climb with no falls or tainting.

When the day was over, I knew better than to suggest we climb for free as equals. Erickson had his hands full anyway with a full-time job and family. Though Erickson wasn't the one to make me into a top climber, to crown off a perfect birthday, he autographed my copy of his *Rocky Heights* guidebook on the very day I became a reckless teenager.

I still needed to find an older partner who would mentor me. Such a person soon materialized in the form of Larry Moffett whom I met on the day of my first lead ever. Among serious climbers, a route is not really accomplished until one leads it. Leading a rock climb also answers the age-old tourist question: How'd you get them ropes up there? As the old mountaineer's saying goes, "The leader must not fall"—advice I did well to heed.

Despite being only thirteen, I was hired at a greasy diner washing dishes for a paltry paycheck to purchase a rack of equipment to lead my own climbs. I hadn't enough money for more than a trifling assortment of strange metal wedges, but, as Reinhold Messner put it, a climber must not "wear his courage in his rucksack." So, a paltry collection of gear was all I had for my first lead on the enormous Third Flatiron overlooking the city of Boulder. Taking the bus from Denver and walking the rest of the way to the Flatirons didn't damper our enthusiasm for the long rock face, a perfect slab, that one crazed individual of years past had even done it in roller skates! It still was not a completely light undertaking as my father recounted from the newspapers that nearly every year some surprised scrambler, often a beer-tipsy picnicker on a lark, went rolling down the face to their demise.

As I neared the top of the first pitch, I pulled up my rope and heard a disheartening *tink, tink, tink,* which was the lively chime of all my protection dislodging down the crack below. I hadn't put enough runners on them and the weight of the rope pulled them all out putting me in great danger—my first lead and I was already facing a ground fall from one hundred feet up. There was nothing but the now useless rope dangling between myself and Red at the bottom of the cliff.

I finished the lead, clawing my way to a little tree where I collapsed. Fortunately, we were climbing what Yosemite pioneer Yvon Chouinard called "the best beginners' climb in the country" since such missteps could usually be survived at that low angle. In fact, after the first pitch, there were hardly any cracks to place gear anyway so we soon accepted the non-existent protection, both doing hundred-foot run-outs above the infrequent anchors on the pitches above.

After several hours, Red and I sat triumphantly on the summit—with no adult support. But our joy was soon forgotten as our rope became tangled up with another party's. After an hour of frustration, a guy from the other team, Larry Moffett, sorted it out. He was patient, kind and his New York goofiness was infectious even while struggling with a huge rope tangle. Moffett said he didn't mind taking us climbing so I took him up on it and he became a regular partner.

When he told stories about the Sixties, Moffett was an incurable romantic. He adored the Rolling Stones and instilled a sense in me that an artist or musician must have "something to say" or their craft is just goods for sale. To us the Rolling Stones said it all.

Moffett also warned me about drugs, but not from the goody-goody Nancy Reagan side of things. He had dropped acid once and lay in a comatose state for four straight days curled up in the fetal position, barely breathing. He never did anything like that again. For Moffett, the Sixties was an era that colored his every thought.

In the Sixties tradition, Moffett was well travelled.

"Hitch-hiking through Europe is the most fun you will ever have," he once told me. "The villages, the mountains, the people invite you to stay in their homes. You don't know what is going to happen next, yet it's totally safe."

The era of idealistic hitching in the States was over. The American road was too scary and regulated but through Moffett's enthusiasm, the charming Europe of stone churches, Roman ruins, pubs, museums, vineyards, and thousands of years of history began to call to me like a dreamy mystery to be discovered. While my classmates dreamed of scoring their first big executive paycheck, I envisioned drifting around Europe's quaint mountain villages, penniless. Poor but, as Thoreau puts his life's goal, "to live deep and suck all the marrow out of life."

On the rocks, Moffett was slow, and we were forever contemplating retreat. He was competent, but it took him hours to complete a 5.8 or 5.9 pitch, often mumbling out loud, and constantly second-guessing his gear placements. He certainly didn't make me into a star, but he was about the best everyman's climbing partner I could have found.

In the summer of 1980, I camped for a few days in Eldorado Springs with a classmate while being guided by Jim Collins. Collins warned us about people at the local pool who did sensory deprivation experiments where they floated in a tank deprived of light and other stimulus.

"Be careful of them. Those people are in a weird cult," Collins said. That from a fellow who had just free soloed the *Naked Edge* and whose fanatical training for *Genesis* had led him to drain the blisters developing on his fingertips on the wall with a needle he held in his teeth!

Eldorado was still in the grip of the 1960's with hippies camped in teepees and "earth mothers" bathing naked in the river holding their babies. To me the 1960s meant cults, Hare Krishnas, people who chant Om, and Charles Manson. In my insular suburbia, we kids were warned about "long hairs" like they were pedophiles. Despite Moffet's perspective, I was still skeptical about that tumultuous decade. I slept "with one eye open" as an eerie spell had been cast over the camping trip. What were these strange seekers looking for in a dark water tank? The cumulative madness of guru cults, wild drug trips and other bizarre behavior gave me the chills.

Drugs weren't going to be part of my story and, if my initiation to alcohol right before my fourteenth birthday was any indication, neither would heavy drinking. I was at the Olafsons', and his parents went out to dinner after Red's mother heated us up some burritos. In their absence, the liquor cabinet stood like a treasure chest at the end of the room.

"Shall we have a drink?" suggested Red.

"Hell yeah!" I was ready to belly up to the bar.

Mimicking cowboys who had just shot some rustlers, we slugged down shots of hard liquor, sampling everything, including Mr. Olafson's $500 bottle of Scotch Whiskey, which tasted like toilet bowl cleaner.

Needless to say, the room began to spin. A warm feeling and giddiness came over us. We were watching *Monty Python's Flying Circus,* and suddenly Graham Chapman's face was sideways. *What's wrong with him?* I thought, but it was *I* who had fallen onto the floor.

Then we tested the tequila. This time my stomach churned, and the fun turned into a sprint to the bathroom. Before long, I retired to the bathroom floor face down languishing in a pool of vomit. About that time, Red's parents came home. Finding me a thirteen-year-old lying in a puddle of puke and unable to stand, Mrs. Olafson was furious.

"It must have been the burritos you made us for dinner," I offered. She didn't appreciate that.

All night I sat on Red's guest bed terrified by the rollicking movement of the room. I thought I'd throw up if I lay down, and I had to grasp the bed's edges to stop the incessant spinning. Besides feeling seasick, I felt dirty, defiled and close to death—alcohol poisoning. The fire-water was bad medicine. I longed for the mountains and happy days in the sunshine far from booze's dark grasp of self-destruction. All I could do was wait for an end to the nightmare.

The worst punishment of all was Mr. Olafson driving me home in silent disgust the next morning in his sleek, black BMW, with fine leather upholstery that I was forever on the verge of puking all over. I braced for the inevitable conference with my parents like a prisoner sentenced to be shot at dawn. It didn't come. Instead, Mr. Olafson disdainfully shooed me out of his car like I was a filthy insect. I couldn't argue. I sure felt like one.

"Slack!" yelled Red.

He clipped a piton placed eons ago by Kor, probably because the exposure caused even the master to overdrive it. Red stretched high for a handhold and then began the long traverse, making an incredible silhouette against the backdrop of the Bastille. Though it was our first 5.10, *Rosy Crucifixion* was our kind of climbing, and Red was making it look easy. *Rosy* had long reaches and traversing moves just like the wall at 7-11. It was situated high on Redgarden Wall, where Kor had hammered in his pitons, arms outstretched like the savior's, crucified against the rainbow hues of the canyon walls. The route is pure vertical and impossible-looking, but just enough holds magically appear in the right places to give passage through the airy improbability—the qualities that put the word "classic" next to it in the guidebook.

As I stepped out onto the wall, the instant exposure formed a lump in my throat. Since *Rosy* traversed above an overhanging roof, it would be hard to get back on the wall if I slipped as there would be nothing to grab onto. I'd be dangling in space, spinning helplessly on the rope. Fortunately, the spectacular moves fit my long frame and flowed beautifully. Panting, I stopped to catch my breath at the end of the traverse before facing the steep crack.

This was the fall of my sixteenth year, the year I saw my greatest advancement in climbing. It started with getting my driver's license on my birthday, then buying a brown Audi that overheated at least once a week to drive to Boulder. With my new wheels, I began to climb regularly. Soon I had successfully lead the crux on *The Yellow Spur*, a stiff 5.9, though still miles from 5.12+.

I was attending Thomas Jefferson Public High School, and I was not knifed by black gangsters as predicted by the rich Kent students, who typically lived in large, beautiful homes but looked out on the world with real fear. Most of my conflicts at T.J. actually came from other upper-middle-class whites. Best of all, classes finished at 1:00 p.m., and I was out of the parking lot by 1:05—not about to waste the afternoon in Denver.

In fact, one hour and five minutes before starting *Rosy Crucifixion, I* had felt crucified in Mr. Foxwood's Sociology class. Foxwood taught there was a strict hierarchy of the strong and the weak and glowed with reverence for the "shakers and movers" of society. Foxwood also lectured that through belief in Jesus Christ, God had made the white man superior to the rest of humanity. Foxwood spent many lectures introducing us to the concept of "The White Man's Burden." He claimed whites had the burden of travelling to the four corners to Christianize, for those who didn't know Jesus would face eternal fire, including those born before Jesus or living too far away. According to him, the world's billions of human inhabitants, from cavemen to present day, kind or nasty, who didn't accept the Good Word were flambéed.

Leading the third pitch—a 5.9—my foot suddenly cut loose, and I took a twenty-foot fall. It happened so fast I could only laugh and pull back on to finish the climb as the brilliant September sun shone over our paradise. The whole wall was alive with a kaleidoscope of color and life. Welcoming birds circled around us in the blue Colorado sky. But looking east to the plains and Denver, a layer of poison gas—the "brown cloud"—waited menacingly in the distance. The toxic urban sprawl, skyscrapers and rush hour traffic came from another world, a stark contrast to the beautiful, rolling buffalo prairies and bright Colorado sun, once Chief Niwot's domain now under occupation by a disharmonious, foreign occupying force. I could feel Mr. Foxwood's lectures were a lie, it reverberated on the golden cliffs of Eldorado. It was a philosophy to degrade others for power and control—originating from a dark and gloomy place I could feel rising through my subconscious European heritage—a place of horrors where it rained, and rained, and rained.

The experience climbing the iconic 5.10 routes of Eldorado Canyon as a sixteen-year-old gave me the nerve to ask Kim, a beautiful blonde, to Homecoming. We had a wonderful dinner and dance and began a romance, but I took her climbing a couple of weeks later and she flipped out.

With our relationship in jeopardy, Kim insisted I attend a Young Life retreat camp at the base of Mt. Princeton (14,254 feet), hoping I would join her version of teen Christianity. She made it clear our last hope to stay together was for me to see things her way. I figured I could sneak away, tromp up snowy Princeton and return for dinner. Instead, the staff locked the gates. The camp became a gulag in Stalin's Siberia and I had been purged.

I had no problem with the church I attended growing up. It was dignified, a large stone gothic building full of sweet old ladies, and the governor of Colorado sometimes attended. It was also socially progressive; Dr. Martin Luther King, Jr., had given a guest sermon when other churches wouldn't even consider racial integration. Best of all, the Sunday school room had perfect windows from which to drop water balloons on the walkway into the chapel. They never suspected what was falling from heaven until it was too late.

The Young Life program began with the counselors weeping, claiming they were "nothing without Jesus." The high school kids wept and wailed too, but I had known many of them since childhood, and they would have sold Jesus out before Judas had his sandals on. For hour upon hour we were forced to sing and praise Jesus till he would have been red in the face.

In my small discussion group, the counselors Brother Kevin and Brother Jordan explained who was going to heaven and who wasn't and that the church sent missionaries throughout the world to help those before it is too late and how lucky I was to be there.

I disagreed so when our flock dissolved, I topped the list for a "special session." Brother Kevin and Brother Jordan took aside their poor lost little lamb—me—into a small, bare white room with no windows.

"The Indians thought there were spirits in the rocks and trees," began Brother Jordan, "and you know what happened to them." Jordan cleared his throat, leaned forward and lowered his voice. His face turned a sickly shade. "It was the will of God that this be a Christian nation. The Indian pagans who worshipped rocks and trees like you are now burning in hell. That is their fate, and I am glad of it. Now why don't you repent and go to heaven, Tom? It's not too late even for a doubter like you."

"I'd rather climb Mt. Princeton, if you don't mind, 'brothers.'"

They disagreed, and locked me in the room.

Presumably, my verbal submission would have been enough to unlock the door but such times, like the Lacrosse coach's tirade, try souls. Locked alone in that room, I felt a kinship with the untold masses who suffered under injustice. I thanked Thomas Jefferson, my high school namesake, a dedicated student of our barbaric European history who stood between them putting hot pokers through my eyes. Furthermore, naturalists John Muir and Colorado's Enos Mills didn't strike me as Satan worshippers any more than did the Dalai Lama. I knew the Native Americans also revered the signature of the Great Spirit on the jagged east face of Long's Peak. They weren't children of a lesser God; they just had fewer guns and were obviously a people of deep feeling and conviction.

I remained a lamb lost from the flock, and thus my first romance came to an end. All the dating drama was new to me, and it brought an emotional pain and isolation I had never fathomed before. I felt betrayed by the blonde; the things I held sacred from childhood began to lose their power. A kind of bitterness came over me, and I fell prey to juvenile delinquency. With some high school friends, we did a dine and dash, ran over mailboxes with a friend's Oldmobile, and got into vandalism and fighting.

A lot of kids were stealing in high school and the rich ones were usually the worst. One guy stole handfuls of ice screws so we could go ice climbing instead of getting out his dad's gold Visa card from his wallet. That was nothing compared to Red's audacity a month previous when he noticed his neighbor's pride in his new ATV and dirt bike resting in their nearby barn. Red and an accomplice boldly snuck onto the neighbor's property, started them up and rode off. Another classmate suggested checking dumpsters behind upscale stores for credit card imprints.

"We can get the numbers off them and order anything we want," he said. "Corporate America cheats us, so let's cheat them instead."

I was not a character from *Little House on the Prairie*, a goody-goody, but I had to get away from such influences before I ending up doing hard time.

Amidst those days of slipping innocence through heartache, assault and battery, and omnipresent dishonesty, I set my sights on *Blackwalk*, a poorly-protected 5.10cR in Eldorado Canyon. Like all Eldorado classics, it was originally a Kor aid route that Jim Erickson had first led free. On that dark section of Redgarden Wall, there are few cracks for placing gear, and Kor's old aid bolt, a decaying quarter-inch bolt he had hastily placed for a quick move of aid, was the only piece of protection. It earned an "R" protection rating in Jim Erickson's *Rocky Heights* guidebook because the leader had to be of a "mature audience" or a master of 5.10, to rationally consider the lead. Jim Erickson took several long falls attempting to lead *Blackwalk* and had to search far for a partner who could second it.

The wall was dark and intimidating as I set off on the unprotected (5.8 X) lower part, belayed by an inexperienced high school freshman. The climb quickly increased in steepness. I made it to the bolt, reached out left for a sloping hold, worked past the crux and weaved my way up, getting farther and farther away from the ancient Kor bolt. The likelihood of such an old bolt holding even a skinny high school kid was a longshot as I got further away. The sensation of danger swirled in my head, but became silent, as I had no choice but to remain calm and focus on the unfamiliar terrain. Higher up, the moves became easier, though I was looking at a forty-foot fall onto the old bolt before I found my next piece of protection. Happily, I sunk it in and carried on to the belay.

Climbing *Blackwalk* changed everything. It was hard to believe that just a couple of years earlier I had been afraid even to set foot on the "Birdwalk" pitch of the *Redgarden Route*. "The white loneliness can overcome the black loneliness," wrote Reinhold Messner. Though *Blackwalk* was an adventure on black stone, the result was the same. The shift in consciousness from the dangerous, but not suicidal, *Blackwalk* had me walking on air for months and cleared the teenage trauma away. I could suddenly think clearly about what mattered—all my trouble had come from being bloated with pride for dating someone I had nothing in common with. I was just riding on the fact that she was good-looking and that symbolized success.

When I needed help the most, the mountain have always come through for me. The two counselors from Young Life and pure science people are wrong—most people can't see it, or don't bother, but there *is* something more than matter and molecules. There *are* spirits in the rocks and woods. Magic has not been completely chased away by our sterile logic in the high, untrodden places. The earth is not without its sanctity if you know where to look, and one thing is for certain: nature is not a false god.

It was my first semester at CU Boulder and I had been bouldering on Flagstaff, a mountain overlooking the city of Boulder, with a strong climber named Justin Kraemer, whom I had just met. As we knocked off boulder problems that I had been working on for weeks by feeding off each other's positive energy, a mysterious man walked by.

"Nice weather we're having," he quipped. The man's appearance made us pause. He was very tall, much older than the other Flagstaff regulars, and his baseball cap and dark glasses looked like a curious ploy to avoid recognition.

"Did you notice something strange about that guy?" I asked Justin.

The man's presence shifted our focus from our own endeavors. Peering through the trees, we watched in amazement as he scampered quickly and effortlessly up several difficult problems. He seemed to know the holds like an old sea captain knows the trade winds.

The mysterious stranger scrambled up a pinnacle and looked serenely into the distance, his face reflecting a distant era of roaming free in the mountains, a time when the world of vertical adventures was new and there for the taking. I will never forget the fearless nobility and unbridled emotion he radiated. I suddenly knew who he was.

"You're Layton Kor, aren't you?" I accused him.

"Yes," he admitted. "Back in Boulder to relive a few memories and see my mother, who is getting on in years."

"Layton Kor!" exclaimed Justin. "Who would have thought I'd meet Layton Kor?"

We couldn't take our eyes off the lanky superman. Kor scrambled lightning fast up another finger of rock and again looked, eyes moist with tears, into the void. The myth of Kor, the madman who had held innumerable climbing partners in constant terror, was also a man of deep sentiment.

"You've always been my hero," I confessed in the parking lot.

"Some hero," Kor replied with genuine modesty. "You boys want to go get some pizza?"

Back in Boulder at a dingy pizza joint, we listened eagerly to Layton's stories of the Alps in the 1960s. He sat nobly in his chair, smiling down on us like a temperamental Greek god. He had removed his sunglasses, and his icy blue eyes sparkled brightly.

"Ya gotta move man, move! One minute the sun is shining on you and then bam!" he slammed his hand on the table for emphasis. "A storm rolls in and freezes your party to the face with three inches of ice. And that's a *summer* storm." He laughed heartily as, true to legend, his idyllic stories turned suddenly to foreboding doom.

I could only gawk while he and Justin discussed plans to climb in the Italian Dolomites the next summer. At the time, I was too unworldly to know where to even get a passport, but they were kind souls, and included me in their discussion regardless.

Later, Kor told stories about working masonry at the Coors brewery in the 1970s, enduring labor strikes, admiring so-and-so's stone work, and determining cement's optimal pouring viscosity. Though the subject would not have interested me otherwise, I still hung on his every word. After all, it was *Kor* explaining the best way to 'butter' the blocks with a mud trowel.

In his account of the hero's journey, the philosopher Joseph Campbell explains how one is often aided by a Jedi-like character, an archetype, or familiar symbol from beyond our time. Throughout my youth, that figure was Layton Kor. Yet, unlike so many of the disillusionments I faced growing up, my childhood champion did not disappoint when I finally met him in the flesh. There was something otherworldly about Kor – a character so real, so concrete, it forced my entire consciousness to wake up and take note. "Some hero," Kor had said to me. Those words and his earthy tone showed the modesty of a man without pretense, a man who, like the title of his autobiography, had gone "Beyond the Vertical."

THE SWEET 1970S DEREK HERSEY-
DANCING WITH THE GODS

A lone and unroped, Derek Hersey sinks his fingers into the cold, orange streaked granite cracks. The wind blows through Hersey's stringy, long dark hair high on Longs Peak's 1,000 foot high Diamond face that sits 14,000 feet above sea level. His appearance is wild like a Tibetan nomad, a non-conformist in any epoch, his laugh is as fearless as the mind that drives his outrageous solo climbs. Hersey is embracing the ultimate climbing experience on any mountain. Hersey has already soloed the Yellow Wall 5.10d and downclimbed the 5.10a Casual Route. Now he is going for the steep and stiff, wide cracks of Pervertical Sanctuary 5.11, a route unfamiliar to him. It is the purest "here and now" act possible: high stakes gambling thousands of feet up a vertical rock face.

Fortunately, Derek Hersey is no stranger to solo or unroped climbing. He does it almost daily and acquired the nickname "Doctor Death" soon after arrival in Boulder from his native England. Rumors circulated he was a suicidal English Lord or Duke. With a working-class Yorkshire accent and background, Derek is just the opposite. Hersey's down to earth love *of life, stays simple and uncomplicated. His room is nearly bare and he is satisfied doing the humblest occupations. There is nothing cluttering his existence such as a serious career or an abundance of possessions to later bring the regrets of a life unclimbed.*

The sky in Rocky Mountain National Park is still clear though it approaches noon, it's a perfect "Diamond day." A day for dancing with the Gods.

ON THE EDGE

I was about to die! My breathing misfired; my mind careened into panic. Alone and un-roped on Fairview Dome's *Regular Route*, I was engaged in a full layback, a push-pull opposing pressure technique quite like climbing a coconut tree. My hands had felt a slippery coating of water in the back of the crack and as my fingers slowly lost their grip, I imagined falling to oblivion hundreds of feet below. This was Derek's fault.

The year 1984, my freshman year at the University of Colorado, Boulder, was indeed "Orwellian." My dorm parking lot was filled with new Mercedes-Benz and BMWs, which made for a reenactment of prep school days. My roommates would talk excitedly for hours about becoming big-shot executives and future earning power *ad nauseam*. As Mark Twain said of his contemporaries in the Gilded Age, "Whereas I merely desired money, they fell down and worshipped it." What had I done wrong to come of age in the 1980s?

The year 1984 saw a revival of Greek life on campus since its near demise in the 1960s. Inspired by the film *Animal House*, I too rushed the fraternities. The parties, symbolism and golden lion statues at the SAE house seemed so cool. However, I soon realized that the re-emergence of fraternities and sororities nationwide had nothing to do with John Belushi. It was more in line with the *Animal House* film's stuffy antagonist Niedermeyer. A resurgence of America's most self-righteous, elitist and, despite lots of cocaine, "Leave it to Beaver" values were upon us.

At the rush parties, I heard glittering promises. Cheap new cars, primo jobs, endless support from the secret Alumnae Brotherhood who were out there in the thousands like an invisible army ready to help those wise enough to join. Getting hazed by spanking our bare bottoms and other degrading acts plus the several thousand dollars a year in dues weren't mentioned. A frat president leaned in my ear: "We will line up the chicks for you. How about it? How about getting laid? It all starts with the secret handshake." It was a lot to pay for a pimp.

I wasn't all that phased, because I didn't move to Boulder to drop acid with the Deadheads, or do lines with the fraternity boys. I attended CU because the world's greatest rock climbing was just down the road. One day while driving to Eldorado Canyon, I picked up a man hitchhiking. He was a thin Jimmy Page look-a-like with long dark hair and a rope coiled across his shoulder. When he got into the car, I had second thoughts. He really smelled.

"W'a' you up to then today, youth?" he asked in a thick English accent. Between his garbled Manchester dialect and bizarre British climbing slang, he lost me every other sentence, but he was very cheerful and laughed a lot. He said his name was Derek Hersey, and he had just arrived in Boulder.

"Oh, you need a climbing partner?" I hung fire. It was one thing to give a stranger a ride, and quite another to trust them with your life belaying. However, Derek suggested *Supremacy Crack*, a notoriously brutal 5.11. I was eighteen and eager to try.

I started to set a top-rope, but Derek stopped me. "Naw, mate, I'll have a go on lead."

He pulled out a meager rack of two cams, and soon his skinny body was swaying gracefully back and forth till he had arrived at the top with relative ease. Derek was one of the best climbers I had ever seen and certainly ever climbed with. A real 1970's free climbing master and minimalist.

Despite Derek's inspiring ascent, I still wanted a top rope for the steep crack. It was a good idea. When I set a handjam, the rough texture of the rock shot misery through the back of my hand. Otherwise, the rock was frustratingly smooth and slippery. I tried to get another jam above a flake, but the crack was narrow and cruel. As I tried to pull up, my hand shot out after only half a move. I went flying out into space, taking Derek with me.

"Weee!" he yelled spinning around and around on the rope shouting and singing.

Who is this madman? I wondered.

Derek resituated his belay and patiently gave precise instructions on the particulars of the crack. My next try, I got much higher but by no means "bagged it."

"That would be a brill solo," he said back in the car.

"What? You would climb that without a rope?" I asked in awe. "If you could solo 5.11s, you would be famous." I had never heard of anyone except for the blonde myth John Bachar in California doing such an outlandish thing.

"Aye, solo is me main gig. That's w'a' I really do best off the top o' me head. If it feels right, it goes."

A month later, Derek soloed the *Naked Edge*. I was floored. I hadn't climbed the *Edge* yet, but I had studied it carefully. I couldn't imagine being alone and un-roped on the overhanging jam crack of the fifth pitch, where a climber hangs out into space above the whole canyon before surmounting the final arête. It gave me shivers of both excitement and total horror—a climber's sweetest nightmare.

Not surprisingly, the legend of Derek Hersey grew. In the months and years following our first encounter, tales of his non-stop soloing circuits and uninhibited laugh became larger than life.

Hersey was like a shining sun in the dark valley of spoiled CU Boulder students. One day he came wandering by a greasy café on the Hill across from CU where I sat with some dormmates. I knocked on the glass, and Derek changed course.

"You *know* that man?" asked one of my dormmates, pointing in horror at Derek, who was squeezing through the crowded entranceway. "I'm not sitting with him."

A moment later, he had reached our table. "Oi youth!" Hersey said sitting down. He turned to the waitress: "Right love, I'll have a greasy plate of food and a cup of bad coffee."

"We don't have that here," she protested.

"Well you did last week! Eh, get it? You did last week!" he elbowed my dormmates, and they started laughing despite themselves.

Hersey casually told me he had soloed every route on the Bastille that morning. I could only imagine the confidence needed to climb that somber citadel *sans corde,* spread-eagled on *Outer Space's* slimy dihedral and airy headwall, crimping *Wide Country's* insecure 5.11 edges, and swinging through the stout 5.11 overhang of *Neon Lights.*

"Another day at the office," Hersey chuckled.

To the amazement of my dormmates, Hersey told jokes that had us all rolling on the floor, before departing to his afternoon job of washing dishes at a restaurant on Pearl Street, cheerful as a groom to the altar. He only wanted enough money to climb. Once Hersey had enough food and beer—especially beer—life began.

As I watched Derek's long-haired form bouncing merrily towards the dirty dishes awaiting him on Pearl Street, talk at our table returned to drooling over Porsches and McMansions. Sitting there a heavy feeling came over me; I couldn't shake the truth that my dormmates would stab me in the back at their first opportunity. Taking a deep breath, I felt grateful there was a Derek Hersey around.

Until that moment on Fairview Dome, it had been a fun-filled summer in Yosemite Valley, California, though overworked as a maid changing sheets in the Curry Camp. Together with Red and two other college students, Matt and Cullum, we threw water balloons at the open sight-seeing bus, and Cullum even pegged a chubby tourist, snapping back his head in surprise. With our supply of clean sheets, we had a toga parade, pushed the whistle-happy new lifeguard into the pool, and were always late to work. Management threatened to fire us, but no one wanted our jobs, so we remained tenuously.

Our coworkers were a cause for concern, however. You'd think a national park would be staffed by nature-lovers going bird-watching and bike riding. Instead, Yosemite concessionaires picked recruits from the unemployment lines of smoky, decrepit coastal cities to populate the employee quarters called "Boys Town." Talk of unsavory deeds and doing time in the penitentiary filled the air. Rangers armed like Storm Troopers routinely raided the tents like in Steinbeck's *The Grapes of Wrath,* and usually found what, or whom, they were looking for. Many employees had no direction, and those who stayed beyond a couple of months were called "lifers." If our workplace was the *Boys Town* of the Mickey Rooney film, Father Flanagan would have been found floating face down in the valley's Merced River.

Of course, we weren't there for the crappy jobs, or starched maid uniforms and slaving in the sweltering canvas tents; it was the magnificent climbing of "The Valley," *the* greatest climbing area in the world. The routes on the soaring granite walls were so huge that many routes took several days to complete. Some nuts even soloed them without a rope.

Solo climbing was a time-honored tradition in Yosemite. The valley counter-parts to Derek Hersey such as John Bachar frequently climbed serious routes without a rope, and Peter Croft had just soloed a long and consistently difficult climb called *Astroman*. So daunting was *Astroman's* reputation that when our alarm didn't go off the morning we planned to climb it, neither Red nor I brought it up again. Just the concept of these solo masters facing certain death from even a foot slipping, overshadowed our pathetic roped adventures as the ultimate experience Yosemite could offer.

On my one day off per week, I was lounging in the parking lot when a backpacker offered me twenty-five dollars for a ride to his car parked in Tuolumne Meadows. The valley was blistering hot, so the cool white domes of the high country sounded inviting, though I had no one to climb with. The hiker filled the hour with pleasant stories, but I felt a twinge of fear driving past Fairview Dome. Red and I had made a roped ascent of the dome's 900-foot *Regular Route* the week before, finding it as intimidating as a game of lawn croquet. As I looked at the cool, shady face, I felt a surging thrill inside that I *must* do it un-roped! By the time I dropped the backpacker at his car, I had shaken off the crazy idea, but, heading back, the enormity of Fairview Dome filled my entire view. Fairview was beckoning me, daring me, laughing at me.

So I found myself high on the cliff, clinging to the slimy, wet crack, moments away from tumbling down the slabs to my death or a future of tubes and beeping machines. But as terror shot through every nerve, *it* happened. Under this extreme duress, time and space swirled for a moment as if in a Salvador Dali painting, and I began to think very clearly. *The Inner Game of Tennis*, from my middle school class taught by the Beatnik, returned to mind.

The concepts of Self 1 and Self 2 ceased to be idle speculation; instead, they came exploding into the forefront of my consciousness. Self 1, after its initial outrage, shut completely off, and Self 2 took over. The corny cliché I became "one with the rock" came true. When facing death, nothing, but nothing, mattered other than controlling a slippery wet finger-lock in the corner of a granite crack. I caked my other fingers in chalk and delicately leaned in to compensate if my first hand came skidding out of the fissure. My breathing calmed, the shaking stopped, and all eternity balanced on simply sticking the next layback by treading the ultra-fine line of not pulling too hard or too little. Through Self 2, I climbed with the precision of a master surgeon. It was a separate reality: a beautiful kingdom hidden beneath our human world's petty concerns like the tourist trap down below.

I stood on the ledge above the first pitch stunned, squinting at the distant snowcapped ranges of the high Sierra. Without a rope, I was committed to the nine pitches above, but the climbing was much easier. As I passed a roped party on the fifth pitch, they nodded respectfully to me, and I felt like I was John Bachar—quickly forgetting the shaky episode below. I also began to appreciate that with rope systems, so much time is spent fumbling with equipment, setting belays and yelling commands. Climbing unroped was pure speed and freedom. So much more time was spent moving and in contact with the rock. I flowed up cracks and corners, my shadow following obediently up the perfect white granite. The wind gently kissed my face, and I hit a stride that could reach the stars.

Suddenly, there was no more cliff. As I pulled over the top, the cool beams of the three-quarter moon became forever imprinted on my mind. I fell flat on the summit in awe and thanksgiving. I felt awake, alive, and happy just to be breathing among the clouds of Tuolumne. The repulsive tourist din of soft-serve ice cream, RV traffic jams and tacky t-shirt shops in the valley no longer existed. Fairview Dome's summit was hauntingly stark and moonlike. The white granite flowed away in a curving arch down unbroken slabs. I stood in the shimmering golden sun surveying the Range of Light that spread in all directions. I could feel John Muir's "heaven that is underfoot." Waves of bliss and joyous hysteria overcame me. As long as the light allowed, I lingered aware every peak, meadow, and needle of a sequoia was a friend. Climbing's true purpose had come through more strongly than ever with these visions of grandiose beauty. The only trouble was that I had to nearly kill myself to get it.

The fall after the Yosemite experience, I spent a semester at CU Denver, which offered yoga. I figured I could get credit for a silly elective P.E. course and improve my flexibility for climbing. Surely, it had to be an easy "A." It was almost a self-dare to take a class that seemed as sissy as ballet or flower-arranging. The first day, I looked both ways before ducking into the dance studio, and what awaited wasn't pretty. The room was packed with middle-aged housewives unrealistically crammed into bulging Jane Fonda tights. In the corner was a curly haired woman who looked like a sickly, pale vegetarian. Most of us were under the impression she was the teacher. I was about to leave and sign up for weightlifting when a tall, blonde woman sparkling with enthusiasm waltzed into the room.

"*Namaste* everyone," she sang out. "*Namaste* is an Indian greeting meaning the divinity within me salutes the divinity within you." Her name was Patricia Hansen, and she was a real "Sixties" yoga teacher, having taught Patanjali's—yoga's first known chronicler—ancient eightfold path of yoga realization for over twenty-five years—before the Beatles even followed the Maharishi.

"Yoga is the science of religion," she continued. "It was developed by the Vedic people who gave special attention to what makes people unhappy who concluded that suffering originates in the mind. Initially the mind has the smooth surface of a lake that reflects the mountains above. But thoughts and desires called *vrittis* disturb the mind like rocks thrown in until the lake's reflection is no longer visible. Yoga is designed to calm the ripples and restore the reflection. Hatha Yoga is the path of physical exercises to prepare the body for meditation and attain the peace all humanity prays for."

We did some basic postures, though I could hardly reach past my knees. While in an upside-down posture, the greeting *Namaste* resonated in my mind like a seed planted from a faraway land. My fanciful imagination envisioned a Gandhi-esque peoples reflecting truth like the mountain lake she described—undefiled humans not those looking for the opportune moment to proverbially "stick the knife in."

Despite that wonderful fantasy, my skepticism returned a week later along with the housewives in their leotards. The class had to get me hooked that day, or I was going to drop it for a class I could at least admit I was taking.

"A yoga posture is an attitude of the mind," the teacher began. "George Bernard Shaw once said that we must constantly keep the mind clean since it is 'the window through which we see the world.'"

After a series of asanas, we began a shoulder stand pose called "the plough." With my toes hovering overhead, the altered blood flow made a dizzying increase of pressure in my head. Hansen talked in hypnotic tones about expanding one's awareness of breathing deeply. My hamstrings were still incredibly tight, but a remarkable sensation of lightness flowed through my neck and upper back muscles.

"The most important approach to yoga is to use an effortless effort," Hansen said. "And let your spine down vertebrae by vertebrae. Now let yourselves go completely limp."

With her guidance, we lay on our backs, and I fell into deep relaxation. Strangely, I felt sleepy but also clear-minded, reminiscent of the day I had soloed Fairview Dome. Indeed, Self 1 was yet again dissolving into Self 2. With the class in a hypnotic state, Hansen began to chant a mysterious verse and afterward translated it to English:

Asato Maa Sat Gamaya,
Tamaso Maa Jyotir Gamaya
Mritoyor Maa Amritam Gamaya

Lead us from the unreal to the Real
Lead us from the darkness to the Light
Lead us from a fear of death to an
understanding of Immortality

Outside class, the sun shone lovingly on my face as I serenely watched students play frisbee. Noises filled the air, the sun's rays ignited a patch of grass, and I felt like I did on Fairview, absorbing the moon's cool rays. So often, climbing has led me from the unreality of daily human life to experience something higher. This Indian philosophy promised to do the same; it was another way to open that door. It was a startling realization that maybe I didn't have to nearly die to experience a higher state of mind. Yet without the Yosemite debacle, I might not have recognized what yoga really is.

Over the semester my fascination with yoga grew. I wanted to put it to the test to see what it could really do, and what better place than on the *Naked Edge?*

Annie Whitehouse, a prolific Boulder climber and veteran of the first American women's Annapurna expedition, agreed to join me on the *Naked Edge* for my twenty-second birthday. This time, I wanted to climb the *Edge* without the taint the first time I climbed it with Red two years before. Climbing the *Naked Edge* with him, the heights got to me on the fifth pitch, and I grabbed a piece of gear and hung on in terror.

Sitting with Annie below the fourth pitch, a sinister chimney waited overhead, hundreds of feet above the canyon floor. I began to feel the pull of fatigue and self-doubt. It was Annie's lead. I wanted to follow the chimney and then lead my fifth pitch easily. My goal was to be calm and cool like Annie's boyfriend, Derek Hersey, when he did laps on the *Naked Edge* without a rope.

With the pressure building on my *Self 1*, I struggled to envision my *Self 2* easily climbing the 5.11 chimney and then leading the awkward 5.11 moves off the small belay to exit atop the strenuous, airy hand crack around the corner. But it is here that the *Edge* takes on its most sinister tone. We would be two insects perched on the dark blade of rock at the top of the canyon wall with mind-blowing exposure. I was quickly losing my nerve.

In yoga class, we had practiced alternate nostril *pranayama* breathing to calm the mind and invigorate the body's tissues with oxygen. So, for ten minutes I sat on the airy perch, covering one nostril to breathe in for eight slow counts then out for eight counts, repeating the routine with the other nostril. As my anxiety dissipated, my breathing cycles naturally extended to ten counts. I began to feel an energetic detachment, and the crazy heights ceased to torment me. I became calmer and able to fully focus my strength to the task at hand.

"Ready now?" Annie asked with a tolerant laugh. She had encountered many esoteric gurus and Buddhist monks on her extended travels through Nepal.

Annie led the chimney slot confidently, and on my turn, I followed it without hesitating, for the *pranayama* had restored my strength, mentally and physically. The dreaded forearm pump had mostly dissipated. My lead went past in a daze, and I soon found myself securely sinking my last hand-jam into the crack and pulling over the top. Finally, an ascent with no taints, but this fact seemed minor compared to the remarkable effects of *pranayama*.

"Be ready! I'm losing it up here!" I yelled down to Red, who was belaying me.

He laughed and shouted up insults. Red was always overjoyed to see me fail, and if he could help the process along, it doubled his pleasure. In the nine-years we had been climbing together little had changed between us.

But by the mid-1980s, the world of rock climbing was changing fast. Interest in long, challenging "trad" routes on Longs Peak's Diamond or the *Naked Edge* was giving way to "sport climbing." The new style, which originated in France, meant liberally placing expansion bolts with screaming power drills hanging on rappel. To someone who had grown up fed on the legends of old-school hardmen like Layton Kor and clean ethics like Jim Erickson's re-vulsion for tainting, the result was a dumbing down. To me, the cliffs looked vandalized by grid patterns of silver bolts. The clip-and-go world of bolted routes was removing the mystery, danger, adventure, and certainly the soul.

Besides the bolting, sport climbing promoted the regrettable fashion of wearing brightly colored lycra circus tights, with a pref-erence for hot pink designs. This skin-tight attire left very little to the imagination, often making it hard to look up at the cliffs. Climbers devoted to this style could have cast as the guitarist, Nigel, in the rock band spoof movie *Spinal Tap*. The neon leggings were less modest than the skimpy gourds that African tribesmen strapped on at the request of missionaries. Importing such a trend back to the U.S. may have been a greater crime than bolting.

Sport climbing shifted the goal of climbing away from gaining a summit or even the top of a cliff. Now finger-wrenching moves led only to chain-link anchors. The basis of sport climbing became merely difficult gymnastic stunts, introspection be damned. Also, the typical sport route was less than eighty-feet high, allowing little sensation of commitment or exploration.

Sport climbers also attacked traditional climbing ethics such as the ground up mentality and certainly the idea that the leader must not fall. They spent shameless amounts of time, even years, working out the moves of a route. This practice of hanging on routes while dogging the moves earned them the derogatory title of 'hangdoggers.' Poor ethics aside, it did raise technical standards through the roof.

Style still counted. Now the climber was expected to "redpoint" a route, a term borrowed from German climbers who sprayed a red dot at the base of routes they had successfully led without falls. Taking years to redpoint a climb was obviously inferior to a fast effort or an ascent in its purest form: on sight. To do a route on-sight means on your first try—a lot harder than rehearsing the moves over and over until they become as familiar as a simple dance routine.

There were notorious holdouts against the new wave, such as California's John Bachar, who subscribed to the traditional give the route a fighting chance ethic in Yosemite. He felt bolting was ruining the aesthetics of the national park and respected a climber who could do a 5.10 in good style more than one who sieged a 5.12 like a medieval rampart. Yosemite had always carried the torch of good ethics, harkening back to environmentalists like John Muir. The bolting wars were upon us.

I had occasionally been tempted to try the new hangdogging style. I was torn between keeping up with the new hotshots and my childhood principles. One day at the base of *Genesis*, I confessed my sinful thoughts to Derek Hersey.

"The hangdoggers cheat," Derek advised. "Wha's the bloody point of that?"

Derek wasn't just another mouth. He had just made the first ascent of *To RP or Not to Be* in a direct challenge to Frenchman

J.B. Tribout's 5.14a bolted route at Smith Rocks, Oregon, *To Bolt or Not to Be*, technically the hardest climb in the country. Derek's was "only" 5.12, but it was dangerous, leading high above tiny brass RP nuts, and he had done it on-sight.

But I was also tempted by some of sport climbing's truly inspiring representatives. In 1985, Patrick Edlinger, a famous Frenchman, had become the first person to on-sight *Genesis* during his first big tour of the States. It was America's wakeup call that we were years behind the French. Shortly after he climbed *Genesis*, I had met Patrick, pronounced "Patreek." He was not the stereotypical red-nosed, truffle-hunting Frenchman with a beret, but tan, muscular and lean with a sharp profile framed by his trademark long blonde hair. *Le Blond*, as he was called, was quite a European media star, appearing often in *Paris Match* and featured on television soloing hard climbs in the dramatic Gorges du Verdon barefoot. Yet despite his accomplishments, he still seemed friendly and down-to-earth.

"You must visit France," he told me. "Aix-en-Provence is very much like Boulder, ze students, ze nature, ze life." Patreek kissed his fingertips in the air, closing his eyes as though remembering far off dreams of steep grey walls and lavender fields.

I promised him I would climb in his legendary Verdon Gorge someday. Though I was a confused and impoverished college freshman and making it to France anytime soon was as likely as leaving the solar system, the image of Patreek kissing his fingertips initiated the dream.

With every climbing magazine littered with photos of lycra-clad lizards on bolted climbs, curiosity got the better of Red and I, and we wanted to try a sport route. For our first one, Red and I chose a newly bolted Euro-style climb called *Dragon Lady* in Left Hand canyon outside Boulder. It was rated 5.12, that mythical, elusive dream grade at which *Genesis* languishes at the extreme top end. I tied into the rope and led out an overhanging section at the bottom. It was immediately strenuous and tore at my confidence to ever do a 5.12. I made it up a few more feet, but my forearms became so exhausted that the tiny handholds began to slowly slip from under my fingers. I reached fruitlessly above for a good hold and strained to see through the sweat stinging my eyes. That's where I was when Red was making fun of me.

I began to shake and swung my right hand up to a chalked hold which sloped nastily downwards and I could only watch my hand slide off in slow motion. After a spectacular plunge through the air, I stopped only five feet above the ground. So much for the "leader must not fall" rule.

"You're always trying to screw with my mind," I complained.

Red chuckled. "You weren't exactly Patrick Edlinger up there."

Red took the lead on *Dragon Lady*, fired the overhang and sauntered past my high point.

"Starts getting hard up here," he sang down well above the sections I struggled on. Higher, he took a short fall, but hung on the rope to become familiar with the holds.

"Hey hangdogger!" I accused as I lowered Red to the ground. "You were cheating up there."

"Oh, come on, the French are climbing 5.14s." Red shot back. "It's time to come out of the dark ages."

"The challenge is gone," I replied. "The soul of climbing will be lost."

"You looked pretty challenged to me," Red laughed.

A week after trying to lead *Dragon Lady*, I was back in yoga class.

"Only now Scientists are discovering facts about sound waves that the ancient yogis of India already knew," Pat Hansen explained. "*Om* is the sound of the universe. Microphones in space have recorded sound vibrations exactly matching the tone of Om. In yoga, Om is the sacred sound from which all things come. Consciousness has its origins in the sound and that is why Om is repeated with great reverence. In the world's religions, Om is the basic vibration of prayers like the A-men at the end of Christian hymns. You might have noticed people hum when they are happy. They are soothing their minds with sound vibration. Mantra is meditation using vibrating sounds. Certain sounds create different consciousness and emotion, the way musicians compose with notes and chords. Gregorian chant is used in Christianity and the Buddhists in the mountains of Tibet often use *Om Mane Padme Hum.*"

After a pause, she continued, "Okay let's try chanting a few Om's. Ready? Oooooouuuummm Ooooooouuuummmmmmn."

What the hell happened to the nice, wholesome stretching? I thought.

The dance studio reverberated with those awful moaning sounds like a brainwashing cult was going in full session. The gym doors were open, exposing us to the ridicule of any passersby. I burned with embarrassment. *Why wasn't I in weight lifting?*

The students repeated "Oooooouuuummm," resembling earnest zombies and taking it as seriously as a calculus final exam. I sheepishly mumbled "UUumnn" off key. After a while my apprehension gave way to suppressed laughter, like in church where something slightly funny becomes hysterical, a comic pressure cooker, because you can't show any signs of enjoying yourself.

A few minutes later, however, chanting Om began to give me a buzz. "Om, Om, Om," I went, forgetting my earlier distaste. A deep calm reminiscent of soloing Fairview Dome yet again, spread through me. I had climbed so well that day, so exactingly under threat of death, and I began to realize this Om chanting could get me there too. What would happen should the twain meet?

I bought a book called *Climbing Fit,* hoping it would give me some answers to beat Red. It was full of boring exercises like sit-ups and pull-ups. Then I found a picture of a short, stocky fellow clinging to the side of one of those indoor climbing walls. The caption

read: the infamous Johnny Dawes in action. *Infamous?* The saluta-
tion to Dawes made me so fumed I nearly threw away the book.
Thumbing through the back pages, I found a thought-provoking
sentence from the well-known English star, Jerry Moffat, saying he
was interested in yoga but didn't know much about it. It seemed
the way to go, along with pull-ups and sit-ups. From that moment
on, yoga became my secret weapon against Red.

I stopped in a Boulder Pearl Street new age bookstore to learn
more. Once inside, however, I felt embarrassed, overcome by the
heavy stench of incense. I searched fruitlessly through row after
row of books with titles like *Discovering Your True Being through
Crystal Awareness* and others written in a style on par with pyramid schemes. The alternative living genre was clearly a world far-
removed from my revelations atop Fairview Dome.

Even though I was obviously very impressed with my wonderful yoga class, the books of that section were, ironically, the most
disturbing of all. Shadowy literature from the crazed and confused
1960s with titles like *His Eminent Spiritual Holiness* gave me the
creeps. All I wanted was a book with more stretches and stuff illustrated with pictures of dorky models in leotards. Instead there were
esoteric promises made by gurus driving Rolls Royce motor cars.

As I hurried toward the exit, an aisle of cassette tapes caught
my eye. Next to a cassette bizarrely titled *Sounds of the Child Within*
was one called *The Eternal OM*. Its cover graphic showed a half-
moon exploding in psychedelic colors. The back cover described it
as "The Sounds of Om made by a fusion of voice and synthesizer in
repetition." There could not be a stranger thing to listen to. *What
the hell? I'll try it.*

"That's a really awesome tape," said the woman at the register,
who sported a tie-dyed dress and dreadlocks.

"Yes, yes, please hurry," I blushed.

In my car, I *had* to hear what it sounded like. "Om … Om!" my
car stereo boomed.

The packaging warned: "Not for use in a moving automobile." *What in the world could that mean? Is it going to hypnotize me?* Someone pulled into the next parking space while my car shook to Om. I turned it off, caught red-handed, and tried not to die laughing.

As the days passed, I found that playing that crazy Om tape was actually a lot of fun. It got me into a relaxed but clear state of mind where I could observe the self-conscious chattering patterns of my thinking. I began to use it before taking exams and found I usually got an 'A.'

A few days later, I found myself once again at the base of *Dragon Lady* with Red.

"I want to lead it," I said confidently.

"Don't you think you are wasting your energy? You didn't look very strong last time..." Red began his string of put-downs. However, that morning I had been playing the Om tape and could nearly tune out the fact that he was there. I continued chanting *Om, Om, Om* quietly to myself.

Om, Om ... I tied into the rope. *Om, Om* ... I put on my climbing shoes. No mental dialogue or desires only *Om ... Om...*

In a dreamy state, present but also removed, I looked down from the second bolt, experiencing only the awareness of a dull throb in my arms. *Om ... Om ...* humiliation or victory became *Om ... Om ...* It was only climbing after all.

The sun beat down as I clipped the third bolt and the fourth. The rock was easing past like a slow river. The crux was a long stretch for a one-inch incut handhold. *Om.* I got it and clipped the fifth bolt. The hardest climbing was below me. In a sleepy daze, I did a few easier moves, but then even the bigger holds became hard to hang onto. High on the cliff, I reached for a horizontal break, but it offered no rest to my bloated arms. Momentarily, I forgot *Om,* read the next move wrong, made a wild lunge, and fell backwards into space.

"Whoa! You almost nailed the route!" Red said in amazement. "Your climbing looked effortless until the top. You blasted right through the crux!"

His compliments were rare, but this was especially confusing. *How can I take credit for that?* It was like I was absent, only observing myself. Unexplainable, but it happened—a breakthrough experience, as Timothy Gallwey describes such moments in his book *Inner Tennis.*

"It was an effortless effort, wasn't it?" I said looking up at the rope blowing peacefully back and forth in the wind.

Red paused. "I've been thinking about taking a trip to France to climb in Buoux. They say you get way stronger in Buoux than anywhere else."

Already enrolled for my third year at CU, I was instantly in a dilemma. It would be insufferable, *the end,* if Red got that much better.

"France?" I asked uncertainly, dreading the idea. "Everyone says they are complete assholes over there. Besides, what about the language barrier?"

"They all speak English. Anyway, I thought you took French in high school."

"I got an 'F.'"

"Oh, it's all the same. We just gotta get there and burn off the Euro-trash."

The next day Red bought a plane ticket to France. He would be there for nearly a year.

As summer waned, Larry Moffett hired me to work in his video store, and I suffered the agony of receiving Red's postcards from Europe saying how strong he was getting. It seemed I could do nothing but feel sorry for myself while he became a climbing star.

After a month, I couldn't take it anymore. I withdrew from school and bought a one-way ticket to Europe. I had been at CU Boulder for three years and it was more socialization than learning, brainwashing to prevent me from someday leaving my cubicle. Over the university library were the words etched in stone: "He who knows only his own generation remains always a child." It was true that all I knew was my own crass, consumer MTV generation. It was time to see the world and get my education.

What was I doing selling out to sport climbing? Going on a trip to Europe fueled by little more than competition and ambition had a dirty feel. If I had run into Derek Hersey in the days before I left I couldn't have looked him in the eye. Boarding the plane, I looked out at the sacred places of my youth, Long's Peak's shape to the north, the Flatirons rising out of the haze ascended by the gods Kor and Erickson I spent my youth worshiping. But as I settled in my seat it felt like the gods were dying…

1980S BIRTH OF THE PHYSICAL EXTREME

JOHNNY DAWES-SICK MONKEY

*O*n a cliff high above the Welsh countryside, Johnny Dawes climbed higher above his last anchor until it was certain he would hit the ground if he fell. His head spun as he rested before the crux of the climb "Indian Face." Then he went for it, risking it all. He had rehearsed and cleaned the holds before the first ascent but with death certain on extreme climbing, the marriage of both danger and high difficulty was born.

The British pioneer, Joe Brown, described Indian Face as "an example of what bold climbs are all about...It is the most adventurous and daring climb in Britain."

It was a golden age of British climbing in October 1986. A time when sticky rubber boots were just come available and climbing advanced to its most physical. Johnny Dawes had an unusual upbringing of privilege on his parent's estate in Worchester, England. He had ample room to roam in nature and "got to know his own intuition." But Dawes doesn't get on well with himself. He was drinking three bottles of whiskey a week when he launched on the suicide mission of making the first ascent of Indian Face.

The self-described "autistic wild boy" was attempting what would be called the most audacious lead on British rock. Audacious because it was about as hard as Genesis, (5.12d) if you got the moves right, but a fall from the crux was death. An unhappy alcoholic with an indifference to his continued existence was the perfect frame of mind for the lead. Johnny is nick-named the "Stone Monkey" but doing climbs so hard and dangerous, he's really a Sick Monkey.

BUOUX: VALLEY OF MY SHAME

I put two fingers into a limestone hole and, being isolated from my other fingers, it put a torque on my tendon like having one's fingers stuck in a spinning bowling ball. The brilliant sun of southern France blinded me. My big feet didn't fit into the strange holes either. Buoux was a desperate place to climb and this route I attempted was one of the easiest in the valley. It was called *Le Dernier Problème des Alpes*, an easy 5.10 translated as "The Last Great Problem of the Alps." A route's name often sets the tone for the climbing, and this one conjured up the drama of the once highly-sought after, unclimbed alpine north faces of the Matterhorn and Eiger. As in skiing, one doesn't feel like a badass linking turns on runs titled *Butterfly* or *Pussywillow*. Names depicting base bodily functions or those that invoke the Prince of Darkness like *Devil's Crotch* or *Child of Satan* lend an air of dignity. Unfortunately, as far as *Dernier* went, the title happened to be sarcastic. It wasn't supposed to be hard, but I hung shamefully on the rope, a dangling sack of potatoes spinning in the wind, as Red laughed.

The day before, after being awake for forty hours straight, I had gotten off the train in the middle of the night in the ancient city of Avignon. Like a shipwrecked sailor crawling ashore, I collapsed against the city's castle walls, which rose above me as they had for the returning Crusaders. As I sat trying to decipher the local advertisements, the street cleaners began hosing down the sidewalk and nearly washed me into the Mediterranean. A café opened in the wee hours; the waiter saw my pack and said he was a climber. I got excited, thinking the waiter could be a new climbing friend and the fabled Buoux must be near. Then the waiter told me to be quiet, wagging his index finger back and forth at me like I was a kindergartner. Being so jet-lagged and clueless, I was probably shouting at him. He was right. We Americans talk far too loudly—a point I can appreciate much more now. Still, there is nothing worse than being scolded by the first French person you meet, especially when he includes that dreaded *non, non, non* finger wag.

I had a longways to go to get to Apt, the small town in the Luberon range that served as a basecamp for the Buoux climbers. "Apt" and "camping" were all I could say to the bus driver despite a whole damn semester of French in high school. I had never been so uninspired by a subject; speaking French seemed sissy and pretentious; it conjured up nothing but images of stuck-up Paris high fashion. Yet, once in rural Provence, I wanted to kick myself for having blown learning the language off.

The bus quickly escaped the tight quagmire of Avignon for a lush Provençal countryside of stone villages and vineyards stretching to the horizon.

Entering Apt, the bus passed sprawling sidewalks of chairs and café tables.

"Camping, Apt. D'accord?" the driver said to me. "D'accord ... d'accord?" he repeated. I was dumbfounded. I struggled in the aisle with my big pack as the whole bus stared. Finally, the word *d'accord* came back from the depths of my long forgotten high school French class. It meant "okay."

True to Red's postcards, the campground was a dump. I found him sharing a caravan with a Norwegian guy named Lärs, a short, stocky red-haired fellow dressed in a permanent frown. As I entered the caravan, he glared angrily at my feet.

"What's the matter with Lärs?" I asked Red.

"He wants you to clean the mud off your shoes," Red explained.

"Oh. Sorry."

I went out and gave them a thorough scraping, but when I returned Lärs was still fixated on them. "Hello. Do you speak English, Lärs?" I asked, trying to be polite.

"Of course I speak English. In Norway we are taught many languages. We are not stupid! Take your shoes off and leave them outside!" he snapped. Then, no longer interested in me, he settled back down at the sorry little caravan table, which was piled high with papers.

"Lärs is making lists," said Red. "He makes lists of the best climbs and especially the best climbers. He is now making a list of the best American climbers."

"Well you can put me at the top; I'm the best from the West," I said for fun.

"I have not heard your name before!" Lärs scrambled excitedly for his pen. "What is your hardest climb?"

"He's just joking with you Lärs," interrupted Red.

While Red made a bland beef stew in the cramped, steamy caravan, Lärs never looked up from his lists nor changed his stern expression. Apparently, he spent untold hours obsessed with the chore, though he wasn't even paid for it. God knows what he was going to do with all his work.

There was no room for me to sleep in the caravan, so I was banished to the dirt outside. Without a tent or pad, I got wet quickly, but at least the ground was soft from many days of rain. The water soaking through my sleeping bag didn't even bother me compared to the feeling that I had passed on seeing castles, palaces, and museums in a frenzy to get there. Instead, I had rushed across Europe like a madman to join a campground chain gang.

The next morning, the sky was still overcast. In front of me, a blonde Scandinavian family sat dejectedly amongst the mud puddles like refugees on their rain-soaked bicycle tour of Provence. Their children ran to and fro smearing dirt all over their faces and bodies. This was one of my first impressions of Europe, and it was hardscrabble grim.

Buoux was nicknamed the laboratory, for all the aspiring climbers came far and wide to hone themselves on its pocketed limestone. It was truly an elite, international scene. I stood in the campground road, recognizing face after face from the covers of climbing magazines.

After a greasy croissant for breakfast, Red and I hitched a lift to the cliffs. Buoux lay in a valley of white limestone cliffs that contrasted sharply with the surrounding green trees and shrubs. The ruins of a mysterious fort stood high on a cliff. It was breathtaking.

Back in the caravan, Lärs laughed his head off when he heard I couldn't make any headway on Buoux's easiest route.

"And to think I was reaching for my pen to add you to my lists," he chortled.

Red and Lärs were redpointing about 5.12c, and the snobbery was endless. They considered any good climber—especially themselves—close to godhood, despite their dubious hang dogging tactics.

Making dinner was a belabored task as Lärs only ate a diet of broccoli. He actually had a scale to weigh it. What would happen if he suffered an overdose? After dinner, those two would grill me on how I did that day and snicker. Every day it seemed I would go and fail on some easy climb in Buoux, and every night, face the music. I was the caravan joke, and Red and Lärs enjoyed throwing me out every night to sleep in the dirt. There was nothing else to do. No cinema, no bookstores just a grimy café called the Gregoise. The little town of Apt was as interesting as Mayberry and nobody spoke English, or even worse, they preferred not to. I could only sulk and repeat to myself "I must get better, I must get better." But I wasn't getting any better. In fact, I was getting worse.

Nothing was going right on this strange new continent, even when I tried to buy supplies. The grocery stores were in the hellish commercial zone of brightly colored warehouse box stores, and inside, there actually wasn't that much food for sale. One third of the shelves were taken up by alcohol, one-third sugary biscuits, and the rest split between somewhat edible food and rows magazines, the majority of them pornographic.

After wandering the aisles flipping through my French phrasebook for the simplest of words, I settled on two baguettes. I gave the cashier, a girl with a frizzed poodle-like hairdo, a one-franc coin and held out my hand for change. She barked gibberish. One franc was all the money I had, so I went back and returned with only one baguette. Now hate and fire really poured out of her snapping mouth. This was the *real* French language, not the "Bonjour, Je m'appelle Sylvie" stuff from high school class. She threw the franc back at me.

"Why didn't you get any bread?" asked Red in the caravan. "We need it for dinner."

"Um, the baguettes didn't look fresh," I said, fumbling an excuse for my clueless state.

"What?" Red was incredulous. "The French bake them twice a day. The bread is the best thing they have to eat here."

"Really? How much do they cost anyway?"

After nearly a week, I finally began to recover from jetlag, and Red wanted to try a 5.11d called *Le Scorpion*. It was an absurdly steep route that began high above the ground on an airy ledge called *La Plage*, or The Beach. *Scorpion* hung well out over the valley, but the holds were jugs—huge, and easy to grip. Still, I had never seen or attempted anything so steep, and the technical crux was fittingly at the end, like the sting in a scorpion's tail.

"One of the Norwegians was so obsessed with flashing *Scorpion* that he jumped for the chains and sliced both his hands open," Red told me. "They took him to the hospital."

"Man, are all Norwegians masochists?" I asked.

"Doing first ascents of the hardest climbs, being winners—what else really counts?" Red replied, going into a typical tirade about the weak versus the strong. Rock climbing was being considered for an Olympic sport, and Red was dreaming about taking home the Gold.

As I started *Scorpion,* hundreds of feet of exposure suddenly appeared below me. The overhanging climbing exhausted me instantly. To be a savvy Francophile, I yelled down *"Bloc."* I had read that *bloc* meant 'hold the rope tight' in a magazine hyping French climbing.

"What does 'bloc' mean?" Red answered to my dismay.

"It means hold him on ze rope," interrupted a young German climber with long red hair, joining us on La Plage. His name was David (pronounced 'Dah-vid').

"Yes, hold me on the rope here, Red. My arms are blown," I said.

"You're only at the third bolt," the German said. "Perhaps you should lower down and let someone strong climb, *d'accord*?" Dahvid snickered.

Red, Lärs and now this new, highly-critical German, Dahvid, were putting the spotlight on me. It was like an awful elementary school gym class again, the athletic kids harassing those, like me, who weren't into dodgeball. Nothing but anxiety that I could only hope to survive and forget. It wasn't even my idea to try a route that hard.

That very afternoon, Red wanted to climb a 5.12a that required a brutal *monodoigt,* or one-finger pull-up. Attempting the 5.12a sent searing pain through my middle finger. I thought I had pulled a tendon, an extremely common injury at Buoux, which sidelined many a top climber for months. The repeated failures once again hung over me as 5.12a seemed utterly impossible, and yet 5.14a's were being done.

To add to my disgrace, I had purchased some blue tights, the kind I made fun of others for wearing, just before I left. To me, these tights were a compromise, not an outrageously bright color, not overly tight, and they didn't fit revealingly around the privates. Besides, they had thin knee pads sewn into them, and I needed something warmer than shorts to climb in when it got colder. I must have been brainwashed by the climbing magazines displaying photo after photo of stars climbing the impossible in lycra, since I believed they actually might help me. But the fiascoes continued day after day, and the tights didn't do a thing. Buoux was *the* place that really counted.

There was another climbing area an hour away from Apt called the Gorges du Verdon with huge gray limestone walls, home of Patrick Edlinger, that seemed like an essential part of the French climbing experience. Red and I met an English guy named Peter in the little youth hostel there. Peter was on his last holiday before joining the military, and he was on a drunken bender.

Peter had refused to speak proper French, replacing phrases like '*merci beaucoup*' with '*murky buckets*' to be deliberately rude. We laughed at his jokes but especially his accent when he told us to "foock off." In slurred tones, he told us of his hatred for the "Frogs," making it clear that he was from the superior race of Britannia, which doesn't have to learn any foreign languages at all since their empire established English as the world language. That silly Brit got plastered and insulted everyone in the hostel, reserving his worst abuse for a walking club of "Krauts" from Bern, Swiss, Krauts – same bloody thing according to Peter, that shared a table with us. They were dull company compared to Peter's off-color joke about a bloke accidentally dipping his toast in a leper's neck. Naturally the Swiss wanted it translated, but how can you explain a joke in such poor taste to the typically stern Swiss people who take everything literally?

After a week in the Verdon, we said goodbye to Peter and promised we'd come visit him at his home outside London. For me, the Verdon was a wonderful change and it was hard to be back at Buoux. The wild atmosphere on the enormous cliffs in the Verdon had wetted my appetite for adventure, so, after only a few days, I'd had enough of Red, Lärs, Dahvid and that caravan.

On every T.V. travel show, Europe was a fairy-tale land. All I knew, however, was that grimy campground and the word for "shit" in multiple languages—reverberating off the canyon walls as climbers fell off their climbs. After one especially provocative taunt by Red, I started packing my rucksack.

"I'm going to Switzerland. The land where mountain climbing began," I announced to Red's surprise. A thrill rose inside me.

In my mind, Switzerland would offer a clean break from the chest-thumping sport climbers. I had also heard that Geneva was a great place to do a semester abroad. With all its alpine mysteries and the possibility of attending school there, Switzerland took on the allure of paradise. It would provide a haven for me and I skipped down the road. I had no idea how to get there, but every step was joyful. At last I was alone on the road with complete freedom to discover Europe.

I put out my thumb for the first time, and before long, two young guys in a zippy, battered sports car picked me up.

"You are going to the station? Be careful of pickpockets," they warned sagely. "They are very good."

I gulped, stuffing my passport and money into my shoe, which made walking almost impossible. My French chauffeurs took me right to the station door. It was the first time I had ever been so much at the mercy of strangers. I felt vulnerable but grateful.

The journey north was difficult. I took a train to Grenoble but the connection to Geneva did not depart until the following morning. I found myself in a strange, cold city with almost no money. I ended up running in place all night in the shadows of a park as the temperature plummeted.

I finally arrived in Geneva, and stumbled out of the train and across the tracks only to be arrested. I was rudely shoved through unmarked doors and down a steep cement stairwell to a tiny office inhabited by men in formal black uniforms echoing the fashion flavors of Hitler's SS.

"Welcome to Switzerland," they cooed sarcastically.

After an hour of searching my pack, asking the same questions over and over again, and laboring over various forms, the police opened a mysterious side door. They tossed my passport, my now empty pack and its contents, and myself out onto the soaking wet streets of Geneva.

"Welcome to Switzerland!" mixed with laughter they repeated as the door slammed behind me.

Geneva was awful. True to story, it was impossibly expensive and the people were so rude I nearly went back to the train police station for company. Maybe the worst thing was the damn coocoo clocks for sale everywhere that kept going off every few minutes. I escaped by hitchhiking up to Interlaken and stayed at a cutesy youth hostel named Balmer's. The Eiger was obscured by clouds lending me none of the scenery that Kor experienced in 1966.

I tried to hitchhike to see the Matterhorn but only the police stopped to give me a lift. Switzerland was alternatively a police state or an overpriced kitschy tourist trap. I bought a train ticket back to France as fast as I could.

A few hours later, I arrived in Chamonix. Instantly, I was over-joyed to be back in the land of *fraternité, liberté* and *égalité*. The yellow head lights, the laissez-faire people and a charming dark-wood youth hostel whose proprietors didn't speak a word of English made me feel immediately at ease.

The morning dawned crystal clear as some Americans from the hostel and I boarded the *Telepherique de l'Aiguille du Midi*, the highest vertical ascent cable car in the world. The cable car creaked back and forth up a precipitously steep climb. We hovered over great rock faces and icy chutes, finally coming to rest on a spectacular tower of granite called the *Aiguille du Midi*. We had entered the world of the mountaineer.

On the shining steel patio, perched atop the granite spire hundreds of feet high, chilly fresh air bit into the lungs. We were nearly nine thousand feet above the Chamonix valley, and the high-altitude sunlight reflecting off the snow was absolutely blinding. Mysterious footprints disappeared over shimmering snow dunes in the direction of Mont Blanc. Precarious jagged rock spires collided with glaciers and dropped away into dark shadows stretching to the horizon.

I couldn't stop gaping at the alpine panorama. My fellow hostel-goers, pretty unromantic corporate America types, were bored. "It's just some snow and rock. What's the big deal?" they said, attacking my *faux pas* of getting excited. To them it was only cool to yawn at everything, put it down and make other travel plans. Mont Blanc, the sheer granite spires and the distant view of the Matterhorn, couldn't compete with the new fall line-up on television.

Those mountain travels had me running out of money fast, and after two days of hitchhiking, it was actually good to be back in the caravan after such a disastrous and expensive side trip like

Switzerland. Despite all my conflicts with the silly climbers, I could finally accept this was where I belonged. One night after a dinner of broccoli stew, when Red had gone out, I broke the awkward silence with the librarian, Lärs. I asked him who was at the top of his list for the best climber in the world? He told me about England's Ben Moon working to complete a 5.14b at Buoux.

"Well, who else is good who does more than sport climbing?" I asked.

"There is one man above all others for the dangerous traditional climbing, also from England, named Johnny Dawes."

"I've heard that name before," I nodded. "'The *infamous* Johnny Dawes' a caption read in a book."

"Yes, infamous is true, more like from another world."

Lärs leaned forward and actually got excited, telling me stories about Dawes like he was a Viking legend, perhaps the furious Norse god of victory, *Odin*, coming to crush dragons in battle. "There are more legends about Johnny Dawes than any other. His bold climbing, wild car driving, and many women. Johnny is different than Ben Moon. He becomes bored and cannot focus when the climbing is safe, but when dangerous ... he shines like a champion."

Lärs went on for what seemed like hours. Dawes clearly thrived on danger; a proud instigator of England's infamous "chop" routes—where if you fall you get the chop. On a Welsh sea cliff, Johnny had led a 5.13a first ascent on-sight with no protection. The holds broke off under his weight—certain death if he fell. The whole route later collapsed into the sea.

"Do you know him, Lärs?"

"No, I would like to meet him very badly. It is rumored Johnny Dawes is coming here to Buoux. It is my dream to shake his hand, a hand that has dared so much." After a reverent pause, Lärs continued, "I am staying in the other Norwegian caravan. You may sleep inside here tonight if you wish."

Yes, the adventurous soul of climbing was alive somewhere, and Dawes, like a dark knight of the north, was descending on Buoux any day now. I hoped to get just a glimpse of him and half expected to hear the James Bond theme playing when he did. Despite the luxury of sleeping in the caravan instead of the mud outside, my rest was disturbed by images of nightmarish chop routes and sea cliffs crumbling into pounding sets of Welsh waves.

The most ridiculous car went up for sale in the campground for $50. It was not the usual tiny French clown car but a large bright pink British Vauxhall Victor with flowers painted all over. The owner, an American named Eric, had driven the car down from Leeds, U.K. The car had no registration or insurance papers and couldn't pass the British safety inspection, so it was a sketchy purchase. The brakes were almost non-existent; it guzzled the $7-a-gallon gas; and handling the right- hand-drive British monster made me feel like a sweaty-palmed sixteen-year-old during my first driving lesson. But for the minimal investment of $25 each, it was worth the risk for some transportation and fun. Dubbed "Pink Floyd" as a salute to the psychedelic pink exterior, the car brought a smile or laugh to anyone who saw it.

The next day Red, and I drove Pink Floyd to the nearest climbing shop, which was nestled in the university town of Aix-en-Provence. Our quest was for Ninja slippers, ridiculous bright green climbing shoes, currently the favorite footwear at Buoux. They fit tightly and could be crammed into the limestone holes to great advantage.

Our pink marvel wobbled down the winding roads of the Luberon, past the remarkable village Lourmarin with its dreamy chateau sitting above green fields. Lakes and vineyards accented the lush countryside, and trees lined the picturesque Provençal roads shading the way. An hour later, we arrived in the center of Aix-en-Provence. In front of us was Aix's largest fountain, where enormous stone dolphins spat water into a pond. Traffic sped around the fountain and down a stunning tree-lined boulevard, Cours Mirabeau, with one beautiful sidewalk café after another. We happily parked on the sidewalk, as Pink Floyd's traffic transgressions were untraceable, and the parking tickets made good scratch paper.

The climbing shop stacks of European gear entrancing me like the Forrest Mountain Shop did as a kid but, best of all, the shop was located across from a medieval cathedral with carvings of saints ascending the archways. Romantic cafes, bars and restaurants lined Aix's narrow, twisting medieval streets, and glamorous boutiques sold ultra-chic and bizarre fashions. French culture stood like the Pyramids of Giza.

"I've never seen so many gorgeous babes in one place," exclaimed Red. "Get your shoes and let's meet some 'birds,'" he added, imitating Peter's slang.

At an outdoor cafe set in a glorious stone square, we chatted with a Canadian girl who was getting full credit at her university back home for studying French in Aix.

"You should sign up for the spring semester," she laughed. "It's just a party."

I was sold in an instant. I could enjoy the good life of Aix and drive up to Buoux other days. No more campground where every night in November climbers passed the evening hours huddled in toilet stalls for warmth.

Back in Pink Floyd we cheerfully tore up the two parking tickets left on the windscreen. The thought of going to school in Aix gave the world a new magic. It was actually cheaper than CU Boulder to do a semester in Aix at the Institute and I would get credit at home. In the coming days, I convinced my parents it would be a worthwhile investment in my education and we could fund it out of my college account. I was all set to begin in early February but what would I do with myself over Christmas break?

I met a Brit in the campground looking for a partner who wanted a belay on a hard route. I wondered if he might be the legendary Dawes. No, he was Mark from London. He had a fast, flashy silver sports car and didn't demand my inflated share of petrol money for the fifteen-minute drive to Buoux and was studying in Aix.

Late in the day, with Mark belaying. Feeling pleased, I started up *Jolinouille*, a 5.11d, the grade "where the big boys start," as Peter put it. I had never completed a 5.11d, but I figured I would get started trying to learn the moves for someday when I was strong enough. My new Ninja slippers fit in the little limestone holes like magic. At the crux, I put my middle finger into the route's notorious *monodoigt*, and simultaneously felt both feet slip. I began to reach for the quickdraw with my free hand, ready to surrender, ready to fall onto the rope, but as I did so I overheard a conversation below. Apparently, Mark knew both Ben Moon and Johnny Dawes, who had just arrived.

"Come on," yelled up Dawes. "You can't stop there! Get your feet back on!"

With one hand inches from the quickdraw, and the rest of my weight hanging entirely off the one finger wedged deeply, I hesitated. It would be so easy, so normal a thing to grab the quickdraw and have Mark lower me off, but having two of the best climbers in the world telling me not to quit was a powerful thing. It was like being an amateur guitarist playing on open mic night when Keith Richards and Mick Jagger drop by. Johnny actually started jumping up and down, telling me to give it my all. Considering my climbing record, especially at Buoux, it was against every probability that I could pull on that one finger and reach a hold above it. But Johnny was there, jumping up and down in the back of my mind as I powered past the holes, and in a blur, I was fighting for air, clipping the anchor chain after on-sighting a 5.11d at Buoux. It was a breakthrough to a new universe due to the magic of Dawes' mysterious inspiration.

The two leading climbers couldn't have been more personable. Moon was a soft-spoken, pale and skinny Rastafarian with a mighty pack of dreadlocks pulled back into an awkward ponytail. Dawes was broad-shouldered, short and dark-haired. He had on a light tweed jacket complete with handkerchief in the breast pocket, as though he was due at a fancy dinner party within the hour.

Dawes gave me a lift back to the campground in his supercharged black Peugeot 205, and I discovered that his driving was just as unhinged, yet just as calculated, as his notoriously dangerous ascents in England and Wales. I had just experienced my greatest breakthrough in climbing and was bubbling with excitement and gratitude, when I noticed French drivers snapping past inches from my window. Sitting in the English right-hand drive, I experienced the full horror of the left seat of Johnny's car as we screamed through the tight bends and tiny roads of the normally tranquil Provençal countryside. Dawes hunched over the wheel, totally obsessed and focused in his own private Grand-Prix video game. He played this "game" with an intensity that alarmed even the reckless French. Dawes got all four tires squealing in a four-wheel drift around a curve and it became obvious to anyone a madman was behind the wheel. The already insane French drivers backed off, enraged or frightened, which was really something to see, and Dawes responded with rounds of diabolical laughter.

INDIA CALLING

Johnny came along with most of the climbers in the campground to Apt's sad *Café Gregois* for lack of anything better to do. In the corner was a video jukebox with a limited selection of horrendous music videos. Multiple nationalities of climbers gathered to pass the evening hours in a warm place and watched the campy videos in disbelief. A particularly atrocious video of Kylie Minogue, the Australian pop star, singing *I should be so lucky* became a sarcastic anthem.

"You lads can take the Mickey can't you?" said Johnny cheerfully. "Brilliant, but this place is boring now. I know. Let's go climb the church."

Outside in the dark medieval streets of Apt, Johnny organized us to make a human bridge across an alley using two people with opposing pressure to move upwards like a crab. I pushed off one wall and he the other, but I fumbled to get a purchase on the wall.

"Damn, I can't."

"Come on, try harder." Johnny could balance on a ledge a half-an-inch wide as though it was a sidewalk. "Put your whole self into it. Come out of your shell!"

Though I couldn't play his game, I began to understand the value of giving something a fully-concentrated, yet playful effort like Dawes did. No matter what he was doing, Johnny gave it his all. He was easily the most inspiring person I'd ever met. He proceeded to climb on stone church walls, balance on chain fences, traverse under bridges, and perform every acrobatic feat – some quite dangerous – Apt could offer. Johnny exploded in a torrent of energy much like Layton Kor's reportedly pell-mell behavior.

Finally, I had met a world-class climber and he didn't obsess over broccoli diets or read training books. His only training theory was to keep it real, go berserk and give it your all!

The next morning, there was a pounding on the caravan door. I sat up and lazily rubbed my eyes before looking out the window. Johnny Dawes was waking *me* to go climbing!

Inside our tiny caravan, Dawes traversed the cheap molding, as excited as a kid on a rollercoaster, his trademark tongue curling over his upper lip. Apparently, the drinks and the three a.m. acrobatics had no effect on his whirling vitality. Dawes brought an energy that changed the whole day—a day about to explode.

"Feeling keen today," Dawes said. "Come on, let's go! Let's go!"

Lärs returned from the open market holding bags overflowing with broccoli. His initial annoyance at finding someone in the caravan with his shoes on disappeared when he recognized Johnny and went "star struck."

"It is such an honor to meet you, Johnny." Lärs stammered, drooling submissively. "Do you have a specific training technique in mind for your climbs, may I ask?"

"No, I just do whatever I feel like. Hey, is this some kind of fucking interview? I just came by to nab Tom for a day's cragging."

"You wish to climb with *him?*" Lärs pointed at me in surprise. A smirk spread across his face.

"Yes, he on-sighted *Jolinouille* yesterday, but most importantly he's a good laugh."

"*Jolinouille?* Zat's 7a. Impossible for him," Lärs laughed. "He has told you a story. He is too weak for 6b."

"I fucking saw him, mate! You rude Norwegian tosser!" Johnny railed at him. "Come on, Tom. Let's piss off to the crags."

Lärs was crestfallen. Like all elitists, snobs, and list-makers large or small, he was made of paper. I watched Lärs crumple as we tore out of the campground in a spectacle of dust and gravel.

"You need some new mates, Tom. Come 'round to our caravan. There's a load of lads coming down from Sheffield tonight."

That day Johnny's wild driving angered more than just motorists. As though possessed by his Formula One racing hero, the Brazilian Ayrton Senna, he spun us completely around in a tight curve using a full brake slide. As smoke came pouring out of the tire wells, a French villager ran outside his country mansion to shake his fist and grace us with that immortal word: "*Merde!*"

Scrambling up to the La Plage ledge, Johnny described his first ascent of the Gritstone chop route *Gaia* (5.12d X). He had to kill a "ladybird," U.S. ladybug, sunning herself on a key exit hold to avoid hitting the ground from seventy feet up. But the death of the bug made him cry. For all his macho leads, Johnny was remarkably sensitive—more a prophet than a Sylvester Stallone stunt-double. Dawes shone with the magic insights that dangerous climbing brings to the human mind, he had mastered what I really climb for: that unexplainable illumination.

On La Plage, Johnny encouraged me to have another go at *Scorpion* but I was pretty lucky with *Jolinouille* which was only vertical with long reaches between pockets. *Scorpion* was still too steep.

"Stop thinking about the grade," Johnny scolded. "It's a just a number. Your human worth is not the difficulty you climb. That's what pratts like that Norwegian think, but free yourself. Each movement is an experience you must get past the surface of. The racecar driver Senna was in perfect harmony with his Formula One engine throttle openings. He knew just when to shift, accelerate, brake.

That's what you need even more than fitness. You must give up trying to control it and become completely in sync with the rock. Try to understand what it is trying to tell you. Think in kinetic motions and shapes, not through words."

With Dawes' instructions in mind, I lurched up the steep moves and found I could do them. The wall overhung the valley hundreds of feet below, but I didn't notice. Five feet from the chain anchors, my forearms screaming, I finally had complete muscle failure and fell. However, I had fumbled the final crux moves, I had pushed it with all I had and nearly made the nasty finish.

"The finish is hard," I said. "One of those Norwegian climbers jumped for the chains and sliced his hands open."

"Yes, that's what I'm talking about," Johnny said thoughtfully. "People like that don't care about the shapes, the process that Buoux has laid out before them. They're desperate enough to hurt themselves because they think success is to knock off another route on their list. They whore Buoux."

"I have to admit, the first time I heard of you was in a book that called you 'the infamous Johnny Dawes,' I was jealous, but now I feel stupid," I said.

"Did you see how fat I was in that picture? Lots of people want what I have, but they have no idea what it is like to be me. Their empty heads just want."

"When I climb with my normal partner, Red, *he wants me to fail.* I start feeling down and wonder why I even bother. The problem is there is usually no one else to climb with and someday I want to burn him off by doing *Genesis*."

"That's the key! He wants you to hate yourself, so you are already defeated. Bashing your esteem is an old favorite from the Empire days, one of our many dirty tricks, like the old 'divide and conquer.' Teaching people shame is the easiest way to control them. Another Empire classic was hooking the Chinese on opium; for you Americans, it was getting your Indians drunk."

I had found more than an idol and coach: we shared a kinship based on a bizarre sense of dark humor, enthusiasm for life, and a desire to break away from all the traditional confines our respective countries offered. Johnny's excitability was incredibly un-British, and I had been told many times that it was my worst quality. One is expected to remain cool and devoid of emotion.

Then Dawes went into a fury on-sighting hard routes, leaping from one hold to another, with ferocious dynamic moves. With me belaying, he made the second ascent of *Mauvais Sang*, 8a or 5.13b, while the overhanging walls sheltered us from a gentle rain. The name, which means "Bad Blood," from a poem by Rimbaud, rang with meaning for both of us with our respective brutal empirical heritages.

Johnny Dawes had arrived like a prophesized superman setting fire to Buoux, but he was nothing like I had imagined, especially in becoming a friend. Dawes was "out there," a refreshingly right-brained individual and *Inner Game of Tennis* incarnate. I've learned that a lot of people write him off as mad, but if you are willing to listen to his ramblings, pearls fell off his plate along with the scraps.

Johnny was right about the British invasion—not the Beatles, but all sorts of wild characters from up north overwhelmed the campground. Many had hairstyles in copies of Bob Marley's dreadlocks. Though the French were mostly cordial hosts, these dreadlocked 'Britafarians' were impossibly rude. As they saw it, climbing was *their* sport and they wanted to make it clear, with echoes of Peter, they were a superior race to the Frogs. To the Brits it was simply tradition. Ever since the 1960s, the likes of British hard-man Don Whillans raised the bar high for British climbers abroad to heap deadly wit and abuse on foreigners during his visits to the Continent.

Much theft is political, or at least that is the prevailing excuse of the perpetrators, in this case the Britafarians. Since Victor

Hugo wrote *Les Misérables,* France suffered from the blind reluctance to prosecute for stealing food—especially Hugo's symbolic loaf of bread. To many naughty Brits abroad, this French custom was a green light to don large down "duvets," or U.S. parkas, with deep pockets even in warm weather and relieve the grocery stores of some of their stock. Some lads even had the nerve to load up shopping trolleys and simply push them right out the "In" door. For those few who were caught, about the worst thing that could happen was the store manager taking their names down and lecturing them in bad English.

The top British climbers were fun and inspiring company, especially Johnny Dawes, but I soon discovered that there was a dark side to his world. I found Johnny crying on a prow high over Buoux.

"I'm bloody finished with this shit, fucking hell!" His voice roared through the canyon. "I'm just a coward. It's those people who work nine-to-five that are the real heroes."

Here was the bravest of climbers, the master of death-defying stunts, having a breakdown. It was like seeing the Wizard of Oz looking cheap and foolish behind the curtain. After leading *Blackwalk,* the somewhat dangerous 5.10cR in high school, I figured that anyone who could face down the terrors of the crags must be superhuman and certainly not prone to such despair.

"Damn Johnny, it's strange to see you crying," I admitted. "You have everything: fame, women, money, that Peugeot. I guess I thought being a top climber could, well, save me from something. I thought to achieve that degree of confidence a person must be onto some kind of salvation."

"Is that what you thought? That's the American mind. Fame can really fuck with my head, actually. All kinds of people telling me I'm great and wanting to be my friend. They don't know what great is. Greatness is crying sometimes. I told you how I cried on *Gaia* because there was a ladybird on a key hold. I had to squash her or die myself. Killing her really upset me in the middle of a dangerous route. It's at those moments I know all life is one, yet I had to kill her and I died a little too. Suppressing our emotions is the British way, living in quiet desperation. You don't know Britain yet do you?"

"No, I haven't been."

"Have you ever heard of 'fagging?' I was sent away to boarding school when I was six. Could you imagine leaving your mum at six-years-old to be a servant to the older boys and buggered and beaten the rest of your school career? I was small, so they brutalized me and told me I was inadequate. They humiliated me every chance they got, trying to make me believe I'm a little elf freak!"

Johnny started sobbing again. It was awful. Apparently, possibly getting raped and abused at boarding school was part of the price of membership in the British aristocracy. The disgusting tradition of "fagging" made his story disturbing yet impressive he survived it. I searched for some light amidst his grim tale and thought about Fairview Dome and what I had learned in yoga class. Within Johnny's despair, I heard a voice calling me to India. I had discovered something special with yoga, tested it through climbing, and began to realize this was the time to do something about it.

"Do you know who Layton Kor is?"

"I've heard the name."

"He's like a Joe Brown or Chris Bonington but in America. One day he quit climbing for religion. I don't want to be a Jehovah's Witness, but his renunciation made me wonder about life beyond climbing. I took a yoga class back home where we learned meditation, and it sent me to another world. I could climb better too. Now I want to go to India someday and see what that stuff can really do."

"Really? How did it happen?" Johnny stopped crying and there was a rise of excitement in his voice.

"Well, one day I did some breathing exercises and then just went flying up a climb I couldn't touch before. The holds just went by. I couldn't take credit for it."

"That's it! It's what happens to me on dangerous solos and rally-car driving, too. The world comes alive. People say I've got a death wish, but there is no death, no life, no good, no bad or evil. When I'm done, they say what a great person I am, but my climbing was done in a dream. I've done bugger all! Yes, yes, yes. Maybe everything is going to be all right!" Johnny jumped up and down. I had never seen a mood change so fast. "Right, now I'm keen. Time for some hard climbing."

We went to the *Rose* area, the most elite of sectors at Buoux, where the wall overhangs formidably, and the *easiest* climb is 5.13b. Dawes attempted the famous *La Rose et le Vampire*, which required successive one or two-finger dynos, launching the climber from pocket to pocket.

Belaying Dawes was like deep-sea fishing. He grabbed the pocket below the crux and shot through the air only to miss and take jolting falls, while I aerobically let out and took in rope as fast as I could.

"Fucking hell!" He would roar with annoyance, impatiently pulling himself back up to his high point, only to jump and miss the hold again. The top-sponsored European climbers with their shiny matching equipment and bright tights watched in amazement at his manic efforts. Johnny climbed with the off-kilter immediacy of Jimi Hendrix's *Purple Haze* thundering at top decibel.

Dawes had borrowed Ben Moon's rope and the white core was protruding through the sheath from taking his violent falls.

"It was brand new, and the only one I have!" Ben steamed. Johnny naturally paid him no notice; the Jim Morrison of rock climbing pushed it to the limit every time.

Maybe I cheered Dawes up, but the image of his tormented, earlier talk haunted me. Dawes was incredibly wealthy: he grew up driving rare Ferraris on his parents' country estate. He was on the cover of climbing magazines, yet even he wasn't free from an inner hell. Clearly something is wrong with Western values. How many of our lauded idols are reaching for a bottle of booze or a vial of pills, sobbing in private? Suddenly it was clear: climbing, like fame and fortune, isn't the ultimate answer. I knew that someday I must travel East and seek these answers through yoga. I shuddered at the perilous journey ahead.

By late November, the infamous Mistral was blowing a freezing wind across Provence, and most of the climbers, including Dawes, had gone home. Ice forming on the inside of the caravan window convinced Red and I to migrate to the British guy Mark's apartment in Aix. As the Mediterranean sun lost its ability to warm rock, fingers and spirits, Mark's offer became too good to pass up. Pink Floyd had overheated so we sold it to some newly arrived Norwegian climbers for $100, and persuaded Dahvid to give us a ride to Aix in his VW bus. Dahvid didn't want to stay. He didn't think much of Aix.

"At least my city Freiburg is half freak and half sissy. Zis Aix is all sissy!" he said.

True, Aix fashion was French chic at its most effeminate; the men hung brightly colored scarves on their necks over pink shirts and sipped $15 cocktails in the fashionable cafes. But with ice forming in our caravan, I was willing to put up with some poseurs for a warm apartment.

Genuinely dejected, Dahvid dropped us off and pointed his camper north toward the German winter gloom to begin his sorrowful journey home to Freiburg to pass the holidays. I could imagine him sitting at his parents Christmas dinner table amongst the decorations fuming and obsessing about climbing. He swore he'd return in February.

Red and I ended up staying with Mark for several weeks. Cafes such as Les Deux Garcons, a former hang of Paul Cezanne, Emile

Zola, and Pablo Picasso, were ideal for watching glamorous French girls. They mesmerized us, tossing their hair about with sunglasses always remaining perfectly balanced on their heads and blowing smoke from roll-up Gitanes cigarettes in great clouds. Aix has been aptly described as a real-life Fellini film with eye-popping glamorous Euro-girls like models from *Elle* and *Vogue.* Yet it had a quiet European charm that oozed an old-world romance like Rick's café in *Casablanca.* It sure beat a night in the toilet stalls of the Apt campground.

Despite the sweet life around him, Aix was lost on Mark. "When I see the white cliffs of Dover, I know I am home," he told us with a twinge.

Studying abroad among the Frogs was a lonely semester for Mark. At the time, I didn't realize how ridiculous his homesickness for England was, especially in winter. He made his island sound like a paradise, a beacon of civilization. Since I hadn't been to England yet, I could hardly disagree. I had to spend the holiday somewhere before my semester in Aix began, so in early December, Red and I decided to go visit Peter and see Britain for ourselves.

France's hyper-speed train, the TGV, took us quickly to Paris, but, even after a long consultation of a metro map and extensively exploring the underground warren of *Le Metro*, we were lost. Red had been to Paris before and thought he knew the way to pass through the capital to northern France and get a ferry across the channel.

I had never been in a big city before, not even our own New York City or Los Angeles. Paris was supposed to be the classiest city on earth, but no romantic icon like the Eiffel Tower could be seen from the claustrophobic tunnels in which we wandered. Alluringly beautiful girls hustled by with bouquets of flowers in their hands, and, at one turn, a whole Rasta band was playing Bob Marley's "Get up, Stand up, Stand Up For Your Rights" for a group of leather-clad youth drinking wine out of paper bags. The music echoed eerily, beckoning us, through the tunnels.

We reached the Gare du Nord, but there were no trains out that night and we forced to spend the night in Paris. We stood in the train station entrance contemplating dark, drizzling streets. The youth hostel was full. We dumbly stared out at the rain, waiting and watching the crowds of people hurrying by. Many of them were of African heritage and they carried the same grace and *egalité* as the French. Red asked a big black guy with a diamond earring if he knew of a place to stay. The man approached us, grinning peacefully, and said that when the station closed at eleven we could sneak into an abandoned train car and sleep for free.

It was only nine, so we stepped outside to see the famous city at last, but still no Eiffel Tower was in sight. Instead, building fronts rose around us while endless rain soaked the streets. No sooner were we on the sidewalk than a screaming girl pushed by with a red-faced guy chasing her. She was running for her life. He jumped to grab her but hit his head on a pole and fell down unconscious. A ring of pedestrians formed around the scene and laughed. Ten seconds on the big city streets and we had witnessed an attempted crime of passion.

We checked for hotel rooms but they were far too expensive. My spirits sank.

Red suggested that we have a beer in a cafe and get out of the rain. So, we entered a grimy street-level place with a line of old men standing at the bar, drinking without having stools to sit on. I dropped our packs at a table away from the crowd while Red ordered at the bar.

"*Non, non, non,*" scolded the bartender, pointing at me and letting loose the dreaded French finger wag.

"We've got to stand at the bar or they charge us double," Red explained, "and these already cost $7 a piece." He handed me a beer in tiny glass.

Reluctantly, I pulled our bags back over to the bar, and we stood there like part of the regiment. The locals were verbally abusing a sad-looking old fellow at the end of the bar. I couldn't understand the dialogue, but the tones were nasty and sarcastic. The bartender joined in, sneering first at the man and then at Red and me for piling our unruly bags on his floor. Despite the crowd of men at the bar, the scene echoed the desperation and loneliness of the metropolis from Hemingway's short story "A Clean Well Lit Place." I wore the innocence of rural Provence around me like a halo, but it was beginning to wear thin. Lined up at the sad bar with a bunch of bastards, I could do without the company and the big city life. I could see why Emile Zola labeled big cities "the holocaust of humanity."

We downed our tiny beers just in time to return before the station closed. I found myself climbing into the stale smells of a boxcar and we crouched down to hide while nearby loudspeakers blared the closing announcements.

After fifteen minutes, all seemed safe, and we stretched out on the seats, proud of ourselves for sneaking a night on the cheap.

I got into my sleeping bag and bridged across two seats. The small gap in the middle didn't support me, but at least I'd get some sleep.

We had just dozed off when we heard a desperate cry nearby. "Ohhhh. Moooon Dieu! Aaahhhhhhhh! Oh ma petite daaaaah,"

Both of us bolted upright.

"What the hell is that?"

"Stay cool," cautioned Red. "The back of the car is full of hobos."

We sat captive while the most lonely, heart-wrenching moans I had ever heard filled the train car. They sounded like the tormented ghosts of a Dickens novel. I wanted to tune them out and sleep, but I was afraid of being jumped in the night. We might have to fight for our lives.

"So are you awake?" Red whispered an hour later.

"You kidding me?"

"Yeah. Jesus, I'd pay anything for a locked room now," he admitted.

"Maybe they're too drunk to be dangerous."

On American T.V., travel shows painted Paris as the city of sophistication, everyone sipping champagne under the Eiffel Tower night and day. We were seeing the other side of the "city of light and knowledge." I lay wide-awake as howls of despair lit up the night and haunted my soul. It wasn't just sleep lost because of some drunken fools; it was a descent into the very pits of hell.

Suddenly, one of our cohabitants abruptly screamed "Sophie! Sophie!" at the top of his lungs. *Who was Sophie, and what regretful past was he confessing to?*

Sometimes the moans and shrieks cut to the bone; the way I felt when I saw Johnny Dawes crying. Why make a horror movie with vampires or with chainsaws and limbs flying? The *real* lost faces of humanity are much scarier.

For me, that night provided a chilling lesson of the bitter remorse felt by those who didn't search for their pearl. I had to find a way out, or I would end up emotionally crippled like the man yelling "Sophie!" During the long, bleak hours, the idea of really studying yoga worked its way deeper into my thick skull. It also seemed important to immerse myself in yoga's birthplace and not be satisfied taking a course back home taught by Americans. I had to really know yoga from its source. It was my second time called.

In the morning, we boarded our train, and, as it pulled out of the Gare du Nord, my first sight of daytime Paris was of smashed-out windows above the grimy station tunnel. The television cameras never featured that on the travel programs either. The scene was a medieval nightmare, and I felt sick to my stomach. Yet as the light of day unfolded, some normalcy returned with the familiarity of travel and it helped me shed my horror. I found that the lessons of Johnny's torment and the desperate characters from Paris's underbelly could be shaken off. India's call loosened its grip. After all, we would see what England will bring. Before I tromped across the wastes of Asia, which I really couldn't afford to do, something more had to happen—something that would send me to India with no turning back.

THE THIRD TIME CALLED

Just getting from France to England was ominous. Our ferry rocked wildly pulling out of Calais. The sad cafeteria, decorated with pictures of miserable, wet fishermen on the walls, offered nothing but soggy, deep-fried food. Spending the previous night sleepless in the Paris boxcar, it was hard to see the cheer in anything. Fish and chips with a rancid brown sauce on the side didn't help. It was an ill-advised diet, especially on a wobbly ferry boat, and I soon felt nauseous.

"Is this really what they eat in England?" I asked.

"Raahhther, old boy," said Red, feigning an upper-crust British accent. "Fish and chips—just like in Buckingham Palace."

"Yeah, that was a royal feast," I said sarcastically, feeling queasier than ever and already chilled by the breeze off the bow. "So why are we going *north* in winter? There can't be any climbing this time of year."

"Because it's gonna be hilarious to see Peter and to party with his mates."

At that moment, the loudspeaker barked: *"All non-U.K. citizens must fill out embarkation forms prior to being interviewed by British Customs Agents."*

After we had labored over the dismal forms for twenty minutes, Red went in for his interview.

"Watch what you say to those immigration pricks," he said wearily on return. When one dislikes authority they can quickly tell, and Red had it written all over him. Though he no longer had his hair styled in a Mohawk, Red made a big point of maintaining his punk-rock persona, which included hating cops.

When my turn came, at first, I didn't see what Red was talking about. The customs officer looked like a wholesome apple-pie middle-aged man in a cheerful white uniform with sparkling gold buttons. He would have fit right in on the *Love Boat* T.V. show, except for the scowl on his face.

"'Ello," I said cheerfully, only to receive his sudden, dirty look.

The customs official gave me the third degree and I found myself agreeing with Red very quickly. For some reason, I had anticipated a bumbling, self-effacing official like Eric Idle of the Monty Python comedy series, and I was dying to say, "I didn't expect the Spanish Inquisition." As I stood there fighting a splitting headache from our rough night in Paris, I wondered why this man was so eager to keep me out of the land of George Orwell, Roger Waters, J.R.R. Tolkien, Led Zeppelin and the Rolling Stones. His grimace gave me the foreboding that maybe the U.K. wasn't the land of uproarious laughter and rock-and-roll after all. Disappointment crossed his face when he found no crimes worth displaying my head on a pole at the Tower of London. He stamped my passport dejectedly.

"Enjoy your visit to the U.K.," he said employing what I had learned is the favored language of police and customs agents abroad: sarcasm.

That was before we even *saw* the damn white cliffs of Dover.

Two hours later, we stood freezing in the chaos of Victoria Station. Signs, ads, colors and noises swirled in the historic station, and we stared open-mouthed at stunning girls chatting with enchanting English accents while snow-white pigeons flew about the ceiling. In the background, Victoria's intercom eerily droned:

Passengers are reminded to Mind the Gap...Mind the Gap... Mind the Gap...

Phrases like "mind the gap" were so strange that British-English felt like a foreign language. We sifted through a mad rush of commuters shooting in all directions while searching in vain for one of those classic British red telephone booths to call Peter. The red boxes were already a relic of the past, as Prime Minister Margaret Thatcher had been modernizing the U.K. by selling them off to our American theme restaurants.

Navigating the huge mess called London did not alleviate my headache. To make matters worse, we found we had to take another train to Gravesend, backtracking an hour south, the direction, from which we had just come. Even though we were finally in an English-speaking country, travelling was still an ordeal, and everything was more expensive than even France.

The British Railway ticket-counter person was a black Rastafarian with an eloquent James Bond accent. Our gold pound-and-pence change shot back at us out of the kiosk with the same "ka-ching!"sound effect at the beginning of Pink Floyd's *Money*, and we realized we were in the land of British rock. The same thing happened using a drab grey payphone, when we called Peter's flat, as the ringtone was right out of *The Wall* album when "Pink" calls home.

"This is the United States calling for Mrs. Floyd from Mr. Floyd. Are we reaching?" said Red into the receiver, mimicking the Pink Floyd sound effect of a nosy and nasal sounding American operator. "There seems to be a man answering."

"Wha' the 'ell?" answered a confused Peter on the other end.

An hour and a half later, we waited for Peter to rescue us from the Gravesend train station in the coldest, wettest wind I've ever suffered through. The town looked as gloomy as its name, the result of its designation as a mass grave site during the Black Plague. We watched the pale orb called the sun set in the clouds to the west. Considering it was only 3:30 p.m., and otherwise rarely seems to come completely out, I'm surprised the English even have a name for the sun. Nearly dark and the biter wind ensured Red and I both had head colds under construction.

Peter took us to his parents' house where his "mum" had prepared a traditional English dinner of roast beef and potatoes. She and his father were very polite, though there was a hushed silence at the table. It was my first time experiencing the zombie-like British reserve. A portrait of Her Majesty hung prominently on the wall and "Liz" the second looked at me very disapprovingly. Peter had been quite the "lager lout" in France, so it was amusing to see him chafing at the bit of self-restraint in front of his parents.

"Could I have some ketchup with my roast beef, please?" I asked at the table.

"Sorry, Dear, you would like what?" Peter's mum responded.

"Some ketchup?"

"Yes, I'll just go see." She went into her kitchen, motioning Peter to follow.

In a harsh whisper that was just audible in the dining room, she asked him what it was I wanted.

"He wants to put *tom-ah-toe sauce* on his roast beef."

"*Tom-ah-to* sauce on roast beef?!" There was a thoughtful pause and then: "He's not staying long, is he?"

"Oi Tom! It's called *tom-ah-to* sauce," Peter blared at me back in the dining room. "We don't put it on a *proper* roast beef dinner here, mate. This isn't bloody Burger King."

His mum placed a bottle of ketchup—sorry, I mean *tom-ah-to sauce*—in front of me, but as I sliced the roast beef and dipped it into the red sauce, I knew I had committed a treasonous crime. I felt beams of hatred aimed at me, as though I had halted the Royal carriage and vomited on the Queen.

The morning after we arrived, I awoke on the couch in Peter's living room to the sound of rain spattering the window with the force of a car wash.

"Doesn't it ever stop raining here?" I asked, fearing the answer.

"You know the difference between winter and summer in England?" Peter replied, "The rain is warmer. Tom, put the kettle on and brew up some bloody tea, if that's not too much for a Yank to do."

I dutifully boiled the water.

"Bloody hell!" exclaimed Peter on his return to the kitchen, outraged to find tea bags floating in the kettle. The Japanese Zen tea ceremony has nothing on the fussy English method for brewing a "proper cuppa." Nothing could be more British than a good brew, I was told, though of course the leaves are grown in the Far East. I also quickly discovered that tea and a jumper, or sweater, provided the only central heating.

"Now get your kit and let's go for a climb," Peter ordered, assembling a special treat of Marmite sandwiches and humming their advertisment: "My mate Marmite."

"What if it's still raining?" Red and I protested. "Won't the rock be wet?"

"Come on you Yankee puffs. The first thing to learn about Britain is if you wait for the rain to stop, nothing will ever happen."

Peter warmed up his rusty car, an "Imperial Princess." It sputtered and coughed, sending a large cloud of silver exhaust across his driveway.

"Is this what Princess Di drives?" Red asked, convulsing with laughter.

"Show some respect for our royalty or piss off!" replied Peter angrily. He was dead serious. Every human being in the world was a worthless Frog, Kraut, Dego or, worst of all—Yank. But, for Peter, the Royal Family was beyond reproach.

Peter took us to breakfast at a truck stop along a busy motorway. It was the greasiest food I had ever put in my mouth, and it left little dots of oil in my tea. Even the toast was fried. We left with a dry, chalky coating in our throats from an overdose of lard.

"That hit the spot," Peter said, gunning the Princess through a roundabout with all kinds of traffic going in crazy patterns. Momentarily forgetting that the English drive on the left, Red and I both screamed like little girls when a truck came straight for us in the right lane.

"Oh, shut up you Yanks," Peter spouted, speeding on through the Kent rolling green countryside to an isolated car park for the climbing area. The gray skies remained, but the rain stopped for a while. It was freezing, and I was wearing all the clothes I had.

It was back to basics English style. No bolts, no chalk and no harnesses allowed. With only a ratty old rope, climbing shoes, one long sling and a carabiner; we were packed for the day.

"The rock is still wet," I objected at the base of a slab.

"Go on you Nancy boy."

Ten feet up, I lost my grip on the moist rock slab and the rope around my waist crunched harshly into my ribs barely caught by Peter's hip belay.

"Damn it, Peter. I can't breathe. This is how people crack their ribs."

When lunchtime came, Red and I discovered that Marmite was some kind of mysterious black ooze between two slices of white bread that tasted like cooked asphalt. We both coughed it out as Peter chuckled. He was delighted to rout the Yanks on some real man's climbing. Though we were both better climbers, Red and I put up with Peter's jeers to get out of that godforsaken wind.

Peter stopped at a chippy, or Fish and Chip shop, on the way back. We sat in the Princess struggling to eat our dinner that oozed large spots of grease through its' newspaper wrappings. Red and I both felt sick. McDonald's was health food by comparison.

"Nothing washes down a good chippy like pints at me local pub, The Fox and Hounds. Let's get a taste of proper lager."

Peter rushed us down the street several blocks from his flat to a cottage with gold letters on the door. His sacred pub was like a grandmother's parlor with dark wood paneling and red wall-paper, a somber temple to Britain's favorite pastime: drinking. In great contrast to American culture, the English would consider it crude to brag about one's money, but they boasted constantly of their drinking abilities, which were often formidable.

Peter's circle included his younger brother James and many childhood friends including Janice who worked there and gave us a warm welcome.

"Cheerio," I said in my best British accent.

"What the foock you on abou' Tom? Don't you know what 'cheerio' means?"

"Um, sure, it means to be cheerful?" I replied uncertainly. By their puzzled expressions I knew I had said something wrong.

"Bloody hell! *Cheerio* is what you say when you are leaving. Promise me you won't say something stoopid like that again! Also, you sound like bloody Dick Van Dyke in *Mary Poppins* when you do an English accent."

As I began chatting, Peter forced round after round of very strong beer in my hand.

"Get that beer down your neck. It's almost last call and I'm not even pissed!" pleaded Peter anxiously.

Drinking in England is a race against time. The pub was slated to close at eleven like every other in the land since Queen Victoria's reign. "Last orders, Gentlemen," announced the bartender, and I found two beers in my hands. With the consumption of one, the pub started spinning. I was that abomination to Britain: a lightweight. I hadn't been so far gone in years, whereas Peter wasn't affected until his seventh pint.

"So this is British living, eh Peter?" I said as we just about crawled back to his house. "I feel lucky to have survived one day of it."

"Aye," Peter agreed. "I think you are too."

Not surprisingly, there wasn't much activity around Peter's place the next morning. Peter planned to take us sight-seeing in London but it took an hour and a half to drag our hung-over carcasses out of bed, catch a train into Victoria, and underground "tube" to Westminster.

London: We were really there. A childhood dream had come true, and I was in a big city for the first time, except for the awful and brief boxcar overnight in Paris. Big Ben framed the station doorway, and the gothic playground of Parliament and Westminster looked regal under the Union Jack.

The place names around London came to life when I recalled Knightsbridge and Saint John's Wood from the old Rolling Stones song "Play with Fire."

Parliament was a grey castle surrounded by moat-like grass. Mysterious black "Jag-u-ars," as Peter called them, and Mercedes with darkened windows entered and exited a side entrance lined with police "Bobbies."

Westminster Abbey soared upwards in splendor. Inside, the names of kings, queens, and nobles were etched over their tombs hewn into the stone floor.

We jumped a moving double-decker bus with an open back and hung onto the bars to Trafalgar Square, as much the symbol of London as Big Ben. Giant stone lions and hundreds of pigeons fluttering around in waves came into view.

"That's Lord Nelson's Column," Peter explained. "Hitler had a place mapped out in his garden where he was going to put it. A couple of climbers scaled it a few years ago to protest Apartheid in South Africa." It was inspiring to think of climbers using their skills as political activists and highlight the world problems like only such stunts can.

Peter walked fast, and following him around London wasn't easy. It was a massive and crowded city. We Yanks nearly got hit by a black taxi before noticing the painted sidewalk lettering that said: "Look Left."

"That sign is for you ketchup eaters," Peter pointed.

In an outdoor shop, amidst the rushing urban mayhem, we popped in to see a video playing of none other than national hero, Johnny Dawes, climbing on the dark rock walls of Wales. There was no escaping that remarkable guy even in a big city.

Piccadilly Circus, however, was just tacky stands selling little bobby hats and toy double-decker buses. The vendors preyed on tourists coming to purchase Rock and Roll history from the Beatles to Punk Rock on t-shirts and tote bags. It was a sour note to be in a tacky tourist dump after an amazing tour of the historical monuments.

"Right Yanks: Up for pukin' yer guts out tonight?"

That evening, Peter led us back to his "local." The usual gang was at the Fox and Hounds and Peter, naturally, bragged about how much beer he could hold.

"Head-butting contest!" announced a very drunk Peter a few hours and pints later at a little table. "Who's first?" Suddenly, he grabbed a young fellow, one of James' friends, and smashed his forehead into the guy's face. Blood shot all over the table.

"Bastard!" shouted the youth. He ran off, blood still pouring through his fingers.

"Peter! What's gotten into you?" Janice scolded. "You just broke his nose!"

"He's a soft shite," Peter shrugged. "Probably a puff anyway."

After that ugliness, Peter was overwhelmed by guilt. Peter looked at the blood on the table, sobered up a bit. It was a turning point in what I witnessed of his macho antics. There was a tear in his eye pondering his role. The fun-loving Peter in France was gone as he struggled with the stress of selling his flat and surviving boot camp at Sandhurst. The Britannia he was so proud of was his master. He knew he would not break free again.

She was dead. My hands were shaking. I looked at them in wonder. Many thousand miles to the west was the sound of my father hanging up the phone.

"D'Anne was killed," my dad had told me. Apparently, my previous girlfriend, D'Anne, had been driving back from Iowa Thanksgiving weekend in a snowstorm. Her car skidded across the interstate into the oncoming traffic, killing her and a father of two in another car.

I began to feel angry. This ghost of an awkward, forgettable relationship, was embarrassing me in front of my new friends in Britain. Then I realized solemnly that she would never bother me again; she was being shoveled into the cold ground somewhere. Those thoughts made me feel even worse than the embarrassment. I could only sit at the table, looking in wonder at my shaking hands.

I had met D'Anne my junior year at CU and she was enjoyable to date, pretty, even a homecoming queen in her native Texas, but

I began to discover she was severely depressed. When we briefly lived together, she started pulling me down like quicksand.

After a hike on a beautiful day, she had suddenly burst into uncontrollable sobbing that sent shivers up my spine. Another day she confided that she wanted to die. I suggested we go for climbs, runs, and hikes—the things that keep the blues at bay. She wasn't interested. There was nothing I could do. She lacked the crucial ingredient in conquering her depression: a willingness to fight.

After some reservation, D'Anne agreed to have an appointment with my yoga teacher.

"A good yoga practice makes you see things in a new way," Hansen explained to her during our appointment. "It makes you want to get right out of bed so you don't miss anything."

D'Anne smiled and nodded. She was amused by the postures, but ultimately, she thought yoga was weird, and most of all, naïve. She dismissed yoga, stayed depressed, and we broke up a couple of months later. I thought I would never hear of her again.

The night of the phone call when I learned of D'Anne's death, at the late hour when graves are their coldest, I dreamed of ghosts and witches pointing crooked, accusatory fingers at me like Dicken's ghosts of Christmas past. I felt terrible, ashamed, prioritizing climbing over everything like a spoiled child. The world was in despair, burning with agony, and I only cared about what it took to climb *Genesis*. It was what I went to Europe for, lived for—revenge for a taunt from when I was twelve.

I awoke suddenly on Peter's couch, simultaneously sweating and shivering. The moon shone on the metal roof of the flat's back shed. The sky was clear for the first time in ten days but the cold English winter night seemed as macabre and horrible as the nightmare from which I had just awoken.

In the morning, Peter fired up his rusty Princess for our coldest day of climbing yet. We picked up Janice accompanied by her baby Anna from her parents' cottage.

"Why are you so quiet today?" she asked. We walked up the path away from the others. Numb and withdrawn, I told her about D'Anne while the cruel English winter winds battered the rocks around us. Janice understood me with a touching humanity. Her own past may have played a role in her compassion. She had had Anna as a teenager, making her an outcast from her "proper" childhood friends. She was a "fallen" one and the only person in our gang who cared to talk about D'Anne's death with me.

Instead of returning to climb with the rest of the gang, I wandered alone up a dirt road into the Kent countryside. Next to the green fields, I saw a man sweeping out the remains of a pub that had burned to the ground that very morning. It reminded me of a quote from the Buddha saying, "We are all asleep in a burning house." D'Anne's death was the spark that lit my house on fire. The flames were spreading, I could feel them; they were going to take down everything I knew.

Farther up the path, I came across a tiny artificial ski hill in a farmer's field, complete with moguls sculpted from white nylon. This surreal image seemed the sorriest thing I'd ever seen. I overheard two Englishwomen dressed in tweed in the middle of the slope prattling on about the finer points of skiing.

"Oh goodness, I've caught an edge!" quibbled one with a particularly prissy accent.

"Dear me, what shall we do?"

The Southern English were certainly desperate for recreation. I sat on a stone wall watching their efforts while my hands continued to shake. The pettiness of this nylon ski run, its occupants, and the world in general overwhelmed me. Yet I realized that I was no better. *I* was the one obsessed with climbing *Genesis*. In realizing that while watching the skiers, climbing suddenly lost its pull. I began to understand Layton Kor's decision to give up climbing completely and search for something greater, describing his change of heart in his autobiography *Beyond the Vertical:*

But it was more than tiredness, more than the ennui that comes from repetition. It was the gradually dawning awareness that whatever it was that I had been seeking in my headlong quest through the mountains, I had not been finding it…

Ironically, as I also pondered quitting climbing, I felt closer to my hero then than ever before. It was my Layton Kor moment.

On the way home, Peter dropped off Janice and popped into a Fish and Chip shop.

As soon as we were alone, Red turned on me. "What's the matter with you?" he asked, as though it were my fault for ruining the day. "Why are you so down?"

"I told you. D'Anne was killed!"

"Yeah, that's weird. Well, don't think about it."

"What? Don't *think* about it?"

"Yeah, man. Just don't think about it," he repeated, grinning. "I'm flying home in two days, and I can't wait to ski the big stashes of *pow* in Aspen. They've already got a good base. It's going to be a killer year to shred."

I couldn't believe it. Red had known D'Anne for the last year. I didn't expect him to break into tears, but I thought he would've shown at least a little remorse or sympathy. Instead, his callous response suggested emotion was for the weak, and the world and its inhabitants were only there for his amusement. At first, I envied his cold response, all tough and unflappable, but then I realized that reaction was because he was dead—dead inside and his remark was a howl inviting me to join him in the graveyard. I thought of Dawes crying about killing a ladybird, or ladybug, the bravest climber among us was, most importantly, also brave enough to be a real human being. While emotional suppression is the English way, it's certainly American too. The cold arrogances that James Dean's character had railed against in *Rebel without a Cause*, come to mind. I realized that throughout my life I had too often gone that route, but D'Anne's death changed all that. Empathy was not a shameful weakness, like Red implied, but the last bastion of humanity.

Though I said nothing, I looked at Red in a new way. We were competitors, ranging from jovial to openly hostile, both wanting the same glory through climbing for ourselves. I tolerated Red's berating all those years because I wanted to beat him on a sportsman's terms, but D'Anne's death revealed something so callous and ugly I thought I might be seeing him for the last time. Strangely, I felt grateful to him as his indifference pushed me to make the choice of a lifetime. My future was sealed by Red's four magic words: **Don't think about it.** This was my third time called to India. I did not refuse.

"I don't want to go to Aspen," I said at last. "I'm going to India."

THE DARK MAN'S BURDEN

The next day, it rained again, but this time it was like being sprayed by a fire hose. Even Peter wasn't interested in climbing. To get ready for Sandhurst, he still had to do endless "press-ups," or push-ups, and go for long runs in the perpetual downpours.

Red and I wandered Gravesend's High Street while Peter did errands. The shops had put out their colorful Christmas merchandise, but the atmosphere was dismal. The contrast between those bright colors and the normally limited English palette of gray skies and green grass hurt our eyes. A giant billboard at the end of the street depicted a skinhead sporting a fresh black eye with the caption: *Teach him to accumulate wealth and not aggro.* Teach him to be a good capitalist instead of a pub brawler I guess was the point.

The constant dampness made me crave the warmth of Peter's tea. Red was counting his remaining time until he flew home to ski Aspen. The winter days were so short and overcast in the far north that Peter said in Scotland they were experimenting with U.V. lights to relieve depression. In that wet, desperate hovel, I could feel the yearning of my ancestors' desire to escape Britain for such simple luxuries as the sun.

Wherever I turned, Queen Victoria's famous quip, "We are not amused," seemed to hang in the moist air expressing their national consciousness. If I joked around or was optimistic, the Brits mostly considered me a fool. It certainly wasn't our romanticized Old West, where never is heard a discouraging word. Instead, I found myself silently agreeing with the line in Pink Floyd's *Dark Side of the Moon*: "hanging on in quiet desperation is the English way."

In Peter's flat, I found fascinating history books written from the English perspective like *The American Colonies: Britain's Vietnam*. I had no idea the British Empire was so vast and powerful. My high school and college American history books never let on how second rate we were for 150 years. The popular English boast, "The Sun never set on the British Empire," was true but I also didn't realize it was so *cruel*. India was the subject of several revealing remarks by Winston Churchill: "I hate Indians. They are a beastly people with a beastly religion!" When officials begged Churchill during a 1943 famine to give food supplies to Bengal, Churchill excused his non-action as culling the surplus population. As a result, millions starved to death despite ample supplies hoarded by the rich and huge stockpiles for export.

From the books I was reading, British colonialism was the story of a serial killer. The Irish Wars of Independence, concentration camps in the Boer Wars, Kenyan massacres, chemical warfare, Afghanistan, Iraq, The depth of it was appalling.

If one argues Churchill was merely a product of his time, "On the subject of India, Winston is not quite sane..." wrote Leo Amery, British Secretary of State for India. "I didn't see much difference between his outlook and Hitler's."

Spurred on by a mood resulting from these revelations accompanied by an increasing revulsion for Western "civilization," my dream of India intensified, but I had to find a ticket that was affordable. One evening, Peter and his Fox and Hounds friends met in central London for a meal at the American chain eatery Bennigans. London was suffocating me in the endless rain, maze of streets, lights, people, and traffic. I felt like if I didn't get out of there, something more than my dream of India would die. And, Christ, what was I doing at a Bennigans chain in England?

I sat apart from the others having drinks and good times.

"Come on, Tom, have a beer," Peter called over.

"Is drinking your pain killer?"

"Shut up and go find that ticket to India, you. Piss off down Bond Street to the 'bucket shops' already,"

I wandered alone through a gauntlet of faces dreaming of having their evening beer and scotch, receding in waves to the suburbs. A little blonde girl coming out of the Tube paused to give me a memorable sneer. The empire had reached her already. Dark business suits danced in and out of the foggy evening. Harrods' shoppers pushed their way past vagrants into the underground tube. The faces of the homeless on sidewalks or busking in the Tube conveyed a misery beyond description. I realized the world was a bigger, more over-populated, polluted, exploited, desperate and nastier place than I had ever imagined back home.

Walking east from Nelson's Column, I searched one run-down bucket shop after another for a deal.

"What are you off to India of all places for? Sounds dreadful," asked a Margaret Thatcher look-a-like in one of the travel agencies.

I didn't care anymore, so I said: "I'm going to shave my head, join one of their beastly religions and chant 'Om.'"

She shuddered.

I accidently drifted into Soho, a seedy hedonistic district of girly shows and topless clubs. I remembered an interview with the Who's Pete Townsend, where he explained that the song "Who Are You?" was addressing God and mentioned the despair of Soho.

How could God exist and there be a place like Soho? It was a good question for those desperate, rainy streets. Who are you? How could you let this happen?

As I wandered London, the real meaning of the White Man's Burden, described to me in Foxwood's high school class, became clear—it was an excuse for spreading our white misery to the four corners of the earthlike the devils we are. In parks, I found shrines to heroes who gave their lives "so that China could remain British," as the Monty Python troupe joked. Across from the Royal Albert Hall stood a memorial exalting British soldiers who had subdued the Chinese and the troublesome darkies in Africa. All under the sun that never set on the Union Jack.

At the sketchiest bucket shop of all, I finally found an affordable ticket on Iraqi Airlines. As I counted out sterling silver bills on the counter, the image of the Her Majesty gracing each note looked up at me as if to say: "India on Iraqi Airlines? Have you lost your mind you stupid colonial?"

Now that I was booked, I couldn't help but wonder what the real Indian people would be like. To help me prepare, Janice, the friend of Peter's who worked at the pub, took me to see her schoolmate, Wendy, a young blonde, who had just returned from India. We sat in the well-furnished parlor of Wendy's parents' home watching flames dancing in the fireplace.

"Brilliant trip," Wendy began, "We saw the Taj, of course, and got up to the Himalayas. Unbelievable and dead cheap, but nearly got our stuff nicked twice. The monkeys were at it every minute."

"Wow, what kind of monkeys?" I asked.

"No, we call the natives 'monkeys.'" She failed to suppress a laugh. "I guess it's not very nice, but it does fit. You'll see. You'll need to watch your kit round the clock. We met a couple who lost their cameras and passports while they slept. The bastards took a razor blade to the tent and nabbed their passports right off their chests, slicing the tent and bags through. India's a dodgy place. Then we met a right load of twats over there with that bollocks about yoga and moaning 'Om.'"

I shifted uncomfortably.

"He wants to know about jabs and pills for India," said Janice.

"You'll have to get loads of jabs up in London. The malaria pills give you brain damage, so there's your choice. The rest make your bum sore for a week. Better to get the bloody disease."

"Which shots should I get then?"

"All of them, mate. If you get stricken, they'll throw you in the Ganges with the other sixty million that kicked it that day."

"Off to India?" asked a stout young man with red cheeks coming into the room.

"That's my brother, George. *He'll* never go over there, that's for sure."

"You're going to be up to your ears in W.O.G.s, mate."

"What's a W.O.G.?"

"A 'Westernized Oriental Gentleman,' that what we call 'em 'ere. Of course, over there, they aren't Westernized; they're just niggers. Bloody bunch of useless, fucking children," George explained, pouring himself a big frothy beer and tuning into a football game.

"We'd better be off," said Janice.

She started the car as I stared vacantly at the neatly manicured suburban gardens down the block. Didn't I start life believing in butterflies and Big Bird on *Sesame Street?*

Growing up in Denver, I had gained my first impression of non-whites in the lobby of a movie theater when I was about seven years old. I watched as the black employees joked amongst themselves with a warmth and love I didn't know beaming the brightest smiles. My father pulled me away by the hand, muttering, "Those people have no ambition." Perhaps that's why I liked them.

Then there was Randy at summer camp. His parents owned the biggest car dealership in Arkansas. He couldn't open his mouth without the "N-word" coming out—friendliest guy in the world, otherwise. I got sick of his racist banter knowing his life was very sheltered and asked him if he actually knew any black people. "My Nanny" he replied. Where would rock music be if Keith Richards never ventured into the "colored" part of town?

Besides fun and climbing, my travels are a search for my roots, an escape from "Old America," but all too often I have found "Old Europe."

Why did I have such faith in a strange place like India? Was I crazy to believe a land of disease, starvation, theft, filth, and millions crammed together could offer some kind of salvation? There was no logic, only a feeling, a calling I didn't understand.

"Are you still excited to go?" Janice asked on the drive back to Peter's flat.

"No, but I have to. I can't explain why, but I have to go."

"You don't have to bloody explain," she replied firmly, "why you'd want to get the bloody 'ell out of 'ere!"

BOOK TWO

Into the Indian Fire

"If you see the buddha on the road, slay him."

THE SALT OF THE EARTH

I'm off to India.

The last thing Peter says to me is him prophesizing: "You will be coming back bald wearing orange robes and moaning *Om*."

"Like hell I will." I respond spiritedly. "Foock off!"

That's how Peter and I say goodbye on this rainy English afternoon.

Peter has given me a present of a money belt to keep my passport and cash strapped high on my waist, so thieves would have to tear it from my dead carcass. He also offered me a few "bob" for the road since I have only $90 to last me for a six-week trip. Somehow, I can't accept it. With a lack of funds, no credit cards and a ticket via Iraqi, the only airline I can afford, this is going to be a memorable trip.

I don't know if or when I will see Peter again. My pack feels heavy on my shoulders as I take a last look at Peter's semi-detached flat with the "For Sale" sign. The sky is getting ready to rain again and I've still got the same head cold since arriving. As I come around the corner, the smokestacks of Gravesend cast a watchful eye down on my load, and the cold, moist wind pummels me.

In the Gravesend train station, locals give me condescending glares. One man sneers at me and my backpack from behind his *Daily Mail*. That will stop once I am on the teeming streets of London—no one looks at anyone in the rush of the big city.

The train grows overcrowded, and new entrants squeeze in with their usual mood of pure irritation. By the time we reach Victoria Station, the car is unbearably packed. I have to fight through riptides of dark raincoats and umbrellas that crush onto the platforms. The pasty-white, scowling passengers embody the meaninglessness of accumulating only wealth. I already look forward to being among the gentler faces featured in Peter's travel magazines.

On the train to Heathrow, the overhead lights flicker on and off, as though the Luftwaffe is raining bombs on the city once more. Occasionally, a train window frames Parliament or the Tower of London in the evening drizzle. Gradually, commuters disembark to miserable looking hamlets decorated by broken windows, litter, and graffiti.

At the last stop, the bright yellow plastic seats of the Heathrow await me. My plane doesn't leave until 6:00 a.m. the next morning, so I get to spend the night on the linoleum floors. Silly shops like Sox Appeal are closing, leaving only the food court. I have no money for a hot meal, so I sit down to eat one of the sixteen cheese sandwiches, certainly not Marmite, I brought from Peter's. I raid the condiments station of the cafeteria, filling my bag with handfuls of ketchup, mustard, and a tasty brown sauce that goes well with the cheese sandwiches. It's the only bargain I've found in overpriced Britain.

I thumb through a terrible paperback Peter gave me. It is about a sea voyage where captain and crew discover an enchanted island. They are greeted by strange creatures, which they promptly kill while saying "Great Scott!" and "Aye, aye, sir." It only gets worse.

A pimply faced young man sitting nearby, also with a big ruck-sack, asks the time and the inevitable question: "Where ya off to?"

Simon is his name and he's off to India on my very same flight. I shake his hand. It is sweaty and he seems very nervous. I find he has good reason. In the tradition of an English Royal Geographic Society explorer, young Simon is planning a three-year trip through India, Thailand, and Vietnam. He shows me his knife collection, which ranges from a small pen knife to a Rambo-sized machete to hack through the jungle like Tarzan. All I have is a Swiss Army knife.

We have hours and hours to kill, so Simon tells idyllic stories about living on the beach in Portugal with a band of English friends. Every week they came up a long staircase to the village for food and water, but otherwise they enjoyed an uncomplicated hippy freedom. Yet Simon doesn't seem to be a hippy. His brown hair is short, and he isn't spacey or drugged out. Instead, there is a wholesome Boy Scout innocence to Simon's get-away-from-it-all adventures. I'm impressed and believe Simon would make a good travel partner after being wary of strangers on the way to a strange land.

The evening grows late, and cleaning crews begin clanging around us. The intercom announcements in icy British accents subside. Together we search for somewhere to sleep, eventually joining a host of vagabond travelers huddling on the floor. Dominating the group is an elderly Scotsman with a sea-captain's white beard spouting apocalyptic conspiracies which is made more dramatic by his fiery Scottish accent. It is a send-off, a graduation speech before going out to experience the real world for ourselves. Soon we spread out to camp on the shiny, hard linoleum floor.

A couple of hours later, the clanking of the graveyard shift cleaning crew wakes me up. There is nothing to do but watch the closest janitor, a portly middle-aged Indian woman, struggling to wax an already clean floor at three in the morning. I can only wonder about her country where I am headed. Cynicism overcomes me as I consider what her countrymen can be capable of when she can't manage to wax a floor. What in the world am I doing going to a crazy country like India, nearly broke before I even get there? I'm having an attack of racism and apprehension reigns in the early hours.

At 4:30 a.m., after about half an hour of sleep each, Simon and I join a sea of Indians already in line for the flight. Most have luggage piled as high as elephants on the airport carts.

For the moment, Iraq has a cease-fire with Iran, but we are still frisked three times, and the airline confiscates our batteries and Simon's entire knife collection. The interior of the plane is decorated with pleasant desert scenes of camels around an oasis. Just as we settle in our seats, the airline announces that it has dumped the entire plane's luggage onto the wet runway. The airline crew orders all passengers out into the dark, misty morning to personally identify their bags. Some refuse, and the crew threatens to leave those passengers behind. There is yelling and chest beating—anarchy, and we are still at Heathrow. The trip is off to an ominous start.

After another thorough frisking to get back on the plane after claiming our now soggy packs, Simon and I find ourselves seated next to a distinguished-looking British man wearing a white suit. He is a scientist named Robert. To my amazement, he claims he was born in India.

"I'm going back to check on my equipment, which gathers atmospheric data," Robert says. "It should be in good nick if the damn natives haven't touched it!"

During the flight Robert shares Indian travel stories, and we hang on the veteran's every word, looking for clues to the tough times ahead. I notice with unease that Robert often portrays a typical racism describing locals like the impulsive *Curious George* monkey.

The plane zooms off, and London's lights recede in the rain below. I can't believe I am on Iraqi Airlines to New Delhi via Bagdhad. Life is certainly getting interesting.

Dawn arrives, igniting desert sands through the bizarre, shafted windows of the Bagdhad airport. *What in the world am I doing in Bagdhad?* The clashing cultural extravagance of airport architecture suggests the Pompidou Center meets Ali Baba. Even the seasoned British travelers on this ten-hour stopover gape in disbelief. The ceiling resembles an enormous mosque shaped by a bizarre collection of steel pipes descending in different lengths.

"Just orange seats like any airport the world over, mate," the man in the London ticket office had assured me when my eyebrows had risen in concern over a long layover in Bagdhad.

The name Bagdhad should conjure images of the ancient wonders of Babylon, Mesopotamia, and the birthplace of civilization. All that bubbles to the surface of my thick mental soup is the theme song to the show *I Dream of Jeannie.* Proof I watched way too much TV growing up and that I have been taught to disregard their culture and people. Even the genie was blonde.

Simon and I pass the night on soft airport chairs, pulling them together to make little beds and forts. I try to shift my long body from its limiting L-shaped contortion to doze longer, but flight announcements in exotic tongues suggest the odd Arabian night is over. Giving up on catching any more sleep, I walk down the long concourse to the toilet past gaggles of squabbling women. They are bundled in burkas like black veiled specters. I have never felt so far from home.

Back at our den, the rising sun reveals archaic, battered maintenance equipment on the runway. I begin to worry about the condition of the plane we will be boarding in five hours.

"Bloody 'ell! Look at that!" exclaims Simon, pointing to an enormous portrait of Saddam Hussein. "President" Hussein is posing like Napoleon, his chin high in an ostentatious uniform covered in tassels complete with hand tucked in his breast pocket and hunting dogs at his feet.

"I dare you to draw a goatee on him," I tell Simon.

"We'd never be heard from again," he whispers back as though eyes are upon us.

A line of ragged Iraqi men, heads wrapped in cloth to later deflect the merciless sun, forms in front of our airport seats. The men look like a simple, gentle desert people happy to pass their days tending their goats. It is remarkable to think how many people at home would like to kill these goat herders. In Iran, we toppled the democratically-elected leader in the 1950s, arranged fake riots that killed innocent people and re-installed the Shah with his dreaded secret police. Ten years ago, when Iran staged a revolution, a heavily U.S.-subsidized Saddam Hussein attacked his unstable neighbor. After untold numbers on both sides died in a stalemate, the respective governments ceased issuing white underwear to their troops, who continually used them as white flags to surrender. President Reagan secretly supplied arms to both sides, but exactly who did he want to win? To use his famous line: Reagan can't recall. My American passport is well put away until needed.

Soon it will be 1989, the end of a deceitful decade led by an artificial president. The change began with Reagan's removal of Jimmy Carter's solar panels from the White House roof. As if on cue, rock music began to fizzle out. The great bands broke up, replaced by less authentic groups more concerned with making videos than writing real music. The show *Saturday Night Live* with its counterculture humor was mysteriously toned down. *First Blood* was a wholesome movie about a disturbed Vietnam Vet, but by *Rambo III*, Stallone became the unstoppable all-American hero returning to Vietnam alone to win the only war we ever lost all by himself. Even worse was Tom Cruise in *Top Gun* glorifying both combat and greased-up young men playing volleyball. The audience cheered wildly as Cruise downed a Russian MiG. Instead of joining their blood lust, I paused to remember the Vietnam veteran counselors at my summer camp who recalled their brutal battle stories with a haunted stare often followed by outbursts of sobbing. One counselor somehow survived even though the U.S. Army had strapped him into a harness and hung him in the exposed open door of a helicopter. They had lost so many gunners it was easier to hang his soon-to-be-corpse in the helicopter than hunt for his remains in the jungle vegetation below. The odds of his not getting picked off by the Viet-Cong were one in ten.

From abroad, especially in front of non-Americans, our patriotic fantasies look even more childish and cheap. "Zees Rocky and Rambo movies are pure American propaganda," commented a French guy who gave me a ride on my travels through the Alps. Though I am experiencing the loneliness of a far-flung voyage, it isn't all that hard to be away either.

"So why are you going to India, anyway?" Simon asks unexpectedly among the seats of the Bagdhad airport.

"Oh, to knock around, see the mountains," I reply without conviction. I feign looking out the large airport windows into the desert because it is hard to explain to a complete stranger an illogical interest in lofty Eastern philosophy, harder still that my trip is motivated by competition and vengeance. Simon acts like it is a simple question. I study him closely, trying to decide if I can trust him. He can't be an Empire Brit if he is going on a low budget, three-year trek by himself through Asia. I look out the window and evade more questioning just the same.

We board the plane, and Bagdhad is soon below us. The flight is uneventful, but Robert tells stories about India that are discouraging enough to make me want to hide in the bathroom.

After many hours, the plane begins its descent into Delhi. The views out of its tiny plastic windows reveal only plains of yellow dirt interrupted by an occasional tree. Buildings become more frequent, but they are mostly in ruins. Our plane makes a rocky touchdown, jolting and abrasive like the Third World we've landed in.

As my fellow passengers realize they have survived, a great squabbling arises as they all push for the door simultaneously. The stewardesses hide from the mosh pit of elbowing and shoving, knowing better than to fight the tide. I don't like what I see. I feel like chickening out and would stay in my seat for the next five weeks if I could.

Outside, blinding sunshine glares off the steel stairs that descend to the blacktop. On the top stair, I pause and catch my first whiff of sweet Indian air. It is magical, perfumed by unseen flowers. Everything is suddenly in color like *The Wizard of Oz* when Dorothy's house lands over the rainbow. After nearly a month visiting England, a *film noir* where it was freezing and raining every day, the sunshine is instantly pleasant. I hope to quickly shake off the horrendous cold I got the day I arrived in London.

Gandhi International Airport is a charred and battered building covered by log scaffolding. Armies of workers in rags climb up and down balancing heavy loads on their heads. Forty-five minutes later, we are still outside on the runway. Slowly, we approach customs, passing a duty-free shop with a shattered glass case displaying only dust-covered shelves of blonde Barbie dolls in saris. A sign points to "Drinking Water" in some far-off corner. Simon goes for some, but I remain suspicious of public fountains.

"You're going to be thirsty mate."

"And you're going to get sick," I counter.

Simon shrugs acceptingly. "If I get sick, I get sick," he replies. "What do you expect from India? Why did you want to come here anyway?"

"If you really want to know, I want to learn about yoga," I say quietly.

"Yoga?!" Simon says much too loud for my comfort. "Why would you do *that* stuff?"

I have to admit that it is a good question. Why do that *stuff*, that hippy nonsense? Red laughed his head off when he discovered a yoga mat hidden among my possessions in the caravan. He said yoga was for only the most debased of homosexuals. Simon too looks at me differently now.

For all my big plans, I am riddled with doubts. Just the other night Peter was playing a John Lennon record, and the ex-Beatle sang: "Don't believe in yoga!" It jolted me. The Fab Four had been to India. *Do I know better than a rock star?*

But I did not come to India to become an herbal-tea-drinking wuss. I have only the memories of Fairview Dome to sustain my faith in yoga, even as I will face India's harsh realities and discouraging sights. "Don't doubt in the valley what you felt on the mountain top," says Cheley's Trigger Bill.

Finally getting our turn at the Gandhi International passport control, Simon and I find that the airline has lost the batteries they confiscated from us in Heathrow.

"Buy Indian batteries. They are very fine made," advises a customs lady in a sari.

Simon begins to sweat over his knives, which are also missing, and is directed to a far-off, run-down little office to protest. Robert has promised to get Simon and I settled in New Delhi, so I dutifully follow him to accomplish one of the most notoriously difficult tasks of the voyage: arranging a taxi into Delhi.

"There are going to be a lot of beggars out there," he warns. "Just follow me and watch your kit!"

We approach the threshold to the real India, a long window symbolizing the final moments of the safety of the airport. Outside, hundreds of eager Indians press their faces against the glass. Robert told us that unwary Westerners were fresh meat, and the sight of all those faces is nothing short of incredible. As soon as we cross the doorway, the Indian people are upon us. I can only duck and dodge through the sudden avalanche of Indians, following Robert's white suit like a ship's bow cutting through the colorful crowd to our goal: a crooked taxi stand hastily built from rotting wood.

"We would like a taxi into..." Robert begins.

"You want buy a wife?" asks a young boy, about eleven, working the stand.

"What?"

"Good woman for you. Nice teeth."

"No wife today, my boy," Robert says, beaming with amusement. "Just a taxi into New Delhi."

"Okay, but you want wife you come here, yes?"

"You'll be the first to know."

Simon rejoins us with sweat pouring in buckets down his face.

"They can't find my knives!" he says in frustration.

"They're waiting for a little *baksheesh*, a little bribe," suggests Robert. "It's a game. All of India is a game. Try that, and you'll be *amazed* at what turns up."

Robert is right. After rupees appear on the counter, "magically" the knives are quickly located by the airline staff.

With the knife question settled, our luggage is loaded on the roof of a 1950's tiny taxi cab called an Ambassador, painted in wild orange colors. Inside, a blue god statue is mounted on the dashboard, and no less than four Indian men are crammed into the front seat. We drive off, but after a half-mile the Indian men stop in the middle of an empty dirt field to change drivers. The "old" driver walks off to God knows where, and another one suddenly appears, joining the group up front. After another mile, the same thing happens again, and another mile later we have yet another driver.

Now there are three "new" Indians up front. They look back repeatedly, snickering at us foreigners and bantering cheerfully amongst themselves.

"Delhi long way from airport," the current driver says, flashing a set of white teeth. "Many rupees for price."

Robert suddenly says something in their language. "I told them we are not tourists and to cut the crap," he explains to us indignantly. "They've been planning to rip us off since we got in the cab. A bit shocked to realize a westerner could speak fluent Hindi, too. I was born here after all."

The crew up front is now quiet, sullen, and pouting. In his white suit, Robert seems like a James Bond god. "You've got to watch it—they prey on Westerners constantly. Everything is a scam. They pose as railway employees, government tourist office staff, even policeman. And never, EVER give the beggars any money."

The road into the capital is no wider than a bike path. We pass golden dirt fields swarming with rag-tag workers and a woman riding a bicycle while balancing an enormous stack of wood on her head. Turning to see her face, Simon and I grab each other like scared little girls. Her face is gaunt and deeply pockmarked from malnutrition. In front of us is the face of poverty, overpopulation, and deprivation, but also our common human roots. She smiles sheepishly at us, honest and true. She is our first real image of the Third World. Her face says to us fussy foreigners: 'I am alive, even if barely.' It is an image that changes a traveler forever.

Her smile is comforting; it reminds me of the uncomplicated regular people I met in downtown Denver as a middle school student. Transferring several buses to go climbing in Boulder, I met many people of different backgrounds and ethnic groups at the bus stops. After the Country Day school, it was refreshing to talk to people who weren't so boastful. The downtown Denver people often amazed me with their kindness, camaraderie and frank, fatherly advice.

"Never join the army, boy. They don't deserve your dirty socks," a jaded vet told me.

"Stay off the drugs and drinking. It ruined me and my family," another man said. "Now we live on the street." It's a powerful message coming from someone who has been there and only volunteers his advice.

It was from them I often learned how the world really is.

The Rolling Stones sang: 'Let's drink to the salt of the earth.'

It is also strange to see the woman on the bicycle after experiencing Foxwood's class, the way he described a pyramid of human worth. She will never be a "mover or shaker" except on her rickety bicycle. Supposedly, she is my burden. I am supposed to lead her into my enlightened Christian world, yet my society would only be interested in exploiting her cheap labor. Now that I am here on this quest, I am her world's burden instead.

Congestion and anarchy mark the rest of the ride into Delhi. The honking increases every minute. It seems here the horn is king. Three-wheeled rickshaw carts swerve and honk furiously to get around tattered buses spewing black clouds of diesel exhaust and wagons pulled by mangy pack animals. *Honk, honk, honk.* Nothing exists above the constant screeching beeps. The urgent, unnerving, raw, full-volume horn blare normally reserved for avoiding a head-on collision at home is constantly present.

Robert directs our taxi to Connaught Place, a comparatively upscale British-era cluster of buildings with white pillars forming a circle around a park. It is the most Westernized area of Delhi. The white columns look like they belong in London except for wandering cows at their base and hundreds of people packed into shanties.

"Here's a simple hotel you can stay in," Robert says guiding us through a dark entranceway. Four flights of dimly lit, decomposing stairs lead to a balcony where an old man greets us with a filthy registration book. We are required to fill out the information in triplicate, completing questions like, "Who is your father? Who is your mother…?"

From the balcony, a putrid, smoldering Delhi spreads out below. The streets are an ant farm of teeming activity with two accidents per minute. We witness a moped broadsiding a rickshaw. Then a horse cart cuts off a motorcycle that rams the median and flips over. No one stops. No one cares. Apparently, serious injuries are rare since it is too crowded to speed.

"Please sir, shoe shining?" groans a man with a shoeshine kit on the balcony. He wants to shine my Reeboks.

"Be sure you use your own lock. Don't let them supply it," Robert warns. "Let's eat, and then I have to go. I know a restaurant where Westerners don't need to worry about the food too much."

We follow Robert closely across a circular park packed with Indians chatting and playing cards on the grass. It is like wandering through the audience of an outdoor rock festival. There is nothing but loitering, loitering, loitering going on in the park. I do have to admit it's nice to see a contrast to my country's psycho work ethic. To always keep anxiously busy is like a stain left on our culture by the Puritans; idleness was a serious offense sometimes punished by death.

On the other side of the park, a little man wheels himself out from an alley to beg. He is amputated at the belly button and rests his half torso on a small skateboard propelled by his finger stubs. He must be missing organs the human body needs to live, but there he is. The sight makes even our hardened veteran Robert stagger and lose his way for a moment. Robert's stiff upper lip fades, and he fishes through the pockets of his white suit to find a stack of rupees for the beggar even he can't refuse.

The further away we stray from Connaught Place, the wilder the sights become. We pass a high-rise building construction site held together by crude wooden-log scaffolding tied with rope. It is the Empire State Building built from Lincoln Logs. With a lack of modern design and machinery, but with plenty of human labor the bulky building's scale look like it outstripped safe construction methods. We look over the sad fence to see many extended families living in the dirt at its base.

Robert says even bottled drinks aren't safe. The soda factory sanitation can't be guaranteed. There is a brand called *Campa Cola* with a logo design mimicking Coca Cola's trademark.

"India threw the Coca Cola Company out. It doesn't taste the same, but nobody cares as long as Coke is gone." Robert explains implying some kind of abuse of power.

At the restaurant, a boy crawls around under our table constantly sweeping with a tiny, short-handled, miserable broom.

"The *masala dosas* are good here," Robert says.

"Do they have hamburgers?" I ask out of habit.

"Vegetarianism is a good thing to do in India for two reasons: It runs deep in their culture, and flies sit on the meat all day."

"Masala whatever sounds good."

I gobble greedily at my dinner, not knowing if or when another Westerner-safe restaurant will show itself. The meal reminds me of my seventh-grade camping trip to the Sand Dunes National Monument in southern Colorado. Mr. Day, our stout American history teacher, made me finish every last one of the sandwich crusts I had left behind from the previous lunch. I had been spoiled by our middle-class pretenses, and at first I hated him for it as the crusts were very stale and covered in sand blown in from the dunes. But Mr. Day said, "Eat all you can boy, like the British are tracking you through the woods, and you need your strength for a good fight. Or you are high on Everest and that's all that's left in your pack." He added urgency, manliness to the affair as I shoved the rock-hard, sandy crusts into my mouth. It was eating just to live, and I suddenly felt different: more alive. While Westerners eat just to please the palate and waste food by the ton, I am eating dinner just to eat like the millions of poor around the world who aren't sure if, or when, they will get another meal.

"Well, I've got to be off," Robert says, suddenly excusing himself. "My friends are expecting me. Remember, if things get kind of crazy, just sit down and remember man is not in charge here, God is."

On his way out, he picks up the tab. We thank him but watch in dismay as his white suit weaves its way out of the restaurant and disappears into the masses. Simon and I are on our own. Our James Bond god is gone.

THINGS THAT GO "HONK"
IN THE NIGHT

"The best thing about India is sipping a martini on the plane as it takes off from this god-forsaken land," cackles a white-haired British man back at the rooftop balcony of our hotel. He has the raspy laugh of an old salt who has been there and back again. I am stunned at this revelation by yet another veteran. The idea of a revitalizing pilgrimage to India is quickly evaporating before my eyes.

The British man is one of a small group of motley Westerners lounging at the hotel, swapping tales. The scruffy travelers come from many different countries, but they all came to be somewhere cheap. Lowly waiters, tradesmen, or students in the industrialized West all can live like kings in India.

Well, kings experiencing some concessions to their castle's comforts. For $1.50 each per night, our room contains one filthy, hard bed, a ramshackle ceiling fan that chugs like a steamboat which is lit by a bare, four-foot-long buzzing fluorescent light. I locate the toilet down the hall; it reeks as though it has not been cleaned since the British left. I am not a neat freak, but the brutal urine stench actually burns my eyes. Not a good toilet to experience the dreaded "Delhi belly" that condemns its victims to be wrapped around it all day. The thought is too much to bear. If I get ill, I'll walk out into the Delhi traffic. Death will be swift.

Just a few hours off the plane, I am already desperately homesick for the West. The vast loneliness of this exotic land weighs on me. Now I feel a true empathy for anyone far from home. I don't fit in with this crew of pirates on the roof-top. The lure of "because it's cheap" travel isn't for me. I'm starting to suspect that India is a hellhole struggling to survive, not a soul-repairing retreat.

On top of all this, I need to contact my mother. In all the whirlwind of London I never called to tell her what I was doing, mostly because I didn't know myself. Now I'm worried she might report me as missing. According to Simon's guidebook, the only public telephone is at the post office, a ten-minute walk across from our hotel. I leave Simon and the hotel and, stepping outside, I'm immediately surrounded by beggars, taxi drivers, and assorted scam artists, circling closer to me, as edgy as hyenas. I break into a sprint across the park.

The post office is a stark white building with ingrained streaks of filth at head height running its whole length. Inside, wall-to-wall patrons yell in mysterious languages into telephones with the frantic energy of traders on the floor of a turbulent stock exchange.

"Oh, Daddums, the Himalayas were magnificent," gushes a British girl into a nearby phone. She and her girlfriend are dressed in saris head to toe. "Yes, brilliant, yes … do I want to see your Polo match when I return? Oh rather!"

Daddums? Hell, if two posh English girls are having a good time so can I. India can't be that bad. My confidence is temporarily restored.

Unfortunately, collect calls are not allowed. Sweat pours down my forehead as I spend a whole $10 of my meager budget for a one-minute call to wake my mother in Colorado in the middle of the night.

"Tom from Delhi, Tom from Delhi," the Indian operator tells her.

"From where? Who?" Mom is utterly confused by the operator's thick accent. Eventually, she wakes up enough to ask why I am in India. Inspired by the English girls, I play down the trip as a lark with a group of imaginary British friends, trying to suppress the fear in my voice. I'm successful convincing my drowsy mom it's what everyone does studying abroad.

It is done, and I walk out feeling better; but my mood is short lived. Outside, the traffic charges like "a mad bull that's lost its way," to quote an appropriate line from the Rolling Stones' chaotic song "Gimmie Shelter." Before me flows a sea of rickshaws thundering like the mighty Buffalo herds once charged across the great plains. Negotiating traffic with no stop lights, crosswalks, or other inventions of safety is more dangerous than the running of the bulls in Spain. Why would the chicken cross the road in Delhi? If one did, he would be Chicken Tikka Masala. Scooters miss me and each other by inches. Robert is right. God must be in charge. My head begins to spin. A crippling wave of terror shoots through me, and I have to stop to gather my wits. There is too much traffic, people, pollution, poverty, filth, and above all honking.

Fortunately, things change around a corner. My eyes settle on the sight of an Indian policeman dressed head to toe in a red suit adorned with gold buttons and tassels and topped by a tall white bobby hat. In that pompous uniform left over from the days of the Empire, he looks more like a circus lion-tamer than a cop. Besides the ridiculous getup, his quest for order is futile, and he sadly knows it. The drivers pay him no notice whatsoever, continuing to honk and crash into one another. It is so damn funny I laugh and laugh, and anxiety drains out of me. I stroll like a new man towards the park. But after a few minutes, the incessant badgering of the locals wears on my nerves and I feel on edge again.

"You want hashish?" asks a taxi driver.

"No." I turn away and begin to jog through the park. To my dismay he parks his rickshaw and gives chase on foot.

"Good hashish! I have," he calls excitedly gaining on me.

"No thanks!" I start into a full run through the crowded park, but he closes in. I'm running fast but so is he. I jump over an entire family building a fire on the sidewalk in front of the hotel.

"Come, you buy!" The driver-dealer follows me in a frantic rush up the stairs.

I've had enough. I whirl around to face my pursuer: "I don't smoke hashish!"

"Okay, why you not say you no smoke hashish?" The dealer turns on his heel and departs.

"Thanks, dumb fucking hippies." I shout down the dark stairway. Foreigners looking for a cheap Shangri-la of drugs, sex parties, and trippy guru ménages have created expectations I will probably have to struggle against the whole trip. I have had enough of Delhi already.

It has become dark now, and on the building adjacent to our hotel roof-top porch a Konica Film advertisement made of neon unfolds its colors. It seems like the modern world's only toehold in India. The company logo blinks on and off in a sad, neon circular pattern with a haunting effect. The surreal, menacing glow appears to say that it would be just as easy to go bonkers in India as anywhere else—in fact, maybe even easier.

The whole country seems to be lit by nothing but bare, dismal fluorescent tube lights. There isn't a pleasing soft or halogen light to be seen, which only adds to the shabbiness.

My contact lenses are being affected by the air pollution. My eyes are blazing red. They itch and burn, but there is nothing clean in the whole country, it seems, to wipe them with. My white t-shirt has turned a grimy gray in the few hours we've been here.

Back in the hotel room, jetlag is taking over both me and Simon. It is just past five in the afternoon, but we are crashed out on the miserable bed oblivious to the clunky fan warbling above. As the night advances, the noise of the honking down below lessens and is further muffled by shutting the window. However, at some level in my waking and in my deepest of dreams the honking of Delhi is always present—omnipresent.

As the whir of the fan enters my mind this morning, I realize we have slept well past noon. Simon jumps up to open the wooden door, letting in a violent intrusion of sunshine.

"Let's check this place out." he says cheerfully.

The honking drifting up to our fourth-story window is already deafening. It is hard to leave the security of even this flea-bag hotel. I stall by getting ready slowly. The madness below can wait a little longer.

Iraqi Airlines requires we confirm our return flights at their Delhi office in person, which has to be done before we can leave the capital. We wander for hours through the chaos of Delhi, searching in vain for street signs, addresses or anything clearly marked by which to navigate. Any people we stop to ask nod and say "yes" to every question and then have some kind of deal "only for you, my friend."

At last, Simon somehow spots the airline's office on a tiny side street. A turbaned guard watching the door with a double-barreled shotgun regards us with suspicion. The guard begrudgingly lets us by. After completing the paperwork, our return flights, mine to London and his on to Nepal, are confirmed. Finally, nothing holds us to this mess of a city and now we can explore the real India.

For all the trouble and expense of coming here, I have no idea where to go. Back in a London bookshop, I found a guide with great advice about visas and immunizations, but then it said: "And we'll even show you where the gurus are." Was even the journey for yoga commercialized too? Was this going to be like the Swiss Balmer's hostel but in India? Enraged, I threw the book on the floor. For an awkward moment, fellow shoppers gawked at my tantrum as I slowly became aware of what I had done, but fortunately, I was quickly absorbed into the protective anonymity of the millions on London's sidewalks. The up-side of a big city.

Mountains have always given me direction. In India, that means going north to the Himalaya. Simon and I thumb through his travel book until we agree on a town called Haridwar at the foot of the great peaks. Now we just need to figure out how to get there.

The Delhi train station is an explosion of action, people, color, and smells, and yet there is a man sleeping in the middle of the floor. He lies there snoring while literally millions of travelers walk inches from his face. Apparently, he's not drunk—he lays there peacefully oblivious and doesn't seem concerned about anything.

From the recesses of a dingy cage, the tired-looking train ticket salesman says it is best to take a bus to Haridwar. Simon's guidebook disagrees. After Robert's stories, we suspect the man is just too lazy to be bothered to fill out all the paperwork to sell us the tickets. He probably only wants rid of us. There is no one else to ask, and since every sign is in Hindi, we are forced to investigate the bus system. According to Simon's guide, a bus leaves every evening to Haridwar. To pass the time, we remember Robert's suggestion to explore the Red Fort at Delhi.

At the Fort, we pay a pittance of an entry fee to find spacious gardens and expanses of grass spreading out to stone monuments ornamented on a royal scale. The ancient Mughal palace of the Red Fort sits within mighty red sandstone walls, and her grounds are deserted compared to the busy streets outside. We have discovered a hidden gem, and I can finally appreciate India's glorious past. For the first time since squeezing into the train to Heathrow days ago, I am not poked, pushed, crushed or crammed into a tiny, air-deprived space. The delights of a seemingly enlightened ancient civilization stand before us in an enormous open-air museum without guards, barriers, or cameras to constrain us.

"Well this is great, but let's go check out the bazaar," Simon says.

"Are you kidding?"

He isn't. Simon is equally excited about exploring the slums of Old Delhi just across the road. There we are ushered through a densely-packed market brimming with rancid odors, noise and confusion. Our presence attracts a great deal of attention, as white tourists rarely dare enter such a place. The merchants' eyes widen on our approach; choking back laughter, they quickly double and triple their prices for us. If there is tuberculosis to be found, it waits for us here. But for Simon, this is the real Indian experience.

Afternoon is waning, so we trudge through more urban mayhem to the dirt yards of the Delhi bus station. The lot is unpaved with an enormous relief of potholes, peaks, and valleys not unlike the dramatic Himalayas themselves. It is a wonder the buses don't get lost among them.

Masses of Indians are loitering around the bus station, sleeping on the ground and starting fires, and almost all are staring at us. There is no ticket office or schedule posted. Simon rushes around looking for our escape bus. Our confusion marks a new high point in my discomfort. *What I am doing here?*

"Haridwar, Rishikesh?" says a man pointing at a bus pulling up.

"That one? Are you sure?" Simon asks.

"No, this bus Haridwar-Rishikesh," another man contradicts. "Be careful of that man. He is cheat."

As they argue in their tongue, the sky is darkening, and I notice many people look like they are settling in for the night.

"I don't think most of these people are waiting for a bus," I observe. "I think they live here."

"That bus no good. He is crazy man," the first man whispers to us sideways. "This bus. Hello, yes come I am your friend. Come this way, please."

He pulls us both by the arm briskly to a far off bus, but it isn't going to Haridwar or Rishikesh. We look around to find that our "friend" has disappeared like a ghost. I check to see if my money belt is still safely strapped around my waist.

"No bus Haridwar/Rishikesh tonight," says a different bus driver. "Of this I am certain."

Simon is sweating again. We don't know what to do. As the evening darkens, the station can be described as something like a biblical plague—robed people, piles of burlap luggage and mayhem. Yet we remain the unwanted center of attention. Eyes fix upon us from every direction; whole crowds now form around us with no purpose in mind except to stare. But the vendors are the worst. Plates of dirty bananas, oranges, candy, or coconuts are thrust in our face. The fruit is covered with filth and flies. The coconut slices are stained a sickening brown. Despite growing hunger pains, we only gaze worriedly at the state of the food.

"You buy. Highest quality fruit," they repeat over and over.

To them even the most destitute foreigner is a Rockefeller. Repeating a polite "no thank you" only encourages them. We stare coldly into space ahead, socially jaded after only one full day in Delhi.

Strangely, I feel the familiar sensation of adventure, for the gnawing of horror in my stomach is routine after a life of climbing. Three years earlier, I ascended Yosemite's Half Dome, big and improbable standing ominously at the top of the valley. I felt so intimidated being on the massive wall that I puked into a chimney. My body cruelly expelled the nutrients and moisture I would sorely miss in the August heat when we ran out of water two-thirds of the way to the top. Climbing up higher severe dehydration gave me muscle cramps that squirmed with a mind of its own.

The tension broke as I ran up the last ledges in the setting sun to the treasure of the glistening, golden summit. The big-wall suffering had been worth it to break into a new world, but traveling in India might not have the same rewards.

Suddenly a bus pulls up and the driver sings out: "Haridwar, Haridwar, Rishikesh."

In a mad scramble, Indians pour out of the woodwork to crush onto the bus. Our luggage has to go on the roof, so I frantically scramble up a rusty ladder with no fewer than fifteen other passengers fighting to do the same. Our colorful packs stand out rudely against the pile of native burlap sacks.

"Not the biggest seats in the world, are they?" Simon comments inside the bus. My legs are crammed against the wood backing of the seat in front of us.

"Keep an eye out for our bags 'mysteriously' falling off the roof," I add.

"Yeah, well, nothing I can't live without."

The hopelessly overloaded bus starts with an awful roar and slowly ambles off, jerking and jolting along. The potholes alone are a challenge for the old diesel.

"Wait a minute!" I say. "Can't live without ... My malaria pills are in my pack on the roof." According to the stories, packs can just disappear into the crowds. I'm sure I've been bitten by mosquitos today.

"It'll be all right," says Simon unconvincingly.

Now we are both sweating.

The bus rattles through streets in no better repair than the bus station. Restless waves of rickshaws, motorcycles, and mule-wagon teams throb in the twilight. And people. There are literally thousands crammed on every block. The bus driver lays into his horn endlessly, but we gain mere feet and inches for his efforts. With no red lights, signs, or rules, the traffic has a Tao of its own, and no mercy for anyone under its heel.

"This place is like the apocalypse," I remark.

"Aye, I've heard stories, but ... fucking 'ell," Simon agrees.

"The end of the world will look this way, everyone lost and wandering. This is the biggest city, right? Haridwar has got to be smaller."

"Yes. My travel guide says, 'Haridwar is the gateway to the mountain gods.'"

"Mountain gods? I'll be happy to see *them*."

Darkness is complete as our bus struggles to escape Delhi's city limits an hour later. Now we pick up speed, and we relax slightly as the bus is honking and swerving less on the open road—well, at least not honking and swerving *all* the time. The driver fights for space on the still-crowded road, overtaking wagons and badgering livestock that wanders into the middle. Our honking only makes lost cows look curiously at the bus; to them we are just another thing that goes honk in the night. Strange human inhabitants roam the night road, wrapped in colorful blankets and oblivious to our presence. What are they doing and where are they going? They are another mystery of the twilight, and I'm certain there will be plenty more ahead.

Driving the bus is apparently a four-man job. There is a cage for the driver, two friends, and a man that squabbles with uniformed officials at random police-barricade stops that seem to be some kind of shakedown. He is the designated squabbler. The drivers change frequently, but they all worship the horn – the louder the better.

Bulging trucks clog the road, overburdened past their load limits. They have signs painted on their back that say "Blow Horn," encouraging their use. Also painted on the trucks' rear, Indian bumper stickers of sorts, say "God is One" or "Love is All."

We pass abandoned building projects with steel supports shooting like hair out of the cement ramparts. Poster advertisements give their bright colors to the dusk, often with misspelled English words, but quick as a blink they are gone.

Simon and I are the only whites on the bus, and at some drowsy hour I feel a hand on my knee which protrudes out of necessity into the aisle, but why the hand? Is it a queer rider copping a feel or a gentle expression of brotherly love? Either way, the thought *Somebody's got their hand on my knee,* nags at me, and I can't relax until I carefully brush it off.

Outside, I can see the moon shining down on lush green fields. They are adorned by big, beautiful trees lush with foliage. It is these open spaces that comfort me most, and I search for places to hide until this nightmarish trip is over.

Hours later, we stop under the cheerful, soft lights of an Indian truck stop. We rub our eyes and descend like spacemen to see literally hundreds of men relieving themselves in the surrounding woods. In my delirium and hunger, I gobble down an egg on toast without a thought for hygiene.

Back on the bus, Simon and I pass out instantly, despite the nearly constant honking and swerving. A few hours later, in the dark depths of night, we are fully awake in sync with English time. There is nothing to do but stare dumbly out the window. Passing through one village, we see twenty beds by the side of the road packed with Indians watching a cricket game on a massive television. In a flash, the surreal vision is gone, as reality and dream blend together.

The bus begins to pass building fronts with fountains and enormous blue statues. They represent Hindu gods with cobras curled on their shoulders, hand-mudras, or symbolic hand gestures, with the palms up, massive quantities of red powder and wreaths on their necks. The images with the powder look like they have been vandalized in the name of devotion. The name "Haridwar" stirs on the lips of the passengers. We are here. The Mountain Gods are waiting for us.

As our bus pulls into a dirt lot, high, dark buildings tower above. Finally, the engine and horn fall quiet, leaving me with a ringing in my ears. Our bags are happily still resting on top, but no sooner do I hand one down than a skinny Indian man quickly takes it and loads it onto his bicycle rickshaw.

"Hey, just hang on a minute," protests Simon.

"Good hotel. You come," the man responds.

"Hotel? How much is it?"

"Good hotel."

"Yes, how many rupees? Rupees?"

"You come."

Everything else at this late hour looks inhospitable. We are in a tough spot arriving at three a.m., so we chance his offer. The sinewy man deftly balances our luggage precariously on his bicycle rickshaw frame, loads us behind and starts all the bulking weight in motion. Our fate is now in this stranger's hands.

After taking us down shadowy, nondescript streets for about a mile, the driver stops us at a barely visible steel gate.

"This is a hotel?" Simon asks.

"Here hotel. Good hotel." The driver bangs on the gate and yells at a man sleeping on the floor three feet away. Only snores are returned. The driver continues to make an enormous racket to no avail. Finally, he hurls a stone at the sleeping man who still doesn't stir, as oblivious as the man sleeping on the floor in the middle of the Delhi train station. Finally, a light comes on in the building and someone lets us in. As we pass, the driver kicks the sleeping man who merely yawns and rubs his eyes.

"Passports tomorrow, come this way," says a tired concierge who shows us to a room. Our chamber has a broken chair and one rock-hard bed to share covered by a filthy, stained blanket. Thankfully, we have our own sleeping bags and fall right to sleep despite a ticklish sensation of microscopic beings performing a miniature circus on my scalp.

Traffic outside awakens us early this morning, but we are re-freshed enough for new adventures. Simon's book says Haridwar sits at the foot of the Himalayas, like Boulder, Colorado does in the Rockies but on a grander scale. The mighty snow-capped Himalayas are supposedly visible from some viewpoints. I am very excited to see the world's greatest range, which until now I have only read about in my Reinhold Messner books. Haridwar is also a holy Hindu site with many temples, one in particular being India's most sacred.

I am all geared up to go Eastern, and this is *the* place to say *Namaste*, if anywhere. I descend to the front desk with my hands clasped to say the magic word from yoga class that suggests a pure, knowing people.

"Namaste," I say with a dramatic bow.

The man at reception is attired in a Los Angeles Lakers jacket and cap like he's at a Fourth of July BBQ. He scrambles awkwardly to return the salute. Hell, he hasn't *Namaste*-ed anybody in years.

Feeling like an idiot, I begin filling out the hotel's tedious reg-istration paperwork. Once again, it is more detailed than a po-lice report: mother and father's names, their occupation, religion, and wife's name, for Indians assume you are married if you are over twelve. While doing this, the front-desk man is flipping cable channels from one shrieking, spinning mad Indian dance video to another. I'm beginning to wonder what happened to the fabled solitude of the Himalayas, much less *Shangri-La?* Is yoga just an-other fairy tale sold to gullible Westerners?

"Lock the windows too," Simon warns back in the room. He has been reading in the guidebook about Haridwar's infamous thieves: monkeys trained to climb in your room and find valuables. "What's more," he adds in disbelief, "they are taught to take *only* cash and decent jewelry."

I laugh, imagining a monkey appraising fine jewelry with an eye glass, but my levity is soon drowned out by the omnipresent honking as we descend to the main street.

Soon, we're outside amid that grinding chaos. On a particularly crowded avenue, Simon buys a bottled orange soda drink from a dirty little wagon. Remembering Robert's warnings, I say, "You're crazy to drink that. The factory must be filthy."

"Yeah, well if I get sick, I get sick."

As Simon enjoys his soda, we watch a monkey hovering back and forth waiting for his chance to grab a banana from a surly vendor twirling a menacing stick. It is the age-old mongoose-cobra standoff. In time, a customer distracts the store owner and in a flash the monkey is screeching joyfully away with his booty.

Without warning, Simon is doubled over in pain. He leans against a wall with beads of sweat rolling down his face. It is a sobering sight.

"Just me stomach. Be alright in a few."

Simon eats a banana, and it soon calms his insides. However, we are both shaken by the unexpected brush with illness.

We wander through the streets toward the famous hill-top temples that promise a great view of everything. On top of a steep green hill ahead of us stands the biggest temple. There are two ways to reach its stark white buildings: a squeaky, rusting chairlift or a long, torturous pathway.

We naturally choose the trail, and it is challenging for both of us. At summer camp I learned "the Everest step," where after every two steps one pauses, shifting all weight onto the leg bones by over-straightening the knee. You breathe deeply, keeping a "steady-wins-the-race" rhythm. Simon blazes ahead but is soon doubled-over, gasping for breath, as I calmly pass him like the turtle and the hare. He regains his strength and repeats the process over and over again. We clearly have competing philosophies. Sometimes I feel like an old fuddy-duddy compared to his charge-ahead ways, but India seems like a place to watch one's step.

Higher up, the wicked cement path, an old ascetic dressed in orange pops out of a little hole where he was tending two Hindu god dolls.

"Om," he says and clasps his hands, bowing to us. His presence is more what I had imagined for India, not the howling dance videos and honking.

We return his bow and continue up the trail.

"What does 'Om' mean exactly?" Simon asks.

"I don't know. I took a yoga class and we had to chant it. It was pretty embarrassing at first."

"Only at first?" Simon laughs.

"Yes." I think back to when that "sound" really did something for me trying to climb *Dragon Lady*. "Only at first."

Simon and I finally make it to the top of the path to find that the temples overlooking Haridwar are actually five stories high with the sweeping stone walls of great fortresses. It is my first contact with the religious institutions of India, and I anticipate this moment as a significant stepping-stone to my future. As we round the final switchback, I see jagged broken glass cemented on top of the temple walls as a cheap form of barbed wire. I don't understand what could be inside to steal.

After paying two rupees to enter, I am astounded to find myself in a carnival with Disneyland long lines. There are serpentine queues of pilgrims waiting to ring bells, and the main attraction is a strange dark box with dolls that must represent gods inside— perhaps Siva. We diligently wait in a line for forty-five minutes, and our patience is rewarded with the honor of seeing a ten-inch blue doll covered in red powder with Hawaiian leis draped around its neck, wielding a trident like Poseidon? Pilgrims who look as though they're pretty short on rupees themselves force coins through the wire bars. Though I am wise enough not to voice my disgust out loud, this is beyond a let-down. I thought it would be full of people chanting Om or meditating.

"Let's go," Simon says. "It's Christmas Eve after all."

Strolling down the steep stairs affords us an eagle's view of chaotic, dusty Haridwar, framed by a far-off mountain range blanketed in clouds. It doesn't feel at all like Christmas in this semi-tropical zone, where Santa's sleigh would be robbed by monkeys the moment he set down. Finally, the traffic slows its clank and clatter as Haridwar goes to bed with the sun.

"I AM MY OWN MASTER"

Christmas morning has us arranging for a bicycle rickshaw driver at the hotel, on the insistence of the proprietor, to take us on a holiday tour of the temples. An hour later, we find our man waiting patiently outside, and we settle awkwardly behind him on a hard little seat. His thin legs ripple into motion without a sigh as he simultaneously lights a little brown cigarette.

Our tour quickly becomes a department-store Christmas parade with us as the main float. As we shuffle along, throngs of Indians turn to stare. Many wave and giggle "Hellwo," sweet white smiles breaking across their faces. We wave back stiffly like the Royal family. There is not another white face in the crowd of thousands.

"Hey, I'm a movie star," I remark sarcastically.

"No wonder celebrities lose their minds with people gawking at them constantly."

"Ironic—all this attention is what people *think* they want."

We come to a steep hill, and the driver gets off and pushes our rickshaw. Having the scrawny driver suffer to get our burger and roast-beef-fed asses up the incline is too exploitative. As we hop off to lend a hand, I begin to realize that Simon is a really decent guy. A lot of people would've gone right on blabbering while the "colonial" had a hernia.

The driver stops at a temple on the edge of town. He smokes at the gate with no interest in accompanying us further. We pay another fee at a colorful booth and go in. These temple grounds are more spacious, but they are also dominated by sets of stairs leading to more sorry little blue dolls locked up behind bars.

For lack of anything better to do, we join a procession of Indians in a long line to ring a bell. A man ahead of us explains that if he rings the bell twice, claps his hands and bows, the gods will hear him. Apparently, we have found God's doorbell.

"With the gods' attention, all I desire shall be granted," the man confidently tells me. When his turn comes a few minutes later, he performs dutifully. Now I am next to hold the bell's rope. That man and several other Indians gleefully motion for me to ring it and clap like it is a dance number. My hands clasp the rope. Suddenly, it feels twisted and wrong.

"Aren't you going to ring the bell? There are people waiting," Simon asks.

"No, I can't."

"Why can't you just ring the bloody bell?"

"I came here to experience something, but ringing a bell isn't it. I can't do it."

I don't wish to offend, but it also feels dangerous to obey. Conformity to symbolic gestures is a kind of death; a non-thinking mode that can so easily be perverted into a rally with torches and uniformed troops saluting their pied piper. No, the bell's rope is a hangman's noose stifling what I came here for. I let go of it.

I wander to the edge of the temple grounds where open spaces unfold past the fence. I stand a long time looking down into a valley as wilderness brings my sanity back. The view of grass and trees extending off into the distance not marred by people is my true Christmas gift. Why aren't the pilgrims looking at nature, where the gods can be heard?

We resume the tour and finally come upon the famous holy river, Ganges—as important to India as the Nile has been to Egypt for untold thousands of years. Hindus have worshiped the river as divine bringing multitudes of pilgrims to come wash away their sins. Faded, red cement steps lining the shores are swarming with believers baptizing themselves.

By the river, beggars holding aluminum bowls wait patiently for a ladle of soup, and I am surprised to see so many smiles. This heart-rending scene reminds me of our own Great Depression. But for the ragged men laughing in line, poverty is a detail, not the ultimate condition of shame. In India, there is happiness even within a soup line, and I have to say I see more smiles here than I remember seeing in Aspen, Colorado, our great benchmark of ultra-wealthy, *nouveau riche* ski towns.

Simon and I duck into a narrow, flamboyantly-colored bazaar displaying an exotic array of brass trinkets, carpets, and clothing. We feel like Marco Polo discovering the court of the Khan, but as the day is getting on, we rush back to resume our tour, heading for the big temples in the main part of town. In an enormous nine-story building that becomes smaller with each level, the world, it seems, is consumed by pilgrims. The temple on the hilltop was a carnival, and now this one is a wild three-ring circus. There is a deafening pounding, making the floor tickle our feet. Upon reaching one of the building's upper stories, we find the source of the racket is three giant drum machines working in overdrive. As if they didn't produce enough noise already, a young man beats a fourth drum in a manic trance. It's getting strange, even for India.

"He's playing the drums for good luck, for that young man is going on a journey," explains an Indian, straining his voice over the hullabaloo. He must have noticed the blatant astonishment on our faces.

"Do you believe it's true?" I ask.

"Oh yes, there is an indisputable link."

I don't understand what the pilgrims expect to accomplish, but I suspect it may not really be all that different than my own love of the crass, noisy excitement most called rock and roll like my first concert by The Who.

After ten minutes, we have to leave the temple to save our eardrums. The Who, the winner of the *Guinness Book of Records* loudest live rock group catagory, was a lullaby in concert compared to the temple drums.

On the way back to our hotel, we foolishly purchase betel nut tobacco and put it between our lips and gums. It is the cause of India's filthy habit of spitting red juice everywhere; crimson stains can be seen on nearly every reachable surface. Our bravado is soon rudely deflated and we are reminded that we are far from home, as we both feel quite dizzy and sick. It is a temporary sensation, but betel nut is off our list for good.

Back at the hotel, twilight descends as fires are lit in the streets below. Haridwar settles down. We order a feast to eat on the rooftop balcony, and it is delivered by an eager-to-please nine-year-old boy. It isn't your Norman Rockwell Christmas with a juicy turkey, but the hot *chapatti* wheat cakes and dhal are wonderful. The low prices and relative peace of the hotel delude us into feeling like royalty. We use the grand occasion to try to unwind and forget our brush with the bizarre temple spectacles that have dampened my hopes for India's spiritual possibilities.

It is impossible not to walk to the balcony railing and gaze down into the tumultuous street below. Simon and I witness a man lean against a wall and throw up—very gross, but his lack of self-consciousness is liberating and puts us at ease. Nobody cares about nuthin'; Indians don't harbor the secret criticisms in their sullen detached ways. It is what people wanted, migrating to the Wild West: the open spaces and freedom to vomit.

A prosperous-looking hotel guest dressed in western clothes about our age joins our party. His name is Rajna, he is traveling from his home near Bombay, has recently been to New York City, and works for a computer company.

"India is certainly an interesting place," I comment. "What do you do in the evenings in Bombay?"

"We watch videos and relax with beer."

"Oh."

We hear a great commotion and go to look over the railing. On the street below, a bullhorn belches out gibberish from a car decorated with flowers like a float in the Rose Bowl. It is packed with men waving their hands and screaming. Large crowds run alongside carrying a banner that reads: "*The Horse Party*." Pure rowdiness reigns for some time. Then the excitement dies down, relatively, until a vehicle goes by from the *Wheel Party* accompanied by the same melee. According to Rajna, it is a political campaign in action. He explains that their Indian government is based on the American system, not the Parliamentary. India, population-wise, is the world's largest democracy.

"All our politicians are terribly corrupt," Rajna tells us.

"What about the Indian people?"

"Out in the country they are mostly ignorant fools ruled by our shameful caste system, and there is little education to replace local superstitions. In many villages, you can still buy protection against the 'Evil Eye' in the local market."

"Well, families are closer here, aren't they? They must have a more tranquil existence than ours."

"Many times, a husband will beat his arranged wife if her dowry is not big enough to buy a scooter. Did you see that red bridge over the river? Last year a man went bankrupt, so he jumped from it to commit suicide and forced his wife and children to jump, too."

"Even here," I sigh.

My naïve hopes are dashed, for it *seems* a gentler place. Of course, I am an idealistic fool to believe people don't suffer from insurmountable problems all over the globe, especially the hoax of class, caste, race. At this moment, I have no hope and hate humanity more than ever and concur with Mark Twain's scathing quote:

> *"I have no race prejudices, and I think I have no color prejudices or caste prejudices nor creed prejudices. Indeed, I know it. I can stand any society. All that I care to know is that a man is a human being- that is enough for me; he can't be any worse."*

Another roar comes from below, but this time it is the movie house down the street. The sound of machine guns and bombs shatter the peace in the already boisterous neighborhood. Rajna says the latest movies of their newly thriving industry are loaded with conservative Hindu propaganda that is shamelessly inching India toward war with Pakistan. It is India's *Rambo III*.

"Movies lie to the people and say their hate is just," he starts in again, "but there is a funny story about the movie houses. Most days it is too hot to close the doors and monkeys become attracted to the noise inside. It is not uncommon to see a family of monkeys sitting next to you eating popcorn from the floor."

"Really?" asks Simon.

"Yes, and the monkeys often become fascinated by the projector and stop the movie by grabbing the reel and running away with it down the street. What would happen in your countries?"

"The monkeys would be shot," says Simon without flinching.

"Our life with the animals is much different. It is not uncommon for a farmer to bring his chickens and pigs and mules on the passenger cars of a train in the countryside."

"Did you come to Haridwar on a religious pilgrimage, Rajna?" I ask.

"No," he laughs, "Only for holiday."

"We saw quite a few temples today," Simon says.

"Ah, you saw the temples of Haridwar. What did you think?"

"Well ... they were decorated nicely ... and had a lot of statues," I say, trying to be polite.

"I hear it in your voices. With me you may speak truthfully. They were silly weren't they? Full of superstition and nonsense."

"Well, they were a bit much," I admit. "I mean one had enormous drums beating for good luck, and there were giant statues of all kinds of eight-armed blue figures and elephant-headed gods. To be honest, I wasn't prepared for anything quite like this. No offense, but it all seems like complete nonsense."

"No, you are right; our religion is based only on superstition."

Hearing this, I instantly relax. I can write off the whole trip as one big mistake. No orange robes for me. "I have to admit that I was curious about yoga, but after what we saw at those temples yesterday I'm just going on home."

"Oh, but the yogis *do* have great powers," Rajna says.

"Huh? What do you mean? You just said it was all silly and superstitious."

"About the religion yes, but every year there is a great yogi festival where they display their abilities."

"You believe in yogis but not in the religion? What's the difference?"

"Religion is the most powerful force on earth, but only for the common people who believe. The suicide attacks on your American Embassy in Beirut were from fools following their religion."

"Well, what are the yogis doing?"

"Yogis have abandoned religion for a personal experience. Religion is from society and from traditions of the culture. To follow a religion is to be forever told of another's experience. A yogi has decided to experience the powers for himself. Another way to say it is religion is an adjective but yoga is a verb."

"What kind of powers do they have?"

"One story is of a boy who played a trick on what looked like a beggar. The boy said, 'Hey beggar, I am a rain cloud' and began to urinate on him from a window. The yogi used his power to stop the boy, which caused him great pain. The boy's mother apologized and begged the yogi to stop."

"Yogis can stop people going to the bathroom?"

"It is a true story."

It reminds me of the first *Star Wars* film when evil Darth Vader began to choke an insolent general without actually touching him physically. The alleged power Rajna described was the dark side of the force in action.

"Wait a minute, Rajna," I exclaim. "You are a modern guy and work for a computer company. Do you really believe that story? Have you seen yogis do these things personally?"

"Oh, yes. At this festival there is a yogi who pulled a train with his penis."

"He pulled a train with his *what?*" I ask in disbelief.

"With his man-penis. I have seen this at the festival."

"Really?"

I can only wonder how to employ that enviable skill, say, the 403 from Dartmouth has broken down just shy of the platform....

"Yes, but the most convincing evidence of all is my uncle who will close the door and practice yoga for two hours each day to come out a very happy man. In this way, I understand the true powers of yoga. You must go to Rishikesh, the next village up the Ganges where there are many ashrams that accept foreigners."

"Well, I guess..." I mumble with a sinking feeling. "Rishikesh you say?"

The next morning Simon and I stroll on the main road towards the north edge of Haridwar and come upon a sign that reads: '*Yoga Lessons.*' It is the first written sign with the 'y' word I have seen in India.

"Here's your place, maybe," says Simon.

We enter a garden, and a bald man about sixty-years old in white robes invites us to stay for tea. He motions for us to sit at a broken-down picnic table. A tray with large glasses made from aluminum soon appears. Flies swarm on the rim of my cup, so I slyly splash boiling hot tea over the rim to sterilize it, pretending to be clumsy.

The man stares at us curiously but makes no attempt at conversation. I feel unnerved by his silence, used to a world of small talk and cheerful chatter trying to be upbeat even when you're not. I begin to realize his silence comes from a deep inner peace beyond any pretense. There is nothing for me to feel self-conscious about—his presence begins to make me feel at ease, though I can't explain why.

"Do you know what that mean?" the man asks us pointing to an "Om" symbol on the crest of his roof.

We shrug.

"Om means God," he tells plainly us after a pause.

"It does?" I ask.

To me, "God" is a confusing and pointless topic. As a child, I was told God was an angry super being with a white flowing beard sitting in a church. But who is god in India? The concept is further confused here as God seems to include a vast host of deities all being more or less equal parts of the whole incarnate. Our Western insistence on monotheism is completely absent, deflating the need for exclusion and fighting. Slaughtering heretics for worshipping the wrong god isn't so easy here, where there are millions of deities to choose from.

The grounds are a shambles of bricks and rubble strewn about, not leaving much room for visitors or conducting yoga lessons. The man also says his yoga lessons are only taught on Sundays. "There are many ashram in Rishikesh for foreign man. They have English better than my bad English."

As we stand up to leave, I ask, "Who did you learn yoga from?" It is an off-hand question, a poor attempt to be polite. "Did you learn from your father or another teacher?"

"Yoga learn? What do you mean?"

"Who was your master?"

Sudden indignation spreads across his face. "I am my own master!" he says fiercely.

His words send chills down my spine. This is what I came here for: to be my own master. The man's words, even born from a misunderstanding, make a deep impression on me. I am inspired by his pure individualism and fiery courage. I can't help but think back to Boulder and to Derek Hersey, who once said, "I'm not an anarchist or anything, but no one tells me what to do," a comment followed, of course, by his fearless laugh.

The day in Haridwar is growing late, so we thank the yoga center man for his hospitality and get up to leave. He won't accept any payment for the tea.

Simon and I walk further away from the teeming city center and pass a stone obelisk that reads: *'All Religions Are One.'* Each major world religion is allotted one side of the marker, showing how their combined meanings have a common goal only separated by distance, time, and culture.

Back home in Denver, my neighbors have a bumper sticker on their car that reads: *And every knee shall bow* in front of a glowing cross. It suggests a subservience to Jesus and the existence of an ever-angry god ready to smite. I think of today's yoga teacher and his fiery words again: "I am my own master." They confirm that yoga can make one strong-willed and independent, and not just exist as a slave to blind faith. True understanding does not lead to subservience, and a defiant willpower not to bow down to any deity, old or new, is strengthening in me. My greatest goal is to someday say those stirring words with that same burning resolution.

Today, Simon and I leave Haridwar for a town called Dehradun. Our plan is to go up to a hill station, a tourist village clinging to a mountain, called Missourie, which is supposed to host incredible views of the Himalayas.

In the anarchy of Dehradun's open-air bus station, we find our ancient "coach" which is soon groaning up wild mountain switchbacks. We are still the only white people around. The passengers are nearly all staring at us again, but our eyes gaze out the window, taking in the strange sights. We pass a school for the blind, but all the students are out in front playing cricket. *How is this possible?*

The turns become even sharper. Judging by the groans and creaks, the bus can't take much more. Painted on the banks of the turns are various safety slogans:

>*Arrive Alive Your Mother and Father are Waiting*
>*Use Your Brakes and Don't Be Sorry*
>*Do Not Bring Shame on Family with Fast Driving*
>*A Smile Takes You Miles*

Our driver must not have read the signs because he takes each curve at maximum speed. My knees grind into the wooden seatback in front of me. I wonder how bruised they will be by the time we reach the top.

The landscape changes as we ascend to another climate zone. The air is becoming cool and fresh, and the forest is giving way to barren yellow hillsides, terraced in local inhabitants' desperate attempt to scratch out a living on the steep terrain.

At the end of the jolting ride we arrive at a small village. The fabled viewpoint is accessed—as usual—by either a rusting but brightly colored chairlift or a steep thirty-minute hike. Eager to breathe fresh mountain air after Delhi and the other toxic cities below, we choose the hike. At the top, we are not disappointed. Dizzying vistas of the world's greatest mountain range stretch into the distance. Simon and I remain on this perch for hours, silent and entranced.

After our fill of Himalayan mountain views, we walk back down the hill to change money in an ostentatious bank boldly decorated with white columns—a remnant of the colonial era reminding the visitor of the British intolerance for the heat on the plains below. Inside, the bank has a Wild West feel with brass cages and wood-paneled walls. We stand at the counter clearing our throats while the tellers, hunched over piles of filthy paper money and worn out tally books, pay us no mind. After a good while, we are told to take numbers and wait, though the lobby is deserted.

"You desire change?" asks one teller when our number is called ten minutes later. "That will be the next window."

"No change today," says the man at the next window, so we return to the first and report this shortcoming.

"One moment please." The man leans over the teller box wall to shove the second teller. The two men exchange harsh, unintelligible words, and then the second teller begins screaming and swearing at the first before retiring into the back.

"There will be change for you, but it will take some time," explains the first teller. "Please take numbers and sit over there."

"But we already took numbers."

"Yes, but they are not numbers to wait for change. They are number numbers."

"Number numbers?"

We sit helplessly on a hard-wooden bench wondering what kind of a bank doesn't have change. We think back to Robert's stories and suspect the tellers think it is just too much work to open the drawer, count out the money and fill out a simple form unless there is something in it for them. But if we are expected to bribe them to change our traveler's checks, we first need the money. It seems like a Catch-22.

We have been waiting some time when suddenly the bank president, well-dressed in a dark Western-style suit and tie, appears and invites us for tea. His office is lavishly decorated in the Victorian style, accentuated by dark wood paneling and marble floors.

"Today is my birthday," he tells us as a ten-year-old boy arrives holding a tray of beverages.

"Well, happy birthday!" we toast him cheerfully with our tea.

"I am thirty-two years old. I do not know whether to be happy or sad that my life is half over."

"Half over?" Simon asks. "No. You must have many good years left."

"Actually, life expectancy in India is just sixty," he says sadly, "if you are a fortunate one."

The bank president somberly continues about how he is trapped in this office, this impermanent world, until he dies. "The Buddha said we are all sleeping in the burning house of our mortality," he explains. He admits that it is obviously preferable to pass one's life in an earthly paradise, however privilege and position are no armor against the ravages of time and a soul unfulfilled.

Simon and I are fascinated by this banker's honest humanity and humility. Instead of our western pretense, he says his deeper thoughts outright. I am reminded of a Bob Dylan lyric that goes:

"We are stuck here stranded, but we are all doing our best to deny it."

We expect the usual sales pitch on the advantages of using his company for all our financial transactions along with the "Cheshire cat grin." Clearly, this is the land where the Buddha left his footprints.

An hour later, we have our money, and we bid goodbye to our melancholy friend. An ATM machine, if they had one, would spit out our money at hyper-speed, but we would miss the president's hospitality and philosophy. Of course, the bank president is right. We human beings bide our time amusing ourselves waiting for the end, but what can we do? I think of Rishikesh again.

Simon and I sit on the patio of a little restaurant and order lunch. Opening my wallet, one thing is clear: I am already running out of money playing tourist. With no credit cards to fall back on when my cash soon runs out, I'm screwed. I sit in the sun sweating over how I can sell off my few possessions. My head fills with schemes and dreams of reselling cheap Indian wares for fast profits back in the West. Then I feel awful. I realize that like so many foreigners my first thoughts have turned to how I can exploit India.

I confide in Simon, adding, "You'd think I was British. Sorry, nothing personal."

"You'll be alright," he replies. "Everything is so cheap. You just have to get somewhere you want to be and stay there."

Simon is right that everything is so cheap. It's like Granddad's economy you only hear about, one penny for a bag of peanuts at the fair, etc., but here we are living it. We spend an hour plodding through Simon's travel book, planning our next adventure. His guidebook claims that Simla is another British outpost and is crowned with so much elegant brick architecture you'd think you never left England. It's the capital of the north circled by idyllic mountains and house-boats floating on pristine-blue lakes. However, this is wintertime in the Himalayas, a ten-hour ride in a clunky bus—a long time to have one's knees crushed. Though it sounds like a nice destination, I secretly wonder if I could stand the ordeal getting there.

Our bus ride down from the hill station can best be summarized by blasting Hindi music, screeching as though it were recorded in a tin can, our driver hitting the stone wall twice, our bus narrowly missing an oncoming one, all under the calm, watchful gaze of a blue Barbie doll-sized goddess with eight arms and legs nailed above the windshield.

In thanks for returning to Dehradun in one piece, I want to kiss the ground in front of the bus station when we finally arrive. I quickly change my mind, noticing that the ground there is covered with trash, excrement, and other foul substances.

According to the best schedule available, it looks like our bus to Simla leaves at 11:30 p.m., so we have more than eight hours to wait. Being the only white people in the whole town, we quickly become zoo exhibits. Large groups of Indians gather around us to begin their unblinking staring contests. There is nowhere to go, nowhere to hide, so we sit on the dirt with our backs against a cement wall, praying silently to be left alone.

"Give to Krishna," a little girl orders us before two minutes have passed. She thrusts a plate covered with dirty coins in our face. She is apparently a Hare Krishna Girl Scout taking offerings of rupees instead of cookie orders. The plate hovers by our noses. "Give to Krishna," she repeats with an increasing firmness. We do our best to ignore her.

"No, thank you. Namaste!" I eventually say, ending the standoff by clasping my hands together in Anjali Mudra, the praying position, in common with Christians, of palms together and fingers pointing up.

She leaves; perhaps that word "Namaste" is good for something. But before we have a minute of peace, a man is growling at us. The little girl stands behind him pointing our way. He thrusts the plate of dirty coins back in our faces.

"You give Krishna!" he rudely demands.

Tension hangs in the air. A crowd, larger than normal, forms around our scene with an unwholesome interest resembling an Old West lynching mob. The Religious Right of India is ready for some justice. It's the world turned upside down, with Hare Krishnas ready to beat us up for skipping the collection plate. We sense a great danger and feel very, very small. Until now, I thought Krishnas were bald, brainwashed nuts beating their drums on the CU campus lawn—nuts, but otherwise peaceful and harmless.

"Ah, Krishna," I say, affecting ignorance. "Very nice."

Our tormentor is taken aback.

"Rupees for Lord Krishna!" he repeats, shoving the plate in Simon's face.

"Ah, rupees," says Simon, catching on quickly. He admires the plate with child-like awe. The "stupid" game is our only hope of escape.

The man whirls away in disgust, and the crowd disperses to gawk at something else.

Simon exhales in relief. "Fuck me. That was an experience."

Just as we begin to relax, a fight breaks out in the street. A teenage boy dressed in rags hits another with a long stick across the back of the head. Dust rises up as the pair struggles to the ground. An excited *rat-tat-tat* of Hindi blares from all directions as passersby break it up. Simon's watch says seven hours and fifteen minutes to go.

Finally, the shadows of the day grow long, and we migrate inside to lounge on the station's brightly colored plastic seats. For dinner we order from the "restaurant," which consists of two guys standing behind a large aluminum pot. The cooks smile tirelessly over their boiling glop. We watch them skillfully flip flat, round breads, the wheat flour generally called *roti* and the white bread version are labelled *chapattis,* on red hot coals until they puff up like balloons, a show not unlike the theatre of a pizza chef spinning the crust over his head to make the perfect pie. Simon and I wolf down the *roti* with spicy *dahl* soup. Dinner tastes wonderful—not all that clean perhaps, but very hot.

After our meal, while I pick up Ray Bradbury's *Dandelion Wine*—which I am reading for the third time—Simon is befriending our fellow travelers.

"This guy is a Tibetan refugee," he tells me. "Check out the way he sits."

An unusually rugged-looking fellow, whose visage and demeanor set him apart from the local Indians, is squatting in his plastic seat effortlessly on his heels. He shares a broad, joyful smile with us.

The man's happy expression makes us ponder the mysteries of not-far-off Tibet. Simon and I also wonder how hard it is to sit on one's heels. A Himalayan squatting competition has begun. I read another chapter of *Dandelion Wine* before the burning feeling in my knees matches the grimace on Simon's face. After five minutes, we call it a draw. The Tibetan man smiles at our adolescent play.

"Let's see what he thinks of Western music," Simon suggests.

I agree and pull out my cassette player, while Simon fits him with earphones. The man laughs sheepishly.

"How about 'Jumpin' Jack Flash.'"

It has to be one of my favorite songs. I became a devoted Rolling Stones fan at summer camp when I first heard "Paint it Black," a song with a sitar and mystical Indian flair. Meanwhile, most of my peers devoured the MTV crap they were told to listen to, miserable new-age bands like A Flock of Seagulls.

The Tibetan refugee nods his head agreeably but remains aloof from any real interest. Then our experiment is ruined by a crowd of Indians appearing to ogle over my cassette player with big eyes. They each insist on holding it and pushing the shiny, silver buttons. I quickly put it away before it can be "donated" to Krishna. They passionately protest—an alarming reminder of the sudden, unnerving excitability of the locals.

These hours after dark, however, pass sweetly. Small fires twinkle like stars down the street and the sounds of soft laughter make a peaceful backdrop as the neighborhood settles in for the night. Most street vendors have a short commute home: they lay out a blanket on top of their carts and go to sleep. Others bed down in the gutter where they themselves dumped refuse all day.

"Do you have an extra jumper I could borrow?" Simon asks. "India is supposed to be an oven, but it's getting bloody cold."

I fish out a sweater from my pack and return to reading. Under the soft, peaceful lights of the Dehradun station, I come to the last *Dandelion Wine* chapter, which begins: "And suddenly summer was over..."

The phrase strikes a chord. Time! Time is running out! This trip isn't a lark. I have to *do something* besides be a tourist. Grinding my knees against a bus seat for ten hours to Simla is losing its appeal. Rishikesh is just over the hill.

The Simla bus arrives as scheduled, and we hustle out into the dust where the drivers are practicing their typical ritual of gunning the engine at maximum revolutions for a couple of minutes before shutting it off. Simon scampers up the back ladder onto the roof and reaches down for my pack. Instead there is only my hand out to shake.

"I'm not coming with you, Simon," I say. My voice shows firmness and direction for the first time in India. "I've got to do something besides be a tourist. I'm going to Rishikesh."

"Right. Wow. Well, this is it then, eh?"

We shake hands warmly. Although I have only known Simon a few days since we were wary strangers at Heathrow, we have developed a timeless, gentlemanly, unspoken trust and friendship forged by being thrown together into the Indian fire.

"I've still got your jumper on..."

"Take it, Simon; you'll need it up north. Good traveling with you." There is a roar and then sudden darkness as his bus pulls away. I never got his address, and he is scheduled to be gone for three years, so it is very likely I will never see him or my sweater again. Now I am at the mercy of a new world, all alone in this dark Indian night.

CLOSE ENCOUNTERS OF THE
FOURTH KIND

The groaning departure of Simon's bus is replaced by the ominous snores, rasping coughs, and mutters of the Dehradun street inhabitants. I can't see a thing, so I carefully place each foot down as though I'm tip-toeing through a room full of snakes until I see a bright light far down the street. My feet point towards the light and when my eyes adjust, I joyously read the word "Hotel."

The front-desk manager is irritable. There is only one room left and his buddy, or probably cousin, is comfortably reclining on the bed watching television at a deafening volume. The lodger protests wanting to remain on the bed and suggests I go elsewhere, but I stand firm. I am not going back on the street tonight. As I drift into sleep, tiny organisms tickle my scalp yet again. Still I am grateful to be here; there are worse places to sleep.

There is no need for an alarm clock where people live by the sun. In the morning, the merciless scraping of throats, coughing and spitting right outside my window gets me up fast. I look with concern at the filthy blanket I spent the night on, wondering if it harbors one of the many foul diseases India has to offer.

The morning front-desk man is dressed head to toe in New York Yankees memorabilia. For fun, I put my hands in Namaste mudra to watch him self-consciously scramble to return the salute. I ask how to get to Rishikesh. He says the only way from Dehradun is by train.

Walking alone for the first time, the unwieldy dirt streets feel more real than ever as I traverse the boisterous town. I find the Dehradun train station all right, but all the signs are in Hindi squiggles. The man at the ticket window says there is no train to Rishikesh. I have to ride to Haridwar on the train, and then take a bus. Though Rishikesh is just over the hill, the journey will take all day.

The train is a steam engine, the kind I took as a child on family vacations for a tourist glimpse of the Old West.

After asking five people if this is the train to Haridwar, I decide to go by majority opinion. The problem, I am beginning to realize, is that the locals are often so agreeable or short on English vocabulary that they'll say "yes" to every question, regardless.

Inside the train car, I locate my seat—a little wooden bench. There is no glass in the windows, only rusty steel bars. It seems I've caught the prison train as I look out between the bars.

As the engine coughs into action, the train struggles at a sluggish pace, billows of steam enveloping the front few cars. Dehradun's dense mess slowly surrenders to a cool, sweet forest. The air is refreshing and the sensation wonderful as the dark tree canopy swallows us.

After only ten minutes, the train stops. Passengers descend to urinate and smoke. There is no apparent reason for the delay, but no one complains. Indians patiently accept life's chaos as though expecting the setting of the sun.

Without warning, the steam engine starts up, belching and gasping. As the train shudders into motion, the passengers who wandered off come alive and dash for the car doors. Everyone is yelling excitedly as though it's all a game.

An hour into the voyage, the train stops for the longest halt yet. Clusters of Indians converse in circles, sitting comfortably on their heels similar to the Tibetan man in Dehradun. Women bounce their babies on their laps. All are happy and at ease, there is no hurry to leave this party in the middle of the forest. I leave my pack propped up where I can see it in the window and cautiously descend from the train to stroll in the forest like a vagabond hillbilly with nothing to do and nowhere to go. I am immediately swallowed whole by the tranquil and mysterious forest. A song by Credence Clearwater Revival I haven't heard in many years plays in my head that starts: *Hey tonight, its gonna be alright.*

Everything is all right on Indian time. Time drips like honey.

My mind wanders back to a day at Lumpy Ridge with my old buddy Larry Moffett when I was sixteen. "Lumpy" sits on the northern end of Estes Park facing Longs Peak and offers hundreds of outings on the granite cracks and slabs. The orange-tan rock, enormous trees and great views of the high peaks make it one of the most beautiful climbing areas imaginable.

That September day found me and Moffett scratching up an obscure climb called *Eumenides* (5.8) on the enormous Sundance Buttress. The guidebook was vague, the route wandered everywhere, and Moffett took forever on lead. However, the warm sun, soft hills of pine trees, and Longs Peak in the distance made the time pass in a sweet dream. The wonderful feeling of time's slow march accented by the aspen trees on the hillsides changing colors at the full height of their glory.

At last, Moffett admitted we were lost on the massive face. We had to do several rappels to retreat, and just made it down as it was getting dark, and, though we had failed on a mere 5.8, I felt an inexplicable joy. If Red heard of our defeat he would be tickled pink, but as Moffett and I basked in Sundance's great shadow, it seemed clear that we were there to experience the natural beauty of the mountains, regardless of how well we climbed.

The train starts up again, recalling me back to India. I run laughing to catch it like everyone else.

An hour later, we are coming into Haridwar. I see a woman reclining contentedly with her children on a mattress under a tree. It is all she has—it is her living room—but she has not yet learned to be ashamed. The bustle of color and noise at the beehive bus station awakens me harshly from the dreamy forest. It is back to helter-skelter modern India. I ask five people, half of them bus employees, which bus goes to Rishikesh; they all offer different opinions.

Thirty confused minutes later, a bus rushes up and the driver sings out "Rishikesh." I tell the driver how hard it was to get here from Dehradun.

"Why not take bus from Dehradun to Rishikesh?" he replies.

As usual, the whole bus stares as though I am a space creature, but the passengers soon find other entertainment. A salesman stands at the head of the bus making a speech in Hindi about a miracle product in the dark bottle he is holding. Although I can't understand a word, it's clear that he is promising absolute satisfaction upon purchase—a snake oil salesman in a Wild West show. His theatre is pure amusement, until I watch some passengers part with their hard-earned rupees for what is probably sewer water. "A sucker born every minute…," as the saying goes.

After a few minutes, the bus driver revs the engine to a deafening volume. The grifter exits and we lumber off. On the road out of Haridwar, I spot the yoga teacher puttering around in front of his house. In this utter ocean of literally thousands of seemingly random people, I find it incredible to recognize someone I have met before. His words, "I am my own master," still echo in my ears. I will do my best to remember them in Rishikesh.

The potholed road winds into more dark, cool forests. A sign in a clearing reads:

Rishikesh is Vegetarian Only:
No Alcohol. No Meat.
Punishable by Fine.

No meat? No alcohol? Prohibition in Rishikesh? I think back to my stay in England, where such ideals seemed inconceivable: hard drinking was essential to the Victorian code. Just a week ago, Peter bet Red he couldn't drink ten pints and several hours later Red returned staggering. Red had downed the ten pints just fine, but the problem was they wouldn't *stay* down. The exalted pub life all too often turned to misery: fights, vomiting, and waiting around under hopelessly grey skies for night to come and do it again. No alcohol? Many people would jump out of the bus, but I'm actually looking forward to alcohol's absence.

Suddenly the Ganges River appears—here it is very wide and flowing with the slow power of an ocean tide. As the bus darts in and out of the forest, the river shifts in and out of view. The air smells lush, and I feel pangs of happiness. But my joy doesn't last. Soon, another overgrown and filthy town swallows our bus. In no time, we are surrounded by clanging rickshaws, mad buzzing swarms of scooters, and piles of trash and excrement.

I exit the bus into a sea of hawkers. The refrain of "Come, come my friend. Special price only for you" washes me down the street. So many rickshaw drivers pester me that, despite my pack, I break into a run down the main thoroughfare. Clearly, capitalism is alive and well in India.

I have no idea where I am going, but I feel this can't be the "yoga" part of Rishikesh. I keep heading up-river past oily, blackened and cramped repair shops. Workshops are spilling onto the sidewalk; men welding scooter parts send great showers of sparks flying around my feet.

On my left is a grimy, closed Red Cross office. I swallow hard. It is a stark reminder that this is the Third World, and I am on my own.

The rush of traffic lessens slightly over a bridge spanning an enormous dry riverbed where thousands of workers, many of them women, are removing rocks by hand. They walk great distances with large piles of rocks stacked on their heads. Shacks and shanty slums show many citizens live in the river's trenches. The mass of workers resembles a colony of slave ants. It is a bleak and brutal sight.

As the views fail to improve, I soon feel like a weary soldier surveying a blood-soaked battlefield. Doubts about India arrive unbidden in my mind. How can a place that can't take care of itself teach me anything? What secrets can Indians be hiding when they live in such desperation?

My efforts to continue upstream lead me into a labyrinth of streets, a ghetto. Open sewers draining down into the holy Ganges host such putrid smells that I have to pull my shirt over my mouth to breathe. Even so, the stench punches at my nostrils like a fist. Here, everything and everyone seems to be covered in human excrement, and I feel certain that it will get on my food or in my water at some point. It all reminds me of the joke in Monty Python's *The Holy Grail*: "How do you know he is a king?" Answer: "He is the only one not covered in shit." In the gloomiest corners of my mind, I see myself covered in sweat, convulsing from dysentery or hepatitis on a soiled Indian hospital bed. How could this country have invented *pranayama*, the special breathing technique, with odors this bad?

Finally, the awful slums begin to peter out, and the Ganges comes closer to the road. I buy a bag of peanuts from a vendor, despite the burning chunk of dry cow dung that sits atop the pile that warms them. Peanuts are a reliably safe food if still sealed tightly in their shells. However, too often you crack the shell and get only a shriveled up nut and a mouth full of sand.

"Where are you from?" asks a man walking in the same direction. He looks more like a western tourist than the typical Indian, and he doesn't seem to want to sell me anything.

"I am in medical school in Kansas, but I am from Iran," he explains.

"Do you like Kansas? I mean, are they friendly to foreigners?"

"Yes, they are friendly. There is some prejudice because of the problems between our governments. But most soon realize I am not a politician, but a person."

I remember back to the Iranian hostage crisis, and how I played jet fighter with my classmates on the playground, bombing the "dirty" Iranians. It seemed my patriotic duty to kill the "ragheads;" society confirmed it. Now I feel ashamed. It had never occurred to me that they were real people like this man.

"What are you in India for?" he asks.

"Well, um, I was thinking about trying some yoga," I respond sheepishly. "But I'm not so sure what to do now."

"Ah, we are walking past a place where westerners are welcome to practice yoga, and here, in fact, is the gate. I have heard it is quite okay."

I look up at the gate and decide I can at least inquire about their programs.

"Thanks then. Goodbye!"

"Good bye and good luck with yoga."

Passing a steel gate topped with barbed wire, I start up a very steep, long, winding walkway. By the time I reach the top of the path, I am exhausted, and I lean against a wall to rest. The noise of the rickshaws has faded away, a sense of peace returns, and there is a beautiful view of the Ganges spreading out below. I continue through another barbed wire gate to see simple, flat-roofed white buildings with yet more barbed wire in curls atop the surrounding walls. I imagine the compound of a brainwashing cult and I feel a chill. I remember Peter's prophecy that I would come back from

India bald, dressed in orange, and chanting Om. I can't let him be right. Such an image seems the antithesis of being my own master. Besides, after having the Denver Broncos pushed on me growing up, I'm sick of orange.

I tread cautiously through a neat garden and past a building titled "Meditation Hall" with an Om symbol mounted above, following "office this way" signs. At the entrance to the office, I almost turn back, but then I think of pranayama on the *Naked Edge*, and, taking a deep breath, I enter.

"Yes, what do you want?" asks a man hunched over a messy desk adorned with haphazard piles of grimy papers.

"Hello. I'd like to ask about taking yoga lessons."

"You want to learn yoga," he says mockingly.

It is not what I expected. Instead of a bearded swami lying on a bed of nails, or a hippy hopping up to give me a hug, I am face to face with the most miserable of all creatures: an Indian bureaucrat. I regret even coming in the door.

"Fill out this form, sign this here and here." There are even more questions than the usual hotel questionnaire form. The paperwork of civilization in a supposedly savage land is giving me a headache.

At last I finish, and the man snatches the form from my hands, saying, "You must pay in advance in Indian rupees."

"Well, I..." It's all happening too fast. My hands shake as I produce nearly all the money I have left.

"Leave your passport here."

I don't feel good about this at all.

The office bureaucrat swears impatiently for a worker to come.

"Take him to his room," he barks.

Am I his prisoner?

The worker grunts irritably but obeys, like a mad scientist's "Igor" leading me sullenly to a room overlooking the Ganges. It is comforting to know that the gate is nearby, in case I have to make a run for it.

The room is bare except for a couple of cupboards and a bed with a wooden frame and cloth-woven hammock-like mattress. I also notice with apprehension some papers and trash left behind by the previous tenant, which suggest a hasty departure, or escape. The rules posted on the wall prohibit music. Will they take away my one great refuge, my cassette player? I hide it as best I can among my few possessions.

Suddenly, there is a rude knock at my door: *Bang, bang, bang!*

"You come office now," snarls Igor. I am surprised he can speak English.

"What is it?"

"You come."

I seem to have no choice but to repack my things and trek across the garden again.

"Your visa to India has expired!" yells the office manager. "You are in our country without permission!" With only a small desk between us, he is shouting at the top of his lungs.

"That can't be right. I've only been here five days now." He reluctantly allows me to hold my own passport. "Here, my visa was issued by the London Embassy a week ago." Sure enough, he had the date of expiry confused with the arrival stamp.

"Go back to your room," is all he says, looking away sulkily.

According to the ashram booklet, the grumpy bureaucrat gave me, meditation class starts at 5 p.m. to be followed by dinner at six. A list of rules states that not attending meditation or yoga class is grounds for being thrown out with no refund. I feel ill. I am forced to participate for the oldest reason in the world: money.

Overwhelmed by anxiety, I unpack my stuff a second time. I am convinced that I have just surrendered the last of my savings to a degenerate cult. Back in a melancholy English winter, the idea of running off to India was a beautiful dream. Now that I am finally here, I can only wonder if the word "ashram" means "insane asylum" in Hindi.

Outside the large hall, shoes and sandals are lined up in rows by the entrance. As I enter, my eye is immediately drawn to a cheesy plastic statue of a man in orange robes on a raised stage—the perfect image of a freaky cult. My unease returns in a flood of nausea. Maybe that Iranian man wanted to kill me after all. I bite my lip and remind myself I have to do this or I'll be out on the street penniless.

Like I always did in school, I make for the back row to hide. As my eyes adjust in the dim light, I see about twenty people in the room. They appear to be a mixture of Indians, Europeans, and East Asians sitting on cushions, many with blankets wrapped around them.

A portly Indian woman comes in and sits on a platform below the plastic statue but above our class. "Get ready and relax the mind," she says with a heavy accent. "Oooooooooooommmmm..." she begins.

The rest of the group joins in, except me.

I feel none of the peacefulness I gained from meditation in my Denver yoga class. Instead, it feels perverse. Sweat rolls down my face; I want to cry for the loneliness of it all. Have I gone nuts? Why am I never satisfied? Why aren't I in a law office getting my career going? My peers are starting to get good jobs, fast cars, mortgages, and even married. *What is wrong with me?*

Instead of trying to meditate, or whatever we are supposed to be doing, I look around the shadowy forms and wonder just how weird the other people here must be. I have always been afraid of nut-cases. The first summer I had my driver's license, I drove up to Wyoming to climb Devil's Tower with a less gung-ho guy from Cheley named Ed. Ed took a lot of allergy medicine that was a derivative of cocaine, and as a result, he was spacey. We just wanted to summit Devil's Tower via the easiest way, *The Durrance Route*, but it was a hard, wide crack and nearly unprotectable with the limited equipment I had. Ed fell, following the first pitch, and his glasses went flying down the crack. He hung on the rope blinking and unwilling to continue. We had just been defeated by Devil's Tower's 5.6 tourist route. But Ed wasn't the only problem. Licking our wounds later in the campground we met a man holding a suitcase full of peanut butter and jelly sandwiches. *Close Encounters of the Third Kind* had come out a few years before using the Devil's Tower as a key part of the story, and this man explained that the sandwiches were for sustenance when the intergalactic shuttle came to pick him up for a voyage beyond our solar system. Even after moving our tent to the other side of the campground, we hardly slept.

As I sit in the dark meditation hall, my mind is anything but quiet. I wonder what kinds of crazy people I am sitting next to. Do they have suitcases packed with sandwiches to visit the planet Nebular with their guru? It looks like it's going to be close encounters of the "fourth kind," since I have to spend the next four weeks living with them.

Such dismal thoughts carry me through the early part of the meditation hour until the door creaks slowly open, and a man stumbles in. He fumbles along the wall and stops in front of me.

"This is my place for meditation. You must move," he whispers in annoyance, ushering me away like I'm a stray dog.

It is the worst of all moments, having to move my place and realizing people aren't going to leave me alone anywhere in the world, even in the counter-culture retreat of an Indian ashram. Disgusted, I move all the way back to the wall in the lonely dark. I hate this place already.

After an eternity of silence, "Oooooooommmmmmmmmmnnn" goes the fat lady, and "Ooooooooommmmmmmmmnnnn" goes the group. The lights turn on, and I limp slowly towards the door. Sitting on the floor in even the beginner's half-lotus pose has cut off all circulation to my legs and, apparently, my brain.

Dinner is served in a separate building on a kind of a porch, where we sit on the ground with our backs to the wall. Workers serve us running up and down the row yelling "subji," offering to scoop vegetable slop onto the army-style aluminum ware in front of us. The term "mess hall" only begins to describe this experience.

"Is the food okay for Westerners?" I ask a silver-haired white lady next to me.

"Yes, it's a *satvik* diet, and the water is okay to drink, too," she replies with an American accent.

"What does *satvik* mean?"

"No onion or garlic is allowed. It is a simple diet, like hospital food."

"Are you American?"

She nods solemnly as though she has taken a vow of silence and turns away. As I eat by myself I feel a grain of dirt in my mouth; hospital food is usually cleaner than this. No meat, no alcohol, no onions, no garlic, and now no talking. I can see this place is going to be a real blast.

"Tra da da aa lala ta da ta," someone is singing. My heavy eyelids part to read 4:30 a.m. on my watch. It seems to be coming from next door.

Bang! bang! bang! on my door. I convulse in my sleeping bag from every rap.

"You are awake, my neighbor? Meditation starts very soon. Do not be late!"

If it starts at five, then 4:58 should suffice, I think drowsily.

I wait until the last possible minute before bravely leaving my cozy sleeping bag. As I shut my door, the Indian sky is still black as ink. Across the river, bullhorns begin a garbled chant. I stagger toward the meditation hall while a fragrant breeze tickles the trees above. I pause to wonder at the bullhorn party now going full blast across the bottomless dark body of the Ganges. It is one of those times when you're not sure what is real anymore. On the other side of the globe, Americans are drinking Coca-Cola, buying Chevy trucks, getting miles plus bonus miles, and eating meal-deals in food courts. This can't be the same planet.

I take a seat in the far back and shiver from the cold. The same lady comes in, moans Om three times, and turns off all the lights except for a dim bulb up front. I twist my body into the pretzel-like full lotus position I learned in yoga class at home. In less than two minutes my knees feel like they're being torn out of their sockets. I surrender and stretch them out straight. Now I am bored, fidgety, and unable to keep my back erect.

In the front row, I spot an Asian man in black robes sitting perfectly straight and still. As the dim light shines off his bald head, he appears strong and eager. *He must be a Zen Buddhist*, I think excitedly. Back in the States, you hear the word "Zen" to describe all the mysteries of the mind. *Here is a professional who can really show me how to meditate!* Full of new enthusiasm, I try to sit up straight again, but my tight leg muscles soon betray me. After five minutes, I slump forward with a backache and regroup to try it repeatedly. The superman up front hasn't so much as twitched the whole hour.

"Om" moans the lady, and "Om" moans the class. The morning session is finally over. Outside, the wind is picking up, and the sky is reddening to the east. I limp out to see the asian man walking "mindfully" around the garden. I approach him respectfully, bowing as they do in Japan.

The man looks at me stone-faced and cold. He is not amused.

"Hello, do you speak English?"

"Yes, I am not stupid."

"You have a perfect posture in meditation. That is remarkable."

"It is hard only if you are weak."

"Oh. Are you a Zen Buddhist?"

"Yes, I am a Zen monk."

"How do you meditate? Could you teach me?"

Evening in Rishikesh

"Our training is most severe. To want this meditation training, you must sit in the full lotus posture for twelve hours at a time. If you cannot, you are beaten."

"What? They beat you?'

"Oh yes, we are beaten every day. To be beaten is a great honor. It keeps the mind focused. The practitioners here are weak because they are not punished."

My heart sinks. The ashram seems like punishment enough to me already. But is spiritual practice supposed to be torture? In Colorado, there is a canyon called Penitente where the early Spanish settlers gathered to whip themselves bloody in self-flagellation. The Spanish settlers seem mad to me. Is that the way? It can't be, and just thinking about such misery makes me feel worse than ever.

I look at the Zen Buddhist and wonder at such elitism in the spiritual world. I ask him. "Is being beaten really what it takes?"

"Oh yes, those that can make Zen have been through great pain. A yogi living on the river has blinded himself putting coals in his eyes to keep them from distracting him. Perhaps he is twenty years away from perfection."

"Twenty years after blinding yourself?"

"Yes, but only if he practices starvation." The Zen monk looks me over and says mockingly, "Do you think *you* want this perfection?"

"I thought I did."

"Bodhidharma made Zen until his legs fell off. You must throw yourself into meditation like to death." Now he looks back at me like I am an insect. "I doubt this accomplishment is for you."

"I guess it's not. I thought it was about something else."

The Japanese man scowls and abruptly excuses himself by basically pushing me out of the way.

I sit dejected in the garden, fighting off the urge to cry. Being inadequate has haunted me all of my life. That it should find me even here, in the world of meditation, begins a familiar nightmare all over again. I contemplate the Zen monk's life of self-denial, enduring beatings, torture and voluntary baldness. *Is being beaten what it's all about?* But his example as a "professional" contradicts my inner instincts. Something doesn't feel right, despite "expert" advice from this man high in the spiritual hierarchy. I begin to reconsider my respect and veneration for Zen Buddhism. In this new light, it doesn't look so different than the elitism and arrogance I faced elsewhere. It's fascism in black robes.

After about an hour of these reflections, I notice the solemn white-haired American woman from dinner walking past. Surprisingly, she waves and says, "Would you like to have a stroll with me? I'm going down to the second bridge, if you don't mind walking with an old lady."

I am curious to discover what is down by the holy river besides the chaos of Rishikesh proper. For example, where the hell are those bullhorns coming from in the pre-dawn hours? We walk down the twisting cement path and turn left onto the main road, where a giant white arch over the road reads:

BE GOOD DO GOOD

The message seems innocent enough, but the arch's imposing 150-foot monumental height suggests to me the ubiquitous watching eyes of a totalitarian regime. Big Brother in the lotus pose.

Further on, we reach a suspension bridge spanning the Ganges. Too narrow for cars, the bridge seems to sag under the weight of throngs of pedestrians fighting to get across. Scooters, many of them absurdly overloaded with luggage, family, and fellow citizens, thrust through the onslaught, incessantly engaging their shrill horns.

"Let's continue up the main road to the second bridge and loop back," the silver-haired woman suggests.

She struts deliberately like she is solving a philosophical question, but for an old lady she can really motor up the steep road.

I find it hard to breathe, much less relax, next to the clambering traffic that sprays plumes of black diesel exhaust in our faces. The air is filled with smoke; there is always a fire somewhere. Pack mules with ridiculously heavy loads of rocks or sand in sad burlap bags are cruelly bent in half as they are whipped along the roadway. Men in orange rags lie around in front of temples like feral cats peering up to see if a meal is coming their way. The degraded state of everything is too much to swallow.

"So how do you meditate?" I ask her.

"That is not an easy question. There are several stages. *Pratiahara* is the first that consists of withdrawing from worldly wandering, indulgence in the senses, and then getting some control over the mind. Choose an object of concentration, or *praktia*. Single-pointed concentration is called *Dharana,* from which the name "zen" is derived."

"What do you concentrate on?"

"I am a Christian. I concentrate on the Christ consciousness," she tells me.

"Is that the best technique?"

"The technique doesn't matter, only the quality of the meditation. Uninterrupted concentration on the *praktia* is the important thing."

Further along the road, dilapidated little shacks line the route. Despite their decrepit condition, the doors are padlocked.

"They need locks on their doors? I thought there was no materialism here."

"Materialism can be two beggars fighting over a bowl," the American lady replies.

"India's not the Nirvana it's supposed to be," I sigh, eyeing the locks on the little shanties. If it wasn't coveting a luxury car like back home it was stealing another's only food bowl.

"People are people the world over." The woman comments.

Pointing ahead, she adds, "There is the second bridge by the colony."

"A yoga colony?"

"No, a leper colony."

I haven't heard of leprosy since Sunday school. "Surely they must have a cure for it?" I ask.

"No cure, only prevention. For these people, it's mostly too late."

We pass a fence over which I catch glimpses of people wandering in a barren yard, their dark skin a patchwork of pink splotches. *What kind of life can a leper have?* I think of Peter's terrible leper joke and feel ashamed that I laughed at it. I am sicker of India and the world than ever before.

We cross the large, arching second foot-bridge in silence, struggling to slip through crowds of pilgrims on their way to the brightly-colored temples on the other side. The sound of bells cascades down from the temple towers. Coming upon a bench, we sit and observe the stage.

"Why do they wear the colored robes?" I ask, looking at a group of Indian men.

"Orange is the color of the holy man, or guru, and the white robes of his disciple signify the renunciation of worldly things."

I watch a young man in white robes attending a bearded man, apparently his guru, in orange. The bearded man snaps his fingers impatiently as his disciple scrambles to please. The young man is certainly not his own master. We continue walking to the quieter side of the river.

"Why are there no young people here doing yoga?" I ask. "I braced myself for wall-to-wall hippies."

"Yes, well, in the 1960s, Rishikesh was packed with Americans."

"Where are they now? I guess yoga and Eastern religion failed."

"No, yoga does not fail people, people fail yoga," the woman says. "It is hard work and very conservative, contrary to what our Sixties-era youth believed."

"Still, you'd think more would be here if there is really something to it."

"Do you think that the thrill-seeking masses would be content with quiet walks by a river when there are exciting gun fights in the cinema? Or fancy cars to drive?" We walk on in silence for a while until we pass a building with noises coming from inside a dark corridor.

"That is a school where they teach Sanskrit, the ancient language of yoga and also the mother-language of English," she explains.

I don't say anything, but I pity her ignorance. There is no way English has any relation to an Indian language, written with squiggles evolving thousands of miles away. I decide she is crazy.

"Aren't you afraid of being in a weird place like India?" I ask her.

"If you have a peaceful mind, most people will not bother you. Don't you see the care the bus drivers take to miss the animals? Do you think they would do that at home? I am much more afraid in Los Angeles or Northern Ireland, where four soldiers march back to back watching for snipers on patrol."

She clearly isn't afraid. She tells me that she lost her job as a school-teacher at age sixty, and, instead of panicking, she saw it as a sign to come to India for prayer—Christian prayer. Next, she will go to the desert in the Holy Land for forty days and forty nights, just as Jesus did.

"It was in the desert that Jesus found his enlightenment," she says.

I am impressed by her efforts to transform herself for her faith. She is following Christ's example literally, rather than popping into church on this or that Sunday, satisfied that heaven is in the bag.

But then she tries to explain the holy texts of India. It is awful. Hinduism is called the world's oldest religion, but in all that time the Hindus don't seem to have written anything *I* can enjoy. Although India's rich spiritual heritage is what brought me to India, the complicated and far-fetched religious stories bore me to death. As Huckleberry Finn said when the devout widow tried reading him the Bible, "By and by she let on Moses had been dead a considerable long time. I don't take no stock in dead folks." I agree. I would rather puke than listen to more of these stories.

Noticing my disinterest, the American woman asks, "Isn't this why you came to India?"

"It's why I *thought* I came. I'm starting to think it will be a miracle if I can get any benefit out of this trip."

"Miracles happen every day, especially in India. Keep your eyes open, and you will see."

NOWHERE TO GO

I have not shaved since England. I try to get cleaned up in my dank little bathroom, but without a mirror, I nearly hack off my lips. A minor cut might mean gangrene and death in a place like this. What really has me on edge is my ignorance about the subcontinent's diseases. On second thought, maybe it's better that I don't know.

I call on my noisy neighbor to ask for a mirror. He's an Indian man well over sixty, very austere in his manners and clothing. He wears white robes and a wool hat and hasn't shaven of late. Instead of a mirror, I get a lecture on materialism.

"It is a mirror that you require? Why is it Westerners require so much more than we?"

Why? His question takes me back to my suburban American upbringing. I can hear the voice of my neighbor, Linda Kinney, taunting: "We have new shoes and you don't, so ha, ha, ha!" as she returned from the mall. It was the first time I heard the *uberjungen*, the superior people, make clear their values. Linda's flowing blonde hair, her shiny swing set, and her piercing scorn comprised some of my earliest memories of our new house on the dusty south Denver prairie. It didn't matter that my shoes were perfectly fine or that my father actually earned more than hers; it was war. Yet Linda's taunts couldn't be dismissed simply as childish rudeness, either. Consumerism was the ethos of both my neighborhood and my nation. Later, the rock band Nirvana would cover its *Nevermind* album with the image of a baby swimming after a dollar bill on a fish hook. Linda, like just about everyone else I grew up with, had that hook firmly lodged in her mouth. In the 80s, people liked to say, "He who dies with the most toys wins." That so-called philosophy describes the world of my youth in a sentence.

I can't defend American greed or consumerism. Unfortunately, the ones who need a good talking-to are unlikely to visit an ashram in India, but I still need a mirror. My staunch neighbor reluctantly retrieves one out of his room.

"Why do Americans not help their family?" he prattles on. "My sons all live at home and we work as one. Some Russian boys have come to India last year. They were such fine, clean people. Why did you not wash yourself at four o' clock this morning? It is the very best time."

"Yes, I heard you."

"I am a school teacher from Madras, so I am always punctual and clean."

"I'll bring the mirror right back, I promise," I tell the scout master wearily. It is strange to meet such dull, conservative people in an Indian ashram of all places.

After lunch, I search the shops down by the river for a shaving mirror and for distraction from this incredibly boring place I now call home.

"You want to try meditation?" asks a little man. "You come and meditate with me, and I show you how."

"Well I don't kn…" I begin to reply when a sweet substance is suddenly shoved into my mouth from someone behind me.

"Good, yes?" asks an Indian man. Slowly I recognize him as the jerk who threw me out of his sitting place in the meditation hall yesterday evening. He has forced a yellow candy into my mouth. I also recognize it as one sold in the market where dark blankets of flies sit the whole day long. I cough and spit it out.

"Yes, yes, come walk with me," he continues, unperturbed by my actions. "You like meditation? Sorry I have to move you yesterday. The meditation place is special place, and one must sit every time same place for good experience." He bends toward me and whispers, "That man who talks to you there is money guru. He wants only money, money, money for teaching meditation, which he don't know because he wants only material thing."

"Oh, well I'm safe," I reply. "I don't have any money."

"No money? Hmm." He frowns.

"Well, I mean, I have no extra money for that. I have just enough to stay. Do you like it at the ashram?" I ask with concern, "Are the yoga teachers strange?"

"Yes, very strange."

"Really?"

"Yes, be very careful of them. Very dangerous persons."

"You seem nice. Could you teach me yoga and meditation?"

"No, no, I am too attached to material things," he replies. "I am not a great master."

"Well I just want to see if I like it. Does it really work? Is there something to it?"

"Yes, yes, yoga can bring many things to you."

"Like what?"

"Money, women … the important things," he says.

That wasn't quite what I meant.

"Yoga is concentration," he continues. "Concentrate toward what you want."

"Aren't we supposed to concentrate on 'Om' or something spiritual?"

"Yes, yes, spiritual thing," he agrees dismissively.

He tells me he is twenty-eight years old and his name is Pradeep Bramachari, the latter term being a religious title. He speaks to me using dated hippy slang that I haven't heard since watching the *Brady Bunch*, saying odd things like "good vibrations." He is wearing the white robes of an initiate and professes to be a devoted Hare Krishna.

Forgetting my manners, I shudder to think I have fallen so low as to pal around with a Hare Krishna. These are the crazies I'd see chanting and dancing with a vacant stare on the CU Boulder campus or pestering passersby at the airport.

"What is the matter, American friend? Do you not like the Hare Krishnas?"

"To be honest, they seem strange in my country, like they're brainwashed."

"Yes, brainwashed," Pradeep considers, "Yes, maybe some hypnosis. Concentration is the focusing of mind like a torch light," he continues. "Yes, be very careful if someone begins to do this." He glares at me with a wide-eyed hypnotic stare, as convincing as a comic book character.

I can't help but laugh. "Yes, I will be very careful of that. Hey, it's almost four o'clock!"

"What happens at four o'clock?"

"Yoga class. We'd better get started."

"Yes! We must hurry," Pradeep says with grave concern. "The teacher will shout again."

I don't need that on my first day, so I set off running up the steep path.

A handful of foreigners are warming up inside the hall. Nearly all of them have gray hair; it seems I have joined a yoga retirement home. As I spread my sticky mat out, I feel spoiled, for the others have only a blanket to do the poses or asanas. There's a noise at the door, and the students stand up straight and respectfully for the teacher. It's Pradeep! He winks at me, then assumes his position at the head of the room. *That guy is our yoga teacher?*

Pradeep's class is a letdown compared to my Denver teacher's. He even gets the *Indian* names for the asanas wrong, and his thoughts seem to be elsewhere.

At dinner, the others keep to themselves. Their cold formality still bothers me, yet I am grateful not to be forced into a community with hokey sing-alongs. I spend my extra evening hours reading and wondering how long it will take for six weeks to go by. This is only the end of the first full day.

My second morning at the ashram begins like the first: the noisy neighbor, bullhorns chanting across the river, and another shivering meditation session, all before five in the morning. Once it's over, I creep back to my room. I don't care if I sleep until lunch.

At noon meditation, Pradeep once again comes in late and tiptoes to his "special place," giving me a comical nod before settling down. I appreciate the distraction. Any clown who dares to fight the tedium is a hero in my book.

"Incredible meditations today! Like floating in the clouds, la de da," Pradeep says afterward in the garden. "Let's go to village. You want a chai?"

"Sure, I guess so. What's chai?"

"First I must find cigarette."

"You want to buy them in the village?"

"Buy cigarettes?" he slaps his thigh laughing. Then he rubs his hands together, looking every direction for prey. "Ah, yes of course, Japanese woman!" He runs up to a door and knocks wildly. An Asian woman opens her door as stone-faced as the Zen monk. In an Oscar-worthy performance, Pradeep prostrates himself at her feet and bemoans his cigarette-less poverty. A smile breaks across her face at his antics, and she returns with a white stick like a Halloween treat. Pradeep backs away on hands and knees, groveling on her walkway and sending passersby into convulsions of laughter.

"You meet my friend, Shanker," Pradeep says ushering me down the path in a hurry. "*Buy* cigarettes?!" he chuckles into the wind like that's the most absurd idea ever.

Off the main road, Pradeep takes us down a street that descends toward the first bridge, pausing at a boarded-up hole in a filthy, crumbling blue cement wall. It literally looks like a fort that kids might make from scrap lumber. Parked outside is a fruit cart labeled: '*Shanker's Fruit Stand.*'

"Yes, welcome," says a voice inside. A young man removes a couple of boards to peer out. He obviously makes his living selling fruit. "Oh yes, I sell only the very finest quality fruits in Rishikesh."

"Shanker sells only the very finest quality," Pradeep repeats.

I look at his wooden fruit cart. It is stocked with the same sorry, bruised and wilting produce as all the other local fruit carts.

"Yes. I see."

We squeeze into the tight hovel. Shanker remains under a filthy blanket while I sit in the crossfire of their Hindi banter. On Shanker's grimy wall hangs a calendar from a Delhi bank. Instead of the pleasant country scenes or images of New England lighthouses normally decorating our calendars, it depicts blue Hindu deities flying like superheroes, lasers shooting through the Om symbols on their palms. I am amazed by the exotic symbolism on an everyday product.

Shanker ignites a blue flame on a gas cooker and balances a large silver pot on top. The stove and its rickety burden sit alarmingly close to my head.

"Chai?" he offers.

"What's chai?"

"Indian tea."

"Sure, if it's boiled thoroughly."

"Hot, hot, yes, yes."

Soon there is a boiling hot cup of chai in my hand, but the filthy glass concerns me. I try to use my clever trick of pretending to be clumsy and slop hot tea over the rim to sterilize it, but it goes all wrong. I spill too much, the boiling tea wets my pants and scalds my leg. The fort is too cramped for me to move, so I end up with a burning leg. Pradeep and Shanker stare curiously at my discomfort.

Shanker's chai is spicy with lots of milk and sugar. It could hardly be more different than the bland English tea Peter made such a fuss about in Kent. I feel privileged, invited to sip chai in the little fort with the locals. Despite my mishap, I begin to feel less like an idiot tourist for once. Shanker's place definitely wouldn't be found in *Let's Go India!*

"You want bidi?" Shanker asks.

"What's a *bee dee?*"

"Bidi, bidi. This one bidi," He unwraps a paper package of brown eucalyptus leaves, rolled up into small, thin cigarettes with a tiny hand-tied pink thread around each one. I wonder who has the job of tying the little thread in the cigarette factory. Pradeep lights one and tucks extras behind his ears. I have a feeling they won't last long. Then he puts one in my hand.

"I don't smoke."

"You don't smoke?"

They look at me puzzled.

"He doesn't want bidi?" Shanker frowns, clearly convinced that I am crazy.

"Ah, no bidi now, but later, yes?" Pradeep suggests, hoping to salvage my reputation.

"Y-yes, later."

The plan seems to have worked. Shanker relaxes, regarding me philosophically. "You come from America. Which place?"

"Colorado."

"Cah-lorodo?"

"Yes, out west."

"Ah, you are cowboy?" Shanker grins, proud of his worldly knowledge.

"Sure," I reply, having decided that agreement is easier than the truth.

Shanker takes my empty cup, first washing it with cloudy, cold water, then wiping it with a filthy rag. It is now more unsanitary than if he had left it alone. The display turns my stomach, and I am no neat freak. I wonder if I'll ever get out of India alive.

"Do you do meditation, Shanker?" I ask to take my mind off of the myriad illnesses I could have just contracted from my cup of chai.

"Oh, yes, every day I sit by Mother Gunga, to make the very highest quality vibrations."

"What's a *Gun-ga*?"

"The river Gunga. Ganges of English," Pradeep explains.

"Okay, you sit by the river, and then *how* do you meditate?"

"Not simple river," Shanker corrects, "*Mother* Gunga. Every day I make mantra repetition. Correct mantra vibration very important. Very powerful."

"Can I ask which mantra do you chant? Which one is best?"

"What do you want from mantra?" Shanker asks.

"I-I don't know. When I tried a mantra at home it gave me a great feeling after a while. I don't know why. I read some books about enlightenment, but I'd just be happy to get that feeling back."

"What do you want from mantra?" Pradeep repeats. "You want beautiful woman or material thing? With mantra you get anything you want."

Anything you want? I look around Shanker's disheveled shack. If these people can get anything they want, why are they living *here*?

"Now you want bidi?"

"Later, please."

"When I was younger my father took me to see the Taj Mahal," Pradeep explains. "I was looking at beautiful girl and wanting her friendship so badly. My father, he sees this and says make yoga concentration on her. Be full of good vibrations and pull her towards you."

"Okay, but is it right to use yoga that way for women and money?"

"Yoga is there for your use. The great emperors of history had this power. Hitler was evil man, but he had incredible concentration. He was a hypnotist of the German people with pure mind power."

"Hitler did yoga?"

"Not good yoga like Indian people, but he knew the power of concentration. He choosed the dark side."

"The dark side?" It sounds like *Star Wars*.

Pradeep examines me through a plume of eucalyptus smoke. "Why did you come to India?"

"To learn yoga, I guess, but I've been having mixed feelings," I confess. "I thought things would be different here. People back at home talk about the power of *Zen*. I wanted to see for myself."

"Now you want bidi?"

"No, thank you. Really, is there anything to yoga?"

I wait breathless for Pradeep's reply. I need to know whether I'm just wasting my time. From watching *Kung Fu* episodes as a kid to my own yoga applied to climbing, I am ready to believe it can do miracles—but what is the secret?

"The power of yoga can do anything," Pradeep states, but without much interest. "I have seen a man in Delhi floating three feet above the floor."

"Really?" Now I am interested; this is what I've been looking for. "I've seen things on television, but it's just a trick, isn't it? Have you seen people walk on fire?"

"Fire? Oh, yes many people," Pradeep affirms dismissively, looking at his watch.

"You're not just telling me stories, are you? How do they walk on the coals without burning their feet?"

"Special mantra," Shanker explains. "The correct mantra must be used to make the mental vibration and so you can do the walking on water, fire, stop the heart from beating, and floating in air."

"Walk on water?"

"Man uses five percent of brain," Pradeep adds. "Yoga can free the rest of brain and you can do anything."

Really? *Really*?!" I am bursting with excitement. This *is* the place!

"Yes, yes," replies Pradeep impatiently. "Now tell us about American girls. Do you think American girls would like me? Do they like Indian man? What do these girls like to do? Would I have success?"

"American girls? What?" I find it an unwelcome change of topic. "I can't believe America is on the same planet as people flying and walking on water."

"Now you want bidi? We must walk back for class while you smoke."

"What are bidis? They aren't hashish, are they? I don't do drugs."

"They are Indian cigarettes approved by the government of India. There is Telephone brand bidis, my favorite, with government stamp. You take two for later."

"Yes, for later."

"I would like to come to America, meet many women and drive a big car on your great American highway, this Route 66," Pradeep tells me as we creep out of Shanker's hovel.

"Sure that's great." I am no longer listening. I have come all this way and risked my neck only to hear how great the States are. If yogic power is for real, then why do Indians dream of Mickey Mouse?

"Do you think I will get to America?"

"Yeah, sure, you'll get there someday."

"Oh thank you. I will call you *chota bhai*, which means 'little brother.' You are American *chota bhai*. Little *chota bhai*," he laughs, making a joke of my towering height.

Pradeep walks me up the path as the December sky darkens.

"See you in class," I call from my porch, watching his figure recede under the ashram from porch florescent tube lighting. As Pradeep pauses to light another bidi, I sense the ruse of it all, and a wave of sadness rushes over me. He is lying; there are no yoga powers. Pradeep is a con-man—a shabby two-bit hustler. I can sense it like smoke from a fire. All his tales are crafted to bewitch gullible foreigners, especially those who smoke.

In the morning, my neighbor wakes me at 4:00 a.m. as usual to get ready for meditation an hour later. It's kind of like getting up to go skiing to be awake in the early dark hours. In class, I can't stay focused on breathing rhythms or mantra repetition. Old ad jingles from my childhood keep spinning through my head. First there is "*plop, plop, fizz, fizz, oh what a relief it is*" from the good people at Pepto Bismol. Then a dog food commercial comes along with a nervous little dog reciting his mantra of "*Kibbles and Bits, Kibbles and Bits. I'm gonna get me some Kibbles and Bits.*" After a while, the refrain at least shifts to a product I used to like. "*Cuckoo for Cocoa Puffs! I'm cuckoo for Cocoa Puffs!!*" shouts the chocolate-colored cereal mascot, Sonny, on his crazed quest for sugary breakfast cereal. I reflect on my situation: sitting in a cold, dark room in India, forbidden from sleep, and psychologically tortured by the sheer garbage I absorbed when there was nothing to do but watch television. Life can't possibly get worse.

Just sitting still is hard. Even in the dumbed-down half-lotus meditation position, which is like Indian style with one foot on the opposite calf, my knees start to throb after five minutes. The Zen monk sits haughtily up front. I always hated a teacher's pet. The hour seems like it will never end. I wonder why I bother trying.

Later, after a nap, I wander down the cement path to the village to get a better padlock for my door and candles to endure the ashram's frequent power outages. Reading my two books at night has been a great help in pretending I am somewhere else.

Only a few feet outside the gate, the beggars pounce. To them, Westerners are eight-armed cash-dispensing gods. The bazaar becomes a gauntlet. They pester me with tales of woe at every turn. Desperate to escape, I search frantically for my objectives.

The shops here are often just crude wooden shacks haphazardly nailed together, much like the psychiatry office where Lucy analyzed Charlie Brown. Some stores are nothing more than a blanket spread on the ground.

Even the best quality padlock I find can be bent with bare hands. I reluctantly part with more of my precious rupees. It hardly seems worth the trouble.

"Little *chota bhai*, what did you come to buy?" asks Pradeep, appearing at my side.

Though I am wary of his ploys, at least he is a friendly face; I can use one in town.

"I bought a padlock."

"How much did you pay?"

Pradeep goes back to the shack where I just purchased the lock. He returns a minute later with a handful of rupees—half of what I had paid.

"You tell me when you buy thing or you pay foreigner price. We go back for lunch."

Going up the path, Pradeep notices my sour mood.

"Why you are so tired, little brother?"

"Just being in India is hard," I try to explain. "So many people … and the beggars. Why are they so annoying?"

"Don't hate the beggars."

"Well, they wear me out. They never leave me alone."

"Love the beggars."

"Yeah, well, what if I don't have any money?"

"Then offer your respect."

Pradeep's advice pierces me. I suddenly feel terrible for complaining about people who are so poor. "Okay, all right. I'm sorry."

"Think always with your heart," he says gently. "Love, love, love all the people and animals and life, for it is all one. Why did you come to India?"

"I took a yoga class in Colorado. I liked it, and it seemed to help with sports. I wanted to find out more. However, just before Christmas…" I hesitate, searching Pradeep's face. It would be nice to detect some humanity before I tell this story.

"Yes, little brother?"

"Do you want to know the real reason?"

"Of course."

I surprise myself by feeling choked up. I begin: "A friend died last month…"

As he listens silently to my story about D'Anne, Pradeep's face shows true compassion. "Your friend must be near," he says. Even though millions die daily in India, he shares my sadness for a person he never knew on the other side of the world, where money, free sex, Mickey Mouse, and the pleasures of driving Route 66 supposedly fall from the heavens.

"You were called to India like a child to his mother," Pradeep remarks, once I've finished. "Now you can suck at the breast of Mother India!" He makes sucking sounds that embarrass me. "A child is happiest, yes?"

"Sure. But what about that Japanese monk with his black robes and shaved head? He isn't here to be a child. He's so intense it's scary."

"Japanese persons," Pradeep chuckles, slapping his thigh, "They have great tensions like your Germans. The yoga process is within. Traditions are a prison that makes men fight. You seem to be free of this and have humility."

"Yeah, well what good is humility? It means that you have been humiliated."

"There is a saying: come hungry to a feast so you can leave full. So it is with mind and soul. Give up your self-importance, and you may fill yourself of wisdom."

"But Pradeep, I can't sit for twenty years in a cave flogging myself or meditating until my legs fall off. The Japanese monk can sit meditating, spine perfectly straight, for weeks without flinching. He has been doing it for years. What do I know? I'm nothing."

"Nobody's nothing!"

Pradeep's response startles me. That was what Johnny Dawes said. I am suddenly reminded of Lärs, the Norwegian man in Buoux, whose image begins to blur with that of the Japanese monk.

"What is required is a pure heart." Pradeep explains softly. "The Japanese man has forgotten our Buddha's 'Middle Way,' just as Europe's knights forgot the love of Jesus in Crusade wars. He needs beatings like the Samurai to overcome his pride. He has the madness of the Kamikaze. You are not soldier man like him. Try to feel love in your meditation and overcome your ego self. With humility, you will go before many others."

Pradeep's advice sounds much easier said than done. "All right," I reply, feeling sorrier for myself than ever. "Anyway, I've got no money and nowhere to go."

"No money and nowhere to go? Hahn, Hahn—yes, yes—you are very, very lucky."

GOOD VIBRATIONS

After the morning meditation class, I notice Pradeep chatting with a silver-haired European man in the garden.

"This is great Italian foreigner, 'Uncle Joe,'" Pradeep tells me. Uncle Joe bows toward me and smiles, revealing many gold fillings. Before Pradeep's introduction he seemed like just another stone-faced European, but Pradeep gets them all smiling.

"Hello, do you speak English?" I ask.

"Piccolo … little bit." He smiles again. "You come coffee?"

"No, I'm going back to sleep," I reply. Pradeep seems fascinated by what is in the town below. To me it is only a collection of dirty shops and filthy cafes full of people who want my non-existent money.

Pradeep grabs my arm. "Sleep, that is not life," he protests. "You have new friend, the fantastic Uncle Joe. You walk with Uncle Joe for coffee. I look for cigarette. Where is Japanese lady this very morning?" Pradeep runs off helter-skelter. I can't help laughing at his antics. Watching him recede up the path in a frenzy, I feel a kinship with the words in *On the Road* by Jack Kerouac's:

"The only people for me are the mad ones, the ones who are mad to live, mad to talk, mad to be saved, desirous of everything at the same time, the ones who never yawn or say a commonplace thing, but burn, burn, burn, like fabulous roman candles exploding like spiders across the stars."

I shrug. "I guess we're going for coffee."

I accompany Uncle Joe to town. He walks very slowly, like he is counting his steps. We pause at an overlook to ponder the flowing Ganges below.

"Buddhist Tibetan," Joe says pointing to himself.

"Oh, you follow Tibetan Buddhism? I learned *Om Mane Padme Hum* in my meditation class."

"Si, si, yes. *Om Mane Padme Hum, Om Mane Padme Hum.*" Excitedly, Joe removes an exotic string of beads from around his neck. He says that he counts one bead for every one of the four words in the mantra *Om Mane Padme Hum.* "Slow, good" he explains. He repeats the mantra, laboring over each syllable, "*Ommm Maannee Paadmee Huhhmmm.*" Then he reflects, "Fast, good too. Everything good," he concludes at last, after trying the chant at several different speeds.

"Buddhism is good for you, Joe—Uncle Joe?" I ask.

"Before Buddhism, emotion problem. Now no problem." He shows me a brilliant smile and shuffles his feet energetically. Uncle Joe must be well over seventy.

I remember taking a series of meditation classes at my yoga teacher's home in Denver. The first class was filled with over-excited, middle-aged yuppie women sitting on the floor forming a little circle. They wouldn't stop giggling. I remained aloof on the couch, feeling sorry I'd come.

"Come sit down here on the floor with us," coaxed one of them as though it was a kindergarten activity.

"Let him stay where he's comfortable," my teacher said. "Meditation can be done anywhere."

"Tonight, let's try chanting meditations," she began. "The first one is more like a prayer from the Tibetan people that goes: *Om Mane Padme Hum / Om Mane Padme Hum / Om Mane Padme Hum / Om Mane Padme Hum.*"

We repeated this for half an hour, and after some time I found I enjoyed it. The mantra chanting was more focused than the absurd operatic tones of *Om* by itself. Repeating the words over and over was hypnotic, like a thundering Led Zeppelin guitar riff, and I came to love it.

Pradeep catches up to us, proudly wielding two cigarettes. One is already lit in his mouth, the other tucked behind his ear. "Come, come my friends, we have coffee? Good vibrations this morning." He charges ahead, his flip-flops snapping briskly on the concrete steps.

In a cramped coffee shop overlooking the Ganges, Pradeep chats excitedly with the owner. He shows off his hard-won cigarettes to everyone, winning enthusiastic cheers.

"Would you like coffee, Joe?" I ask.

He frowns. "Indian coffee no good."

"You like espresso I'll bet. Good and strong."

"Espresso, si."

It would be amazing to have an Italian coffee. Now I dream about a French chocolate croissant. I have to purge those thoughts from my mind.

"I am a mountain climber. I want to go to the Dolomites, your mountains in northern Italy. The *Dolomiti.*"

"Si, *le Dolomiti.* I am yoga teacher in Venice."

"That's nice. Do you have a family? Do they practice yoga with you?"

"Wife no yoga, only parties and fine clothes. Italian no like Buddhism and yoga. Italian people proper." Joe pauses to pantomime a man adjusting an imaginary tie, a man infused with pride. "European man cold."

I nod knowingly. *Proper,* one of Britain's favorite words, and "cold" both can describe much of my experience of visiting Europe. I had been shoved, sneered and yelled at by inhabitants of that illustrious continent for what they considered a lack of properness all while shelling out stacks of play money to meet their ridiculous prices.

Pradeep is talking to a fellow with wild dreadlocks, who looks like Bob Marley and wears the orange robes of a holy man. "Good vibrations," Pradeep says pointing to him.

"You buy for me shoes!" demands the man abruptly.

Sandals are pretty cheap, and he is a friend of Pradeep's, so in the spirit of generosity, I agree.

Pradeep pats me on the back and says: "Good vibrations from American brother."

"What time shoes?" the man asks.

"How about two o'clock this afternoon?"

"We go now," the man grunts.

I wonder with concern what I have gotten myself into. In any case, my money is carefully hidden in my room, so I am off the hook for the moment. "Um, no, two would be better," I suggest.

"Two o'clock," the Rasta-man mutters and sits down as though he is waiting for a bus. "Two o'clock," he repeats staring at his watch.

As promised, I return at 2 p.m. with the rupees equivalent of two American dollars for the Rasta-man's sandals. He grunts at my approach. I suspect he hasn't moved since the appointment was made.

"Well, are you ready to go shopping?" I say, trying to be cheerful.

He only grunts again and leads me across the footbridge into the dense bazaar market along the river. At a store, he stops and points to a pair of sandals hanging on the wall.

"This one," he says.

I inspect the intended sandals while the Rasta-man chats in Hindi with the shopkeeper, who points at me and laughs.

"These are too expensive for me to buy. I am low on money this trip," I explain. "Sorry." I suggest some other sandals—not the cheapest ones either.

"No good." The Rasta-man handles the first pair stubbornly. "This shoes."

"Look, I'm seriously low on money. These are reasonable sandals."

The two men sneer at me as though I am just off the farm.

"More rupees!" the Rasta-man demands. "You pay!"

I'm starting to get sick of this guy. "Sorry, this is all I have," I tell him resolutely. I wait awkwardly while he jabbers with the shopkeeper in their baffling language, eyeing me with contempt.

"He say you have more money in your room!" thunders the shopkeeper in surprisingly clear English. "Go boy. Go get money!"

That's it. I've reached my boiling point. "No!" I bark, hot anger flashing across my face. "Take this and get some shoes." I give him enough rupees for the cheaper sandals. "If that's not enough, then you can shove it!"

The two men's snickering suddenly changes to surprise. I realize, that to them, all of us Westerners are seen as pigeons, rubes, soft chumps. They consider the alternative-living visitors to Rishikesh to be especially exploitable, organic-tea-drinking wusses who, out of guilt, offer up anything to even the rudest and most ungrateful native. Maybe I come from the land of plenty, but, as I'm beginning to discover, I pay a price for that.

A ray of sun invites me outside. *"Namaste!"* I say sarcastically as I leave.

Tired of *all* humanity, I turn to nature, like I have done a thousand times, with no regrets. Strolling by the river, I enjoy the wonderful warm sun on my face. The sandy shores and gravel paths in the forest soothe my nerves. It is a beautiful day, and I refuse to waste it in the dirty realm of man.

The next day before lunch I tell Pradeep what I think of his bullshit "good vibrations" Rasta-man.

"Acha—good," he exhales, laughing heartily. To him every-thing is a game.

But as we walk across the ashram grounds, we soon find our-selves in a serious situation. A gang of rhesus monkeys surrounds us. These beasts are infamously aggressive, the Hell's Angels of furry creatures, who normally remain in the trees only because the groundskeepers throw rocks at them. Not a great relationship. At our approach, some of them begin to growl and bare fangs.

"Monkey very dangerous," Pradeep tells me calmly. "We must treat very carefully."

I've heard most monkeys here have rabies, a mere inconvenience at home, but a couple of days to certain death in India if you can't get the unbelievably expensive shots immediately. Remembering the grimy, closed Red Cross office that I passed on my arrival in Rishikesh, I begin to sweat. One chomp from Curious George and I'm dead.

"Stay relax and don't look them in eye," says Pradeep. "Listen, one day I am sitting on my bed and many monkey come in my room and inspect my possessions. If I quarrel, they would have bite me. I had to sit with very quiet mind. These are the yoga powers you wish to know, in action. Quiet yourself completely."

So we begin an exercise in passivity. Pradeep pretends to in-spect his fingernail, humming softly to himself. I follow suit. The monkeys come so close to us that I could reach out and touch one. We pretend not to notice their presence and certainly don't make eye contact. After an agonizingly long time, something in the dis-tance interests them more. The ring of monkeys slowly leaves.

"The ancient yogis in the forests lived with many dangerous animals, but they used their good-vibrations powers to be friend with them," Pradeep muses. "But caution is needed as they are still dangerous. And so it is with people. Some only curious, some dangerous, but all must be handled very carefully."

I think on Pradeep's words and realize how poorly I have dealt with people in the past. Proof enough is the encounter with the Rasta-man just yesterday. They show me a bad side, and I lose my temper. I am a reactor and not a thinker. I never imagine a step ahead and rarely restrain myself from being an ass, as we were just forced to do when threatened by the monkeys. It's time I learned to handle animals as well as humans more carefully.

At lunch, Pradeep introduces me to some of the other foreigners staying at our ashram. Most are Japanese.

"Kon-nichi-wa," Pradeep says to them. He pours on the charm, no doubt hoping to secure a steady supply of cigarettes. They smile sheepishly and wave back, covering their giggling mouths.

There are a couple of "Sixties" Americans left over in the ashram from the days when the founding guru recruited disciples from abroad. They seem lost since their leader's death. However, they know Colorado from their days of hippy drifting across a wild and free America.

"I remember when Crested Butte still had wood plank sidewalks and a sheriff with a handlebar moustache," one of them tells me.

Crested Butte! I can only salivate for mountain towns, blue skies, and open spaces of the Wild West where there is room to walk on the sidewalk—home where people don't stop everything they're doing to gape vacantly at me.

"When you get to a small town say to the locals, 'Hey this is a nice place,' and it will open doors for you," advises the American man. "But I mean, if it is a dump, don't say that, don't say anything at all. Get the hell outta there," he laughs knowingly.

Sitting on my other side is an Icelandic woman whose hair and face are as pale and bleak as her climate. She spends her time having her fortune told by the local palm readers, drinking the 'magic cure' water bottled from the Ganges, and searching for a guru.

"They see all and know all," she proclaims dreamily.

I feel sick. After being brought up in the cynical West, I am now thrown in with the empty-headed counter-culture ready to believe anything. Perhaps the worst thing about staying in an ashram is that I will be associated with their dull gullibility.

After dinner, I pay Uncle Joe a visit in his room. Despite our inability to converse past a few words, Joe wants to teach me about Buddhism. I appreciate his concern for my well-being, but the subject doesn't hold much interest for me. Back home, Buddhism seemed like the most pretentious topic possible. In a college course on Buddhism that my friend took, the professor shouted at the class, "None of you are fit to lick the Buddha's boots!" Boulder is full of wealthy white "Buddhist" kids swearing that the Tibetans could control the rain. As if they knew. While in Buoux last October, I began reading the supposed classic *Zen and the Art of Motorcycle Maintenance*. At the point where the author states, "all is a manifestation of Lord Buddha," I threw the book against the wall.

Still, I let Joe loan me some Buddhist books as if I am doing *him* the favor. On my way out, I start to give him a hug like I feel I am supposed to do being here. He looks at me in horror. *What the hell am I doing?* All the New Age nonsense swirling around yoga has me mindlessly conforming to some hippy ethos that doesn't fit. The Italian man may be cold, but hugs are the other extreme. Indian yoga isn't a cute spa package of essential oils, aroma therapy, and phony sentimentality.

THE RUBBER GURU

*B*ang! Bang! Bang!
Pradeep knocks wildly on my door. It isn't time for lunch yet, so I just want to sleep.

"I don't have any cigarettes!" I yell instinctively in response.

"Come, my American friend. Many of us go to see a great yogi across the river."

"A great yogi?" I feel reluctant but curious.

"Yes, he has many amazing powers. You want bidi? Yes, yes, come on. Come."

I leave the security of my room to face a small group of Westerners assembled like a kindergarten class under Pradeep's command by the gate. We begin a slow march to the other side of the river, frequently interrupted by Pradeep stopping to add more recruits.

At a coffee stall, an Italian fellow mingles into our assembly. He has gone totally "guru" with flowing beard, twine sandals, and white robes—a dark-haired Jesus. Unlike Uncle Joe, he is taciturn, though his English is reasonably good.

Pradeep leads us into the jungle surrounding Rishikesh on a footpath that becomes progressively faint.

"Wait here," he says, stopping us at a gate nearly hidden by dense foliage.

After some time, Pradeep returns. He takes us into a courtyard of rundown cement buildings where an Indian man, also with long dark hair, a beard, and heavily soiled white robes, is waiting towards the back ready to make his grand entrance.

"Here, as promised, is fantastical guru you have been waiting to meet." Pradeep introduces him as though he is a carnival side-show attraction.

Bowing, the guru clears his throat, shooting a mucous ball in a ten-foot arch into a bush.

"Chai," he barks to a young girl working in the gardens. She scrambles nervously off. Then the guru pulls Pradeep aside, and they conspire, laughing and pointing at our group. This guru strangely reminds me of the Yosemite ex-cons I met—the same criminal strut, the exaggerated swinging the arms to show you are ready for a fight.

A few minutes later, the girl returns with a tray of aluminum cups. The long-haired Italian elbows his way to the front. He appears particularly eager to engage the guru in conversation. Bending down, he touches the guru's feet in a traditional gesture of respect. The other foreigners queue up behind him for their chance to sit on Santa's lap, but I hang back, skeptical.

I find myself face-to-face with Pradeep.

"I get a strange feeling from your friend," I tell him. "He really has great powers?"

"Great powers," Pradeep replies with conviction. "He is a fine teacher. You having doubt? Come see pictures of a yogi master!"

Pradeep opens a photo album sitting on a nearby table. He shows me faded pictures of the guru in his youth contorting himself into ridiculous shapes. In one photo, he stands with his toes pointing an absolute 180° behind him.

"How did he get to be that flexible, Pradeep?" I ask. "I sprain my ankles all the time; that would never happen to him."

"Concentration, mantra, and turning a little bit every day," Pradeep explains. "Do you want to study under him?"

"No, I'm not cut out for this stuff. It doesn't feel right." I look back at the line of enthusiastic disciples waiting to meet their new master. "The other people are so eager. They should go before me."

"What do you say, little brother?" Pradeep eyes me curiously.

"Pradeep, I can't even touch my toes. I don't deserve enlightenment, whatever that is. Besides I'm terrible at yoga."

"We will talk at the river, American brother," Pradeep says. His voice is somber, drained of its typical used car salesman tones.

By this time, the Italian man has finalized plans to live and study under the great rubber teacher. The guru demands cash up front. He licks his lips as the Italian counts out paper bills from a wad tucked in his robe.

"Pradeep, is your friend a good man?" I ask as we scramble down the trail.

"He is good at yoga stretching."

The image of the payout stays in my mind. "Did he pay you to bring us here?" I ask accusingly.

"Yes, it is how to take money. The ashram pays for nothing after my room. He is great instructor." Pradeep looks me in the eye. "To you I talk freely. You are different from the foreigner people."

"Me? Why? What have *I* done?"

"In your Bible does it not say: *He who is last shall later be first?*"

"I don't know. I was throwing water balloons out the window in Sunday School."

"Yes, yes, naughty like Lord Krishna!" he pats me on the back affectionately. "But your Bible does say this, and so you have said back there. You would let others be first to enlightenment."

"But I don't know anything about enlightenment." I think back to a lifetime of misbehavior. I was the only kindergartner riding the school bus who did not get a little toy for being good. "I'm pretty sure I don't deserve it either."

"These Westerners do not know. They only *think* they know. Their minds are full of strange ideas. No room for anything else. They grasp at anything in front of them. And you have said the greatest thing possible: You don't deserve enlightenment. Your ego is small like Indian man's."

"I'm sure I don't deserve it, if there is such a thing," I reply. "I wish I'd never come to India. What about those people you tricked, Pradeep?" I ask. "It's wrong to mislead even foreigners. Is your friend going to help them understand yoga?"

"Foreigner or Indian. Person can only be taught what they are ready to learn. He can teach what they believe is yoga. Could you feel Italian man's arrogance? A person who grabs for truth so quickly is not ready to understand. It is the best place for him."

"So people end up where they deserve?"

"There is many corrupt guru everywhere, but that is not the important thing. Man comes with big ego and big ideas to sit with a true guru and learns nothing. Man with no ego, like child, learns from all people, good or bad."

I'm beginning to understand what he means, but it doesn't change my feelings. So many pitfalls await. The Italian man has come all this way and now…

"I never want a guru or be a part of this bullshit," I tell Pradeep angrily. I am almost shouting. "I don't want to be on the Rishikesh gravy train. It's all a show to con us idiot foreigners, but I can't leave here, because I'm out of money. I'm a prisoner."

"Yes, you are very lucky foreign man."

This time being called "lucky" makes me mad instead of charmed, and I storm away from Pradeep. *Lucky?* How could I be called lucky when I've lived so many nightmares, so many failures?

I wander along the sandy bank of the Ganges feeling sorry for myself yet again. The memories of anguish flood back, and I remember vividly the summer of my seventeenth year, when Red and I went to climb the greatest wall in Colorado, the prize I'd longed for since childhood: the Diamond of Longs Peak. So intimidated was I that I insisted we take absurd amounts of gear. Our massive packs crushed us all the way up the trail. Our bivouac was a night of horror with the moonlight illuminating the enormous Diamond face—huge, vast and vertical without compromise. *Are those clouds? Is it going to rain?* I wondered, squinting up at the dark sky. Late in the night, I said to myself: *I hope so.*

The next day, on the great wall, I felt like puking. The Diamond was too big and I, even at 6' 4" too small. It got late but Red remained undaunted. He wanted to keep going, come what may.

At last I managed to talk Red into a retreat. It was time to, as King Arthur ordered in Monty Python's *Holy Grail,* "run away!" Once we were finally down, Red refused to speak to me. Our big chance to climb the Diamond, and I had blown it! If I couldn't even get up the easiest route on the Diamond, I'd certainly never free climb *Genesis* or do anything to be proud of. Indeed, the great test had come, the holy Diamond and I crawled away crushed and defeated. There was nothing lucky about me; my climbing career was as successful as an NBA player trying to win the Kentucky Derby on a donkey.

Here beside India's so-called sacred river, I only want to walk alone, soothing myself in solitude away from the dirty world of humanity and humiliation and try to forget. But one is never alone in India.

Nighttime brings a heavy homesickness that oppresses my soul. I miss everyone and everything, even people and places I couldn't stand before leaving. The pain and loneliness stabs at me.

I am realizing that my life in the West was actually pretty good. I knew the secret of staying in touch with nature; I could earn money and even drive on the freeways. So what the hell am I doing in this dump, eating *subji* with grits of sand in it?

In the morning cold, I struggle to endure the knee-pain of another pre-dawn meditation. I count the minutes until it is over, craving the toasty-warm sleeping bag back in my room and a door that can lock out everything.

Unfortunately, I am easy prey. It takes me extra time to unwind and un-numb my stiff legs before I can limp to the exit. Pradeep is waiting for me. "Come little *chota bhai*, let's have coffee," he says.

"I'd like to sleep a bit more first. How about I meet you down there about nine o'clock? Where are you going to be?"

"Are you sick?"

"I hope not."

"Come, come, life is outside. Not alone in room"

"Okay, okay," I surrender. "Let's go dig it," I say for fun, mimicking Kerouac.

The sun is painting upper Rishikesh pink. At the river, steam mixes with smoke from gas stoves, charring great black boiling pots in the air above the open chai shops. Though it is just after 6 a.m., excited chatter echoes from everywhere, especially from Pradeep. He knows everyone and skips from one person to another, laughing and joking.

We continue over the bridge past the Chottiwalla Restaurants. Years ago, the siblings who inherited this popular establishment quarreled and split their kingdom in two. Outside, two Sumo-wrestler-sized men painted chalky blue stand like giant glazed doughnuts in front of their respective eateries to attract unwary customers. Even in the early shivering hours, they are available for pictures. As I linger in front of this bizarre scene, one of these mascots hands me a printed note declaring that his is the *real* Chottiwalla Restaurant and that the other is a cheat. America's famously wacky-theme restaurants have nothing on this.

We drift over to some cafes more likely to receive the first rays of the sun. While Pradeep is away chatting, two Indian thugs insist on sitting with me.

"What is your father's address? I have some business with him," one of them firmly demands.

I give them a bogus address, and they slink away with their prize. I consider idly that even if I did give them my father's real address I don't think they'd get very far with him.

Pradeep returns looking concerned. "Bad vibration men. Did you give address?"

"No, I lied."

"Ah, lie very good," Pradeep nods in approval.

We finish our coffee and walk along the riverbank as sunshine begins to warm the Indian day. As the final mists are lifting from the Ganges, Pradeep hails an Asian girl sitting on the steps with some friends.

"You are well, Japanese sister?" he asks. She looks miserable. Pradeep listens to her latest story sympathetically. They discuss strange spiritual concepts that I don't understand or care to.

As we walk onward, Pradeep tells me that he is concerned about his "Japanese sister." "She says if she not find enlightenment soon, she kill herself," he explains.

"Do you think she can find it?" I wonder.

"No, very dangerous. Japanese girl learns meditation from the money guru that tried to take you the day we met. He is no good, and when her money is gone, he throws her out."

I feel a shudder go through me and the accident on the Bastille comes back to mind. Japanese sister has crashed and burned, writhing in agony, but in a spiritual sense, screaming in pain on the road, her spine broken.

"Why are the foreign people so desperate?" I ask. "Isn't just doing the stretching exercises and meditation enough?"

Pradeep sighs. "Japanese girl has crazy life with many drugs and boyfriends. Many foreigner come to India and want enlightenment quickly. When they fail, they try harder or punish themselves. Many have a big arrogance. A German man comes, and I read his poems. Every word from a dark mind. Perhaps he was unhappy his great Emperor is dead!" Pradeep chokes on his laughter.

Germans. I shudder at the thought of encountered them during my time in France with nuts like Dahvid. I ask Pradeep whether there is any hope.

"Yes, little brother," Pradeep starts." The true guru-student relationship is very deep and meaningful, but many want the guru to do all the work. They are like the people who throw their troubles on the back of a god. To find a true guru is not stand in line waiting. It happens when the student is ready."

"A man in orange robes magically appears?"

"A guru is not always a man. All life is guru. Man with big ego learns nothing. But yes, when the time is right, guru come." Pradeep pauses thoughtfully. "Just be sure you can recognize him."

It is 5 a.m., and even though I am sitting through another cold morning meditation, I find myself nearly breaking a sweat despite an ad going through my head singing, *This Buds for you, For all you do the King of Beers is coming through* ... The agonizing sensation in my legs from being twisted is nothing compared to my emotional turbulence. I feel I am in great danger from getting hooked on a guru, getting sick, bitten by monkeys, and/or running out of money. So many missteps, false practices, await. The memory of the climbing accident I witnessed at the base of the Bastille when I was twelve hits home again. Even though I sit on the obviously safe carpet, wave after wave of fear crashes through me: I'd rather have the Budweiser Clydesdales pulling the beer wagon, but the kitschy image is gone.

Today is the last day of 1988, and I'm finally feeling a little better than when I arrived a few days ago. It is becoming clear to me why the hippies went home. The way eastern philosophy is sold in the west is a lie. Yoga isn't an empty-headed joke or a free love party. Nor does it provide easy answers. At its core, it requires a lot of discipline to face the pain in one's heart, head, body, and knees.

The books people here encourage me to read are no help. The Hindu religious texts like the *Bhaghavad Gita* are difficult to enjoy despite the epic battle scenes. The more secular yoga books are no more inspiring. Their stories of yogis in extreme self-denial and self-torture, and their descriptions of complicated philosophical systems regarding transcendental meditation, chakras, karma, hallucinatory experiences, and leaving the body – it all leaves me with a splitting headache. I don't believe or disbelieve the stories; I simply find them tiresome.

Uncle Joe's books about the Buddha are about the most dismal things I've ever read. "All life is suffering" is his notable quote. That enlightened saying only presses down on my spirits. And then there is the dreadful concept of reincarnation. The Christian Bible is harsh enough—it enforces all the suffering in *this* life time—but Buddhist literature predicts nothing but misery for *many* lifetimes to come. In fact, Buddhism seems to suggest that thousands, maybe millions of lives have to be lived in increasing piety to find enlightenment. That requirement ensures that very few of the earth's billions even have a chance, and those who do write books to torture the rest of us. Lifetime after lifetime we get to enjoy the Buddha's claim that all life is suffering all over again.

Anyway, to me, these complicated ideas and philosophies I read about feel no more genuine than the Christian doctrine back home. I remember Pat Hansen's original description of yoga back in my Colorado class where the mind is like a placid mountain lake that reflects the mountains above. If thoughts and negativities like greed, desire, perversion, fear, stir the surface, one can no longer see the reflection above. Human egos stir the surface of their mind's lake, so why not just work to calm the lake? This is the common goal of world religions in reality. Throw out rituals, reverence, intellectual gymnastics, outlandish theories and these books to focus on calming the lake's surface.

A NEW YEAR BEGINS

I t's New Year's Eve, 1989, and, believe it or not, there aren't a lot of wild parties in Rishikesh. The American lady says there will be a talk on world peace at the ashram next door, which is known for devotional yoga. I have looked over the fence to see buildings painted in the bright carnival colors, and resident enthusiasts singing and chanting to a blue deity. At many yoga centers, both in India and abroad, yoga is not carefully enough separated from Hinduism. There are stories about practicing with yogis up into the mountains who insist you fast for weeks and drink a frothy glass of your own urine every day. Forced vomiting and cleaning one's nostrils out with a piece of rope are part of the fun too.

I realize I am very lucky to have found a non-denominational place that is quiet. The buildings are plain, painted white, and no one really bothers me so long as I'm paid up. Pradeep and the lady who presides over the meditation class are the only other "authority figures."

It is early evening, as I stumble up the steep, pitch-dark cement steps of the neighboring ashram. The lecture hall is filled with about fifty people. As I approach, I notice the designated speakers queuing at the microphone, but what really catches my attention are several orange-robed men seated outside. They remain aloof, shy, gently nodding along with the higher sentiments of the discussion, but without fraternizing with the masses. Finding them more interesting than the proceedings, I sit nearby, away from the action. Their solemn, honest faces and standoff-ish ways impress me. Their temperaments challenge the notions I am often told that a spiritual person is a meek, deluded sap who does as instructed. They lend a dignity to New Year's Eve missing from dropping the ball on Times Square.

New Year's Day dawns clear. There are no classes scheduled, so I decide to explore the countryside. My feet lead me up a steep paved road into the foothills. The mountain air smells fresh and cool. Naturally, this area is less inhabited, and I am finally alone. But just as I start to feel at ease, a bus screeches past in an explosion of noise and exhaust. Though I am well off the road, the driver gives me a long blast of his horn, obviously enjoying his monstrous noisemaker. I jump a foot in the air, automatically returning his salute with our Western hand mudra called "the finger."

At a little roadside shrine with the typical blue dolls behind a dirty screen, I spontaneously choose a trail into the woods. Tall trees line the way as the path winds across a hillside and comes out in a meadow.

I can breathe again! The horns, pollution and swarming throngs of India give way to the wilderness that begins to restore me. I wish I could pass the remaining month right here in this meadow.

After only a few beautifully relaxing minutes though, I hear the sounds of a heavy animal tromping through the dense foliage nearby. The crunching stops, and I feel eyes upon me. Could it be a tiger? Panicking, I start to sweat, and regrets pour out. Am I to die for taking a stroll? Cautiously, I backtrack to where I can see the little shrine, which now seems to promise security. The sight floods me with relief, but I also feel a nagging curiosity. To glimpse a tiger would make my trip.

When I was fifteen, a relative invited me to vacation with his family in the Tetons. He was an accomplished sportsman, but subscribed to the traditional American notion that wilderness must be subdued as in killing off the bears—for our own safety of course.

In the Jackson Hole Town Park, long-haired college-aged hippies were holding signs that said "Dump Watt" to protest James Watt, the reckless Secretary of the Interior newly appointed by Reagan. Like most Republicans, Watt wouldn't mind if the national parks were sold off and bounties put on the animals. The protest kids looked like disheveled pot smokers. I was written off as "one of those."

But my relative was a kind man, an armchair mountaineer, and he graciously hired me a guide, none other than the famous Yosemite pioneer Chuck Pratt.

Pratt and I climbed the *Guides Wall,* a long, beautiful 5.8 multi-pitch route overlooking Jenny Lake. As we were hiking down, Chuck was telling me about his most memorable climb, the first ascent of the *Regular Route* on Yosemite's Fairview Dome at age eighteen, when we were startled by a noise on the trail ahead. Pratt pulled me into the woods.

"Moose!" he explained, "It's best to step aside." As he spoke, two giant bulls, each with enormous racks of antlers, lumbered up the trail. They were magnificent.

My boyhood experience in Jackson increased my appreciation for the majesty of the wild animal kingdom, while also raising my awareness of its vulnerability. The animals on our planet face an uncertain future due to an unsympathetic humanity bristling with greed. For the survival of the animal world is it so hard to step aside?

So I find myself, like an idiot, back in the meadow, hoping to see a tiger. A sound in the woods leads me across the path.

Thinking I am somehow invisible, I tip-toe a hundred yards into the tight woods. Suddenly, a sharp crack of underbrush behind makes me freeze in my tracks. The animal has cut me off from the open meadow. Now I am the hunted. *You fool!* I curse myself. Sweat pouring down my face, I turn to face my fate. Astonished but relieved, I find it isn't a striped Lord Death. Instead, I see the silliest looking cow in India, beautified with multiple flower necklaces, stumbling clumsily through the trees.

The next morning, yoga classes are in session again, and I am massaging my knees after another painful meditation session. The hall has emptied out except for a strange European man. His bulky brown bathrobe reminds me of the monks pictured on the cheese packets in France. As I wait for my circulation to return, he engages me in conversation.

"You are the new American, I presume?"

"Um, yes, I guess I am. Hello. Where are you from?"

"I am a monk from Holland."

"You are from a Christian order?" I ask, surprised.

"Yes, of course," he replies matter-of-factly. "How are you finding your meditations?"

"Pretty slow," I admit. "So, how is it allowed that a Christian do yoga and meditation?"

"Well, we are learning in Europe that meditation and yoga has many advantages for reaching the Christ Consciousness."

"But I thought your religion considered all this yoga stuff evil," I say on the attack. "You Christians have always tried to keep people in line by scaring them with stories about hell and the devil."

"Ah yes, I have seen the devil many times," he replies, chuckling.

His response throws me off guard. "Well, I don't believe in a red man with wings and a pitchfork," I counter.

The blood flow has returned to my legs. Before the monk can reply, I leave abruptly, laughing to myself that a grown man should believe in such nonsense. The devil, indeed! Yet the words *"I have seen the devil many times"* continue to haunt me.

Suddenly, as I round a corner, I see, clear as day, Darren, the guy who sat behind me in high school study hall. I know the image is not real, but it possesses a power of its own. Grinning widely, Darren tells me, just as he did one day in study hall how he got a sophomore pregnant. *"She's having my baby. It's so goddamn funny."*

Then Darren disappears. Shocked by this memory, I see the monk's words in a new light. The conception of a pitchfork-toting devil in a red jumpsuit may be a cartoon depiction, but the evil forces inside people are real and transcend religions and time.

The revelation brings to mind other childhood experiences. I think back to a Sunday afternoon when I was thirteen. I was standing at a bus stop Denver after climbing in Boulder. The sky wasn't dark yet, but there were probably no more buses coming, and it was getting cold.

A taxi stopped, and the passenger, a black woman, insisted I get in.

"You look just like my boy," she said sweetly. "I worry about him so. Just like my boy."

Without hesitation, the woman paid the driver to take me to my mother's house in south Denver.

If Darren was a real-life devil, then she was undoubtedly an angel. Pure goodness was working in this woman whom many of my white Christian neighbors would have condemned just on account of the color of her skin.

As a child, I was taught when praying to a wooden cross, a Roman electric chair, I was communing with good, and that evil was the fault of a literal devil. I realize now that good and evil are both very real things, though they do not resemble such trite, material constructs. Rather, these forces are present in everything and everyone, and they exist above and beyond faith, doctrine, and religious divisions. People love to blame a scapegoat for what

they've done, and why not the devil? But as the Rolling Stones im-
ply in their classic single "Sympathy for the Devil:" *I shouted out,
'Who killed the Kennedys,' when after all it was you and me.* I'd rather
give credit for good or evil where credit is due—to the person
responsible.

Seeing Pradeep strolling in the garden nearby, I walk deliberately toward him.

"What is on your mind, *chota bhai*?" he says, eyeing me curiously. "Something has happened?"

"Yes Pradeep," I tell him. "I have just seen the devil, and he
looks like a hell of a lot of people I know."

After lunch, I go up to visit Pradeep in his room. He was absent
from lunch and afternoon meditation. In fact, Pradeep seems to
miss a lot of activities when the office people don't notice.

When I knock on his door, Pradeep is sitting on his bed with
a book.

"I read this Bible again," he tells me, glancing up. "Very good
vibration."

I examine his version of the New Testament written in that mad
Hindi script. "You can understand those funny symbols?"

"Yes, Hindi language. Fifty-two characters in our alphabet.
Japanese has over 3,000." He pauses. "What you think of Christian
things?"

"I don't like them."

"You don't like the enlightenment of Jesus? He was a great
yogi!"

"How can you say Jesus was a yogi?" I ask, dubiously.

"Oh yes!" affirms Pradeep confidently. "Yogis have superhuman powers. A great yogi can survive slow bleeding through his
concentration. Yes, Jesus was the highest possibility of man! Many
think he escaped after his torture and came to live in India!"

"You think Jesus was a man?"

"God or man there is no difference. Yes, the struggle for enlightenment is man's greatest adventure and accomplishment. Like Krishna, like Buddha, Jesus was once a young man like you who struggles with the dangers of this life and finds his enlightenment."

"Most Christians wouldn't like you saying that," I warn him.

"Saying what?"

"To say Jesus was a man and not the one and only son of God. And to compare him with Krishna and Buddha?" Feeling overwhelmed, I bury my head in my hands.

"What is wrong?"

"India is so tolerant. You don't understand what many Christians can be like."

"I understand the mankind. Here also, some are not tolerant. Gandhi was assassinated by our Hindus."

"Yes, well, most Christians believe you either follow Jesus or burn in eternal hellfire," I shoot back.

"That is strange," he reflects, unperturbed. "In India we believe there are many ways to enlightenment, to Heaven, to Nirvana."

"And according to most Christian doctrine," I continue echoing Foxwood's lectures from high school, "the millions of Greeks, Romans, Chinese, Africans, and whoever lived before the time of Christ are in hell right now—even the kindest, gentlest ones. How do you think Christians in the West feel about the elephant god and chanting Hare Krishna?"

"They smile," he states simply.

"I doubt it." An image comes to mind of some imaginary rednecks whooping and hollering as they drag Pradeep behind their pickup truck to "straighten out" his crazy ideas on the Gospel.

Observing my cynicism, Pradeep reflects, "It is great sadness that your culture have only this one yogi. India has countless saints and sages to revive ancient knowledge and explain again and again to the modern people. You must help your culture to understand this knowledge. You must make it alive again for your people, or you are all lost."

"You don't realize," I say, shaking my head, "a few might understand, but most wouldn't, and some would even like to kill you."

"Why?"

"For not believing what they believe."

"Then kill me," Pradeep replies, his voice rising. "What is my death? Violence comes from fools. They see only ego: 'I am...' 'You are...' They fight over stone piles and cement palaces they call sacred. These people speak a language of slavery, a language that makes prisoners chained by lies. I wish to speak the language of Mohammed, Christ, Buddha, and Krishna's truth: love, the language of the gods."

Pradeep falls silent, but his eyes are still flashing. I have never seen him so animated. I find myself reflecting that I don't really understand Christianity, though I still suspect the clowns who presented it to me at home don't have the slightest clue either. More and more, it appears to have a tremendous amount in common with Indian spiritual traditions. I also realize with surprise that, not only does this Hare Krishna respect the inherent faith of my heritage more than I, he has given me a new perspective on it. Pradeep and most of his countrymen do justice to Gandhi's famous claim, "I am a Christian, a Moslem, a Hindu and a Jew." Seeing religion through the eyes of a people accustomed to spiritual universalism, I begin to wonder whether there might be more to Jesus than an excuse for rednecks to kill people. I am reminded of Martin Luther King, Jr., inspired by Gandhi, who was in turn inspired by Thoreau to change the world. Perhaps I can't write off Christianity as *all* lies anymore.

With no meditation or stretching classes, Sundays at the ashram are quiet, but the little library is open. I still have three weeks left here and want to learn more about the strange powers of yogis that

Pradeep has mentioned. I look for books on yogi magic among the tattered stacks; most are a disappointment.

"What are you looking for?" demands the large woman who presides over meditation class. She is the only one in this dusty, cluttered room. It seems no one else ever ventures in here.

"Do you have any books about yoga powers and mysticism?" I ask hesitantly.

"Yoga powers?" she echoes mockingly.

"Yeah, the weird stuff yogis can do. People here swear they've seen yogis fly and all kinds of stories. I don't know about that, but even on American television there was a program about a yogi who could slow his heart rate and be buried in an air-tight box, holding his breath for ten minutes straight. How can people do stuff like that?"

"No, you don't want these books!" she snaps. "Make another selection."

Even on the other side of the globe I am finding that a librarian is a tedious animal.

"Why not?"

"They are ego only."

"They are the highest potential of mankind," I counter, borrowing Pradeep's rhetoric.

I brace for an argument, but, instead, the woman furtively looks both ways to be sure the coast is clear. Then, she leans forward to whisper, "Okay, I will tell you something very special. When I was a little girl, my father was a doctor, and I often rode along on calls to the countryside. One day we went far back into the remote jungle to see a patient. I don't know if it was black magic, but a holy man in that village walked on top of the water. I was only ten years-old, but I will always remember what I saw."

"He walked on water … like the legends of Jesus?"

"Yes. These things are possible for the yogi, it has long been known. And many more powers."

"Then you think they are true."

"I *know* it is true, but … you must be careful! It is only ego! Perhaps a teacher will use his powers to arise faith from his students. But even this is nonsense. There was a bridge in this village a hundred meters down the river. That is the best way to walk on water." Then, drawing up her figure, she adds dismissively, "What is so exciting? When you learn to direct your mind, anything is possible."

I find myself spellbound by the story of her mystical encounter accompanied by her nonchalant attitude. It is a marked contrast to Pradeep's salesmanship.

"I just can't believe this stuff is possible," I exclaim, my voice trembling with excitement. "It's incredible to think about. In the West people don't believe in anything but money."

"*Samadi* is the Sanskrit name for a state of meditation," she begins again in her thick accent. "Thoughts are energy waves and their transformation will activate powers. The memory gets sharper, in everything one's performance is improved, the power of charismatic speech comes. All *Siddis* are special powers but their purpose is not ego. You must not seek them but if they come you must not believe you are superior. Always be humble, polite, and receptive. The goal is to be free of past impressions, *samskaras* we say, like self-importance."

"So there really are powers?" I repeat.

"Yes, well, make your selection; the library is closing," she says sharply, breaking my spell.

Outside in the garden, I come across the stern old American woman. I wonder what she will say on the subject. Settling down next to her, I tell her about my conversation with the librarian.

"Do you believe in yoga powers?" I besiege her. "Do you think it is possible to walk on fire?"

"Where I grew up in South Carolina, we used to walk barefoot on the asphalt in summer."

"Yeah, but those aren't burning coals."

"The asphalt of a Carolina summer can melt into the ground."

"Have you seen anyone here walk on hot coals?"

"I've seen many strange things," she tells me calmly.

"Really? Really, like what?" I lean in closer.

"A beggar died last night," she responds flatly.

"He died?" This is not what I wanted to hear.

"Yes, under the bridge."

Now I understand, and I instantly feel ashamed. Most of what the librarian had tried to teach me went over my idiot head. Mysterious powers from the beyond, real or imagined, doesn't mean beggars won't still die under bridges and colonies aren't filled with lepers. I fall silent.

The next morning dawns beautiful, and I am eager for any change from ashram life. I have heard that there is a high mountain temple above Rishikesh where you can see the pantheon of the Himalayas and Nanda Devi, the highest mountain in India. I would do anything for another good view of the world's greatest range, and a little tourist excursion sounds too good to pass up, so I plan to leave before breakfast.

Overhearing my plan to visit the temple, the Swiss man insists on making me a ridiculously precise map. He sweats and labors over the details, while I stand impatiently by. I find him tedious like his exacting countrymen with their wristwatches and coo-coo clocks. Precious time passes as he draws exactly how many meters to walk for the hiking section.

"Your country is like my Switzerland," he remarks. "We spend more on luxuries and guns than to feed the poor or cure disease. I am very ashamed of our Western ways."

Now I feel silly blaming him for my Swiss disappointment. Of course, his presence at the ashram shows he is no more like his countrymen than I to Ronald Reagan.

According to his plan, I am to hail a bus and ride up the hill for an hour to a stop where I hike the last three kilometers to the viewpoint temple. After walking a short distance up the road, I successfully stop a packed, creaky old vehicle. Every brown eye stares unblinkingly at me. I squeeze into a row, my knees grinding mercilessly against the wooden seat back in front of me as we lumber up the steep, winding road.

Wild, dirty children along the roadside gasp as the bus passes, as though it promises salvation. Spotting the silly white foreigner, they squeal with delight. Women work in fields terraced into the mountainside. With enormous bushels balanced on their heads, they parade down the road wearing heavily soiled, multicolored saris, great ringlets of golden jewelry cascading down from their noses. In the bleak villages nearby, their husbands idle in chai shops, playing cards, and smoking bidis.

After about twenty minutes, the scattered dwellings recede into untamed countryside. By the time I reach my stop, the road is surrounded by green forests, and the sweet mountain freshness fills the air.

The cool breeze and the shade of the woods are refreshing. I am alone for the first time since my "tiger" sighting a few days ago. In the absence of bullhorns, screeching PA systems, and honking, my ears continue to ring. In the cities below, India's dense population—the teeming millions—are crawling all over each other like ants. I have escaped, if only with a day pass.

After following a dirt path for some time, the white Shiva temple suddenly comes into view, rising from the hilltop with the commanding presence of a German castle. A short walk brings me to the base of a long set of white stairs extending up to the temple. Although I'm grateful that there is no chairlift option to reach this temple, I am beginning to feel weak from skipping breakfast. The pure Himalayan sun glares on each step, making me long for sunglasses. I ascend slowly and dizzily, clutching the hand railing.

The climb seems arduous, but not in vain. As promised, Nanda Devi appears over the top of the temple stairs. The peak rises majestically in a distinct sharp blade, as though it would slice the heavens. At 25,643 feet, Nanda Devi dominates the skyline, but it is also surrounded by other distant, mysterious mountains. This soaring vista is better than I ever could have imagined. I stand regarding it silently, overwhelmed by its pure and sudden beauty, and feeling like the luckiest traveler alive. I can relate to the lyrics of the epic Led Zeppelin song "Kashmir" which plays in my head as I gaze into that very region in complete wonderment.

After some glorious minutes, my reverie is interrupted by two grim-faced Indian men who appear through a door in the temple wall. As I watch, they turn their backs on Nanda Devi and the Great Range, and, bent with determination, scrub the brass trinkets intended for the temple's Hindu rituals. I feel the moment's magic destroyed by the great enslavers of mankind: the specters of pointless ritual and duty. Around the world, masses just like the men at the temple above Rishikesh voluntarily imprison themselves, polishing statues or performing other pointless duties and rituals. *Is the key to making God happy pretending to be busy?* I wonder.

I descend the hill behind the temple wall, searching for privacy to absorb the staggering view. Finding a place in the dirt, I spontaneously assume a cross-legged lotus position. After killing my knees these last weeks to accomplish this feat, I am finally beginning to appreciate what it is for. It really is the most comfortable and stable way to sit, especially with one's back straight.

Gazing up in the light blue sky, I can feel the pale white moon's coolness and the craters pop out in relief. It feels so close, so real, this heightened awareness of the moon's subtle qualities. It is the same beautiful moon that greeted me atop Yosemite's Fairview Dome, and it brings the same sense of peace. Now I am witness to my thoughts and breath that keeps me in the here and now. I ponder on what one might call the Zen of climbing when free soloing like Derek Hersey does as the ultimate stay in the present experience. For me, it is much harder staying in the present in a cushy, carpeted meditation hall—a far cry from hanging by the finger tips with eternity waiting below.

Suddenly, I hear laughter from above. Glancing up from what I thought was a solitary, secluded space, I see a modern Indian family dressed in Western fashion. They are pointing at my crossed legs and laughing uproariously. So I'm caught red-handed in the lotus position, proof that I am just another foolish, deluded, desperate Westerner throwing myself at their corrupt gurus. To them, no greater idiot walks the land. It is an odd experience to be mocked by the Indians themselves. Apparently, there is quite a movement among many modern Indian citizens to turn their backs on their own rich heritage of yoga philosophy to embrace the glittering tinsel of the West. Building their economy at all costs and an arms race with Pakistan seem to be their most pressing goals.

The day is slipping by into afternoon, and I am feeling weak from hunger. Leaving the temple complex, I return down the steps and follow the deserted road, mile after mile, wondering where the bus is. I start to worry about getting back before dark—or at all. I need diversion, so, taking inspiration from Uncle Joe, I begin a game of putting my left foot down for Om, right for mane, another left for padme and hum. The walk becomes a meditation, and I fall into a beautiful, peaceful rhythm. I suddenly feel the endurance to stroll all the way back to Rishikesh in this trance. Just as I begin to enjoy the process, however, a bus comes grinding by. I reluctantly hail it.

"Rishikesh?" I query. The driver looks confused. Foreigners are not normally wandering alone in the middle of nowhere. The bus is going the right direction, so I stuff myself in.

The bus stops again and again, picking up even more people until I am crushed from all sides. Claustrophobia overtakes me, and I seriously regret not walking back with the fresh air and open road, even though it would be dark long before I returned.

A woman on my right holds a baby who is shrieking louder than the bus horn. My ears tingle painfully. I try to concentrate on a spot on the seat. The shrieks stop because the baby is throwing up thick, yellow bile on my pant leg. The parents look deeply concerned, as though the baby might die soon.

I feel awful for the baby and also terrified that I might catch something from the projectile vomiting. I had been so happy out on the road. With every passing mile, more sweat pours down my forehead. I am drowning in this pit of misery.

Close to Rishikesh, I hail the driver to stop. I unfold my legs only to find they are asleep. I fight to get off the bus. I never want to be a tourist in India again or to whine about the bus service back home. Delays and poor scheduling pale compared to babies throwing up on you.

"Did you see the temple?" asks the American lady on my return.

"Yes, the view was wonderful, but what a bus ride back. I was so packed in, it was hell. This world is a hell."

"No, no, it's a beautiful, beautiful world," she says softly.

"Yeah?" I feel annoyed. "How beautiful is baby's vomit, and poverty, and pollution?"

"Jesus said: 'The poor will always be with us.' If you wait for people to change their ways, you will be waiting a long time. Rise above it all. Rise above the muck like a lotus flower. You will see it is a beautiful world."

"But I don't see beauty. I see babies puking. I'm not a flower. How will I ever see a beautiful world—if there really is one there?"

"It is there. Keep going with what you are doing here. The yoga and meditation practices will continue to purify your mind so you can meditate effectively." She pauses. "I would also suggest giving up swearing."

She must have heard me swear with Pradeep, who relishes learning new Western expletives.

"Swearing is the first sign of a dirty mind."

Sitting in the evening meditation class, painfully bored with following my breath or repeating the old 'Om Mane Padme Hum' I think on the day's events and the American woman's advice. Part of me wants to tell her to go get stuffed. She's so goody-goody I always feel like I'm talking to a prissy mother superior. Tonight, however, the awful experience on the bus makes me consider what she said. There seems to be a consistency, a pattern emerging, in what I absorb here and in the lotus rising above the muck of the crass worldly elements of life.

Once, on a climbing trip to Hueco Tanks in Texas, Red and I crossed into the adjacent border town of Juarez, Mexico, and asked what there was to do. After a couple of beers, we found ourselves in a whorehouse. It was full of sailors and sketchy-looking, border characters waiting their turn. The place made my skin crawl. A sort of moral alarm clock went off in my head, and I wanted to get the hell out, but Red lingered. It seems people born into so much money suffer from a desperate boredom, and a Mexican bordello was *somewhere* he might not be saved by his parents. In the States, if he pushed it too far, any charges would be dropped with a phone call to the right person from his parents. Fortunately, Red came to his senses, and we left.

Since my arrival in India, I have heard over and over again that retiring from worldly desires and impure behaviors is the way to beauty. The people in this ashram have voluntarily removed themselves from the excitement of the cities, the safety of their prospective countries, the familiarity of friends and family. I can relate, as every summer, I personally couldn't wait to escape from the comforts of "civilization" to live in a creaky cabin.

"All life is suffering," said the Buddha. At first reading, that sentence seemed incredibly depressing, but it now occurs to me that the Buddha meant rising above the worldly human condition of whorehouses, bars, fighting, desire, resentment, jealousy—all the necessary elements of a primetime T.V. show. I realize I have been trying to transcend worldly life by climbing a rock above our stifling cities and leaving mankind's ugliness below. As C.G. Jung wrote "People get dirty through too much civilization. Whenever we touch nature, we get clean." The American lady's words seem to make sense, so I decide to do what she suggests. I will try to purify my mind and see what happens. Maybe attempting to rise above the vulgarities of the world *will* take a person somewhere. Not swearing seems like nitpicking compared to the wholesale decadence of a Mexican whorehouse, but I recall my yoga teacher's advice from George Bernard Shaw, to keep the window we see the world through clean. I guess I can give up a few "fucks" and "shits" here and there.

A BIG BROTHER IN PRADEEP

Some nights, when the happy Indian sun is far away, I have terrible dreams. These nightmares are not about werewolves and vampires or other imaginary fears. Instead, they are memories from my childhood, but with powerful new undercurrents of human tragedy and despair. It seems my daily yoga activities are stirring them up. As I toss and turn in my cot, the memories form in menacing clouds and fall like buzz-bombs from the overhead Luftwaffe.

Tonight, I am at the bus stop on my way to elementary school. I see vividly the vacant face of the girl who lives in the house behind me. Katie is slightly retarded, and she walks with a pronounced limp. Because of her condition, the *uberjungen*, the ruling class of neighborhood kids, often make fun of her. Today, these wolves surround her, circling ever closer. She seems to have stirred an impulse deep in their blood.

"Loser! Retard!" they shout viciously.

"Goo, look at me. I'm Katie the fucking spaz," taunts a model, straight "A" student.

"Stop bothering me," she pleads.

"Or what, goober bitch? What are you gonna do? Drool all over me?"

I awake suddenly, wide-eyed, the image of Katie's panicked face still haunting my mind. Now, in these dark hours, I see this episode for what it really was, another chapter in the endless history of witch hunts, evil, brutality, and hate. Are people bred, like dogs, through the impressions of our past? Is the horror from the white European past, the medieval police state of Christendom, the cause of the paranoia and mistrust that lingers today? Or is it some kind of Social Darwinism?

As I lie awake, I wonder about such things. If we are free from such influences from our horrific European history, it is disturbing to think that people would *choose* to treat others so cruelly.

Though I felt terrible for Katie, I didn't throw myself into the fray and take on the bullies. The neighborhood kids had society's endorsement. Moreover, with my long, lanky body and big feet, I was only one step away from the bonfire myself.

"Some are born to sweet delight, some are born to the endless night," Jim Morrison sang, paraphrasing William Blake. Katie was born to the endless night. A few years later she drank an overdose of anti-freeze and died. End of the night.

Morning meditation has just ended. As usual, I didn't really meditate; I just looked around, fidgeting in the dark. At the same time, after such a restless night, I almost fell asleep. Pradeep has dragged my listless soul to a café.

"Pradeep, I'm having nightmares about home," I say. "Is this what meditation does?"

"Dreams from America?" Pradeep looks wide-eyed. "Yes, yes. An American taxi driver of this New York City comes here. He tells me he sees two men at a table. One man takes a knife and kills other man. Why? Why?"

"I don't know. New York has a lot of people."

"Delhi has much more people and little violence. It is ego working. Your country understands much science and computer but not ego."

I frown, trying to visualize this distinction.

"People problems are same," he continues. "In America, man works like robot in factory for big car, big house, to be important man. They are free but make themselves slaves, slaves to ego. Self-important man is doomed with arrogance and dark poems."

"They don't care," I interject, suddenly reminded of my fellow students from Kent Country Day to CU, prepped for future corporate careers. "They want to win at all costs."

We sit in comfortable silence for a moment. "You are different, little brother, than most foreign man," Pradeep says, peering at me curiously. "They come with strange ideas in the heads."

"I guess it's because I've never been good at anything," I offer. "I've been humiliated so many times it's not a problem."

Pradeep laughs. "You are lucky. The humble mind is close to God. With this mind you can learn *the* secret. You have good vibrations, *chota bhai*. You are not a 'great' man."

His words trouble me. I've always wanted to be great. I dream about being a great climber, a prominent lawyer, or politician. It hurts when I think success won't happen.

As if reading my mind, Pradeep explains further: "Desire, only ego desire will bring hurt. Stop these things, and you shall be the right kind of great man."

I shake my head, "People are horrible to you when you don't excel at something. Why can't I do anything very well? What is the key?"

"Concentration; concentration without ego will bring what you want. This success you wish for is a toy to play with, for one day you may also find people are bad to you when you do something well. It was your destiny to suckle at Mother India's breasts because you are sick by American ego. Yes? That is true greatness. The greatest man has a desire for liberation from the ego. The lotus flower, the holiest symbol of the east, rises above the muck and mud to be the symbol of illumination. You have many nightmares? Many people have insulted you, yes, little brother? This is the muck that you must let go and let settle to the bottom of the pond. These dark things have the nutrients you need to rise from. The people who have insulted you, you must thank. They do you great service."

"Thank them for humiliating me?"

"Yes. Does rich man come to a poor country like India?"

"No, he goes to Aspen."

"Does rich man have good vibrations?"

I pause and think of the heaviness I felt around the super-rich kids and adults like Mr. Olafson. "No, probably not very often," I respond, starting to realize what Pradeep is saying. Despite the world's lust for the good life, Aspen, or even life in a castle, can't keep out depression and despair.

"Yes, man cannot meditate without humility. The door for liberation is open to person like you before all of these 'great' people."

"For me?" I am stunned. It seems so ironic, yet the very people who seem to embody success also have the biggest egos. It is true I avoid their company; however, I feel none of the liberation Pradeep speaks of. Aspen still sounds a lot better than this dump right now. The world still seems a shitty deal.

"Imagine you are a *great* man full of ego. Perhaps you would be cruel and humiliate others chained to your pride."

I think for some time. Would *I* have attacked Katie if I were popular? Maybe if I wasn't a tall moron I would be another tyrant, a self-satisfied jerk. What if I was an Olafson or born into a royal family?

"Come, little brother, that is not your fate," smiles Pradeep, reading my mind. "You are a lucky one."

"I still don't know what you mean by being *lucky*."

"Perhaps you are luckiest of all. Let us look for a cigarette from foreign person."

After lunch, I follow Pradeep back down to town. We pass a small man dressed in dirty rags and a mischievous grin, his wares spread out on a blanket. He calls out: "Hello, foreign brother! Which country? Yes, yes, you come, come."

"Good vibrations," says Pradeep, introducing the bony little man as an esteemed colleague. "You must respect the magic of the Chapatti Baba."

The Chapatti Baba takes a deep theatrical bow. I remember him calling to me as I walked by other times. Of course, I ignored him then, another of the millions of beggars at work, not a magic Chapatti Baba. Everything is different when Pradeep is involved.

"Which country?" he repeats.

"America."

"Ah, American brother, please come here. I have something for you. Come, come."

"Why do they call you the Chapatti Baba?" I ask, attempting conversation. "Do you cook Chapattis?"

"No," he replies, flashing a great, bright smile. "I am making the magical beasts from the Chapatti flour for American man's joy and amusement." He holds up a hardened clump of dough brightly painted with large eyes and rosy red lips, proclaiming, "Behold, brother turtle!"

It looks like kindergarten quality work, maybe deliberately so. I laugh in spite of myself. Encouraged, the Chapatti Baba makes the turtle's head move by jiggling it on a stick running through the shell. He beams a great smile. He is having more fun than a kindergartner.

In seconds, a large crowd of local Indians gathers, piercing me with unblinking, third-world stares. Even in the face of all this awkward and unwanted attention, I can't help but enjoy the show.

"And here is the deadly cobra," the Chapatti Baba continues, picking up a blue figurine and moving its head in and out. "'GGGRRRRRRrrrrr!' He growls at American man."

I have to admit, it is a great sales pitch. "Okay, okay," I laugh, "how much do you want for the snake?"

The man looks surprised. "For my American brother, a free snake." He gives it to me.

I am suddenly ashamed of my assumption that his act was a con, and I also feel silly holding the toy snake. As the crowd begins to break up, I notice a little boy peering longingly at the toys from behind his mother's sari. She begins to pull him away. *What am I going to do with a clay snake?*

Impulsively, I stop the woman, placing the small toy into her little boy's hands. I watch his face light up like a Christmas tree, and the whole crowd smiles. His mother thanks me repeatedly, clasping her hands together. I haven't felt so good in years. At the same time, this encounter makes me realize that I am not naturally generous. I want to blame my Western "grab all you can" heritage, but instead I must acknowledge that my selfishness is no one's fault but my own. Now though, surrounded by sweet Indian smiles, the lightness of benevolence seems to raise me effortlessly above the heaviness of greed. It is a better sensation than having all the crown jewels of England; they may be pretty stones, but they are hard and cold like their owners. This little man grinning over his creations has taught me much, and I resolve not to forget this flash of joy again.

Other people may start their spiritual life claiming they saw a crucifix in the sky, or Jesus or Mother Mary speaking to them from a flood of light, or Lord Siva dancing on a cloud, and that was the beginning of their faith. For me, however, it is the feeling that I would like to quit my previous life of selfishness for this odd feeling of generosity. It's not a negative feeling but a realization I have been missing out on something. Missing out on a lot.

"Thanks, Chapatti Baba," I tell him warmly as we leave. "Your toys *are* magic."

I have been here two weeks and have only two weeks to go. It feels easier being at the halfway point—like there will some kind of end to all this. I can make it if I can keep going day by day.

At lunch, a newly-arrived Belgian woman sits to my right. She is working on her PhD in religious studies. Excitedly, she tells me that she has just come from Varanasi, where she watched thousands of corpses burned and thrown into the Ganges. She asks me when I am going to see it.

"Are you kidding? Get on a bus for fourteen hours to see *that*?"

"But it's essential to Hindu belief!"

"I'm not a Hindu."

Something between confusion and exasperation crosses her face. "Then why are you here?" she snaps, abruptly moving to sit somewhere else.

Her question reminds me what an outsider I am, first at home and now here. There is a difference between me and the majority of foreigners who filter through the sub-continent. The really low-minded visitors come for the plentiful drugs and sex slaves. Others wander aimlessly as New Age nomads captivated by cheap drifting. Those with a dull, stable life at home seem to seek the excitement promised by colorful travel brochures. Their kind isn't moved by the culture as much as a when-in-Rome exotic travel package that allows them to "tick" India. The Belgian religious scholar regards her trip as a fact-gathering mission, analyzing the natives and their faith much like a biologist might study micro-organisms. I am another type of traveler altogether. It doesn't give me a thrill to watch bodies burning, to be trampled in a festival, or dowsed with colored powder. How can I explain myself? It doesn't matter: I am broke, and staying put.

After lunch, I chat with one of the many ashram cooks—there are always twelve Indians doing the job of two. I am agreeable and don't mention the sand that was in my subji today that almost broke my tooth. The cook is about my age but short and already balding under his white cap, and he doesn't smile.

I complement him on his cooking. "Will you open your own restaurant someday?"

The cook laughs, knowing I am pandering to him in the tradition of Pradeep con man ways, and clearly he finds the imitation funny.

"Do you like yoga?" I ask him.

"No," he replies matter-of-factly. "Yoga stupid. I like woman."

The cook walks on, leaving me to contemplate yoga's unpopularity. Maybe he's right. Perhaps it *is* stupid. Turning down the path, I spot another bald man in front of me. It's Pradeep. He's just shaved his head completely except for the little "Krishna tail" hanging in the back. The new hairstyle makes him barely recognizable. He is going down to the river and invites me along.

"You don't mind to be with a Krishna?" he asks with wry smile.

"With you, something interesting always seems to happen."

Reassured, he leads me down the path. "Come, come little brother. We meet people, talk of spiritual things, feel great love."

Immediately, I feel my frustrations bubbling up. "Love is easy to talk about," I sigh, "but it seems like few people really like yoga."

"Yes, yes, true yoga is interesting for the very few," he responds.

"Also, the books I read about yoga say your mind should be silent. Why do those people start bullhorn chanting at 5 a.m. every morning?"

"That is a preliminary stage of spirituality," Pradeep says. "For common people, fear and attachment keep higher experiences away. They believe Ganesh, the elephant god, will clear their path of obstacles to enlightenment. They do not realize that Ganesh is within. They are not ready for silence."

"Then the noise, singing, and outward worship are artificial?"

"Of course. It is a misunderstanding, for the joy of the people. They give their spiritual work to a god to be done for them. Worship is a form of meditation. But on high level it is a mistake, one must make extrovert to introvert. The gods and temples are only symbols of power."

"What is the point of all that symbolism? It just seems confusing."

"Symbol like Ganesh exist because the multitudes cannot read," explains Pradeep. "It was the best way to make them understand. Unfortunately, they begin to worship the symbol itself and fall into the spiritual slavery. The symbol cannot do the work to be done. Only the devotee can do this, and it requires the strength of an elephant." He pauses. "To abandon the ego is not easy. That is why it is greatest triumph of man," Pradeep says punctuating the air with his index finger.

At the river, Pradeep stops to talk to some wealthy Indian pilgrims. He gives them stock orations about spirituality, performing his duty as a Krishna tour guide, but I can tell that he is bored.

Pradeep sees a man in orange robes and comically tries to touch the man's feet, a symbol of worship. The man dodges Pradeep and tries to touch Pradeep's feet instead. It's a game of who's the most humble and won't allow their feet to be touched. Like kids they laugh; their playfulness is a joy to watch.

As we near the first bridge, Pradeep introduces me to a young shopkeeper who sells brass trinkets to pilgrim tourists. The same junk is in every other shop along the river.

"Nice souvenirs," I say politely. The shopkeeper chuckles knowingly. Business is bad. Everything is slow until a good Hindu festival, when tens of thousands of pilgrims descend on Rishikesh. I can't help think of the similarity of the tourist economy in Estes Park, Colorado waiting for summer season when chunky Texan tourists swarm the streets.

I'm still not a habitual bidi smoker but I am starting to enjoy the occasional one, especially socially, as we sit smoking bidis in front of the young shopkeeper's souvenir stall. It feels like quality teenage loitering. The shopkeeper even reminds me of one of my high school friends, same face and hair, only darker. He smiles and nods with a deep, silent, ecstatic peacefulness, and nothing needs to be said. Their company is bliss. There is no criticism, no social discomfort, no "bad vibrations." Backstabbing seems non-existent. I can now sit silently with them not searching for some inane conversation topic to bargain away the time. I have crossed the line over to the natives.

Pradeep spots a knot of giggling young Indian women watching us.

"You must say this words to Hindi girls: *Maya Tamara Chuta Marunga.*"

"Maya Tamara ... what?"

Pradeep starts giggling too. He tries to make me memorize the words again and again, only to burst into hysterics, too weak to continue.

"What do those words mean?" I demand suspiciously. Knowing Pradeep, I'm sure they are sexually charged and taboo. The girl's parents could demand marriage on the spot.

Instead of giving me an answer, Pradeep only laughs harder.

I feel my friendship with Pradeep growing, and we chat as equals. I find myself constantly laughing at his outrageous sense of humor. I'd be a fool to believe half of what the scallywag says, but at times he is as passionate and rebellious as the characters played so convincingly by James Dean. Pradeep is becoming my *bhaiyaa,* my older brother.

Later that day, I invite Pradeep to my room to listen to some Rock and Roll.

"You have Western music, my little brother?" Pradeep handles the cassette player like a holy relic, pouring over my measly possessions.

First up is "Jumpin' Jack Flash." The turbulent strum of guitars leaves Pradeep in awe.

"I like that song because it's about having a bad start, but things get better," I tell him. "I think that's happening to me. Rock and Roll is about the closest thing to religion for many back home."

"More, more," demands Pradeep greedily. "What else you have?"

As the newly appointed ambassador of rock, I hop around frantically, locating tapes and rewinding select songs to lay out the West's thoughts and dreams for the crazy Krishna. Pradeep's excitement reignites my own passion for great classic rock music. I want him to appreciate its inspiration, its energy, and its lunacy. I want him to understand that holy edge where self-consciousness and criticism are replaced by the outrageous like The Who's lead guitarist Pete Townsend's smashing his guitars, or drummer Keith Moon driving a car into the Holiday Inn swimming pool.

My musical tastes had formed just as classic rock began to die. The Who's farewell tour marked the end of an era. The frantic vitality of Townsend was being pushed aside for music videos, synthesizers, and sterile drum machines. The Grateful Dead with their seemingly obligatory L.S.D., was uninspiring to me—more like country-western than rock. Some of my favorite music was orchestrated under its influence, much better than the cocaine fueled 80's songs, but, as Pete Townsend's Indian mystic Mehr Baba warned, "Drugs can open some doors, but their continued use will only lead to madness and death."

Punk rock music was too much, nor did I appreciate the new genre of heavy metal. While I loved the unbridled energy of *The Who: Live at Leeds* and the hard, pounding riffs of Led Zeppelin, I couldn't cross the line to the thuggish simplicity of heavy metal champions Def Leppard and Quiet Riot. It was Viking junk that made perfect fodder for the humorous film, *Spinal Tap*.

But any genre was respectable compared to what sophomore year roommates listened to at C.U. Boulder. We had long arguments about the viability of MTV stars like Cyndi Lauper, Duran Duran, and Madonna—awed mostly by her commercial success alone.

"But she's fake," I protested repeatedly. "She doesn't even write her own songs!"

"Yeah, so what? She's making millions doing it," they responded. It didn't pass the Sixties test of having something to say, but it was selling like hotcakes, and that was good enough for them.

Playing my favorite songs for Pradeep could not feel more different than my frustrating musical encounters back at home. After a while, I get out a particularly special tape. "This is called *The Wall* by an English band named Pink Floyd," I tell him reverently.

I first heard this album when I was listening to the radio at age twelve. Introducing it, the disk jockey had real fear in his voice. I immediately took notice. The songs were brooding and uncompromising in their sentiments. In a way, the whole album seems to embody the haunting refrain, that recalls the vacant minds of people like my former roommates: "Is there anybody out there?"

The song "Mother" begins in solemn acoustic verse; easy to mistake for a goody-goody ode to mumsy... until Roger Waters asks softly, "Mother do you think they'll try to break my balls?" Soon after, David Gilmour's ethereal guitar bursts forth, with never heard before guitar tone, into a breathtaking solo. Later in the album, Pradeep and I listen to "Comfortably Numb." Though I've played it hundreds of times, it makes my blood run cold. The song develops on two levels: a sad disillusioned set of verses sung by Roger Waters and then David Gilmour's transcendent, hope-filled chorus. The ballad ends with Gilmour's exhilarating guitar solo of the gods, elevated to the higher register, releasing all the inhibitions and horror of the human psyche.

When the album was released, I was stuck in my first year at Kent Denver Country Day. The lyrics from across the ocean took me to a new world. Amidst the conservative tension of prep school, I wondered who could write such provocative words as "dark sarcasm in the classroom." Their author, Roger Waters, seemed like the last foothold of humanity, and he became a new hero in my pantheon, in the manner of George Orwell. Now, as I sit with Pradeep, I reflect on the album's gloomy references to a descent into fascism, drugs, and madness, its essential Englishness, and that ever-present question: *Is there anybody out there?*

"This wall is symbolic, *chota bhai*?" Pradeep suggests, looking very interested.

"Yes, I've read *The Wall* album's concept interpreted as the protector of the ego. Every time someone hurts you, another brick is put in the wall until you are safe, until you are 'comfortably numb.'"

"But you cannot see over this wall."

"I suppose not, but you don't know what people can be like in the West, Pradeep."

Pradeep dutifully adores the album, disturbing though it is. "That is Englishman?" he asks as the last spooky melody fades into silence. "Play music from American man."

"Okay, here's perhaps the greatest American band: The Doors."

Once again, the choice is a success. "Yes! yes!" Pradeep yells during "Break on Through."

When I play "The End," however, he shouts, "This is the song! I have found it!" Putting his hands over his ears and closing his eyes, he passes into a trance-like state. He clutches his fists and rubs his temples, moaning along with the music: *This is the end.*

Pradeep unselfconsciously shakes and wobbles in time with the hypnotic tempo that I can hear tinkling softly through the headphones. I giggle as he carefully repeats the lyrics, swooning in amazement.

Throughout the entire, lengthy piece, Pradeep remains wholeheartedly lost, hypnotized by the Great American Poet. I watch as his movements meet the changing tempo of the song, the slow Indian sitar like verses later speeding up to a frenzied jam, shattering in climax, and then returning to relive the song's soft opening phrases.

"It is the apocalypse!" Pradeep yells abruptly, clearly unaware of his volume through the headphones.

It's an insightful comment, considering the song's use in the film, *Apocalypse Now.*

"American music!" Pradeep exclaims after the album ends, holding up the tape in reverence. "India people sing happy songs about flowers. This is darkness and end of world coming!"

"Well, that was Sixties music," I explain. "Now Rock and Roll is nearly dead."

"No more American rock music?"

"Not like The Doors anyway. The times have changed. An Irish band, U-2, tries to carry the torch, but most people from the 1960s now laugh at what the early bands did."

"Yoga was popular in this revolution, yes?"

"Sort of." I think of my own mixed experiences back home. The 1960s are long gone, the big sell out affirmed by movies like *The Big Chill* about former 1960's activists aging and settling down to embrace the new conservatism around them. "But most people think yoga is weird, and certainly against wholesome American values."

"Yoga is 6,000 years old!" Pradeep says in disbelief.

"I was lucky to find yoga through rock climbing." Surveying my stack of tapes, I add, "Do you want to hear the *Om* tape I brought from home?"

"Ah, yes, the great power of Om's vibration."

As he listens, I can faintly hear a chorus of powerful voices chanting, "OOOOOOOMMMMMNNNNNnnnnnnnnnnn…"

Pradeep shakes his head affirmatively. "*Hahn*—yes. Each country has good and bad. America has nuclear bomb and OM tape. India has yoga and poverty, a perfect balance." He gets up. "Thank you, little *chota bhai*. Now I am having good dreams tonight."

Pradeep leaves singing, "This is the end, my only friend…" as he trails off to his room.

The next morning, the sky is overcast. Despite the cold, I decide to go for a stroll down the ashram path towards Rishikesh. In town, I see the Chapatti Baba in his usual place, absorbed in making his absurd toys. He is wearing an American high-school letter jacket. The sight is bizarre but warming.

"Would you like to join me for coffee or chai today?" I offer.

"It is possible," he says, as if he has to cancel a board meeting first. The Chapatti Baba clears his appointments, and we settle into a small chai stall by the river.

"Do you remember when the British were here, Chapatti Baba?"

"Yes, very dirty-minded people," he laughs. "Many years ago, I am young man, and they tell me I am a beggar, for my clothing is soiled. This I tell them: My mind is clean, but yours is not." He pauses reflectively. "Do you like meditation, young man?"

"Yes, mostly, so far," I respond uncertainly.

"The slowing of the mind is man's greatest pleasure. Do you know why many do not like meditation? They cannot stop the restless mind because they do not have karma. They have been immoral in the life, and when they try to meditate nothing happen, or they feel pain. A person first must give selfless service to others before something happen in meditation." He considers his chai cup thoughtfully. "It will not happen without selfless service and working to lose self-importance. To do something well, you must realize: 'I am not the doer. I am not the body. I am not the mind.' Do you understand, young man?"

"I think I am starting to. *'I am not the doer,'*" I repeat, fascinated.

"Yes, not the doer. Man is more than body, more than possessions, more than accomplishments. Man is divine beneath these worldly things. Meditation is not doing, it is observing. Witness the mind without controlling thoughts, witness the breath without controlling air and you will be driven deep into your meditation."

"Technique is not meditation," he continues. "Technique is merely a boat to cross Gunga. Many techniques to meditation, but technique not meditation," the Chapatti Baba laughs. Then he leans forward, again pointing his finger upward. "Never listen to man who says there is only one way or he knows best way. We are all traveler of eternal path. Every way valid, even making my wonderful Chapatti toys valid, but have no attachment to techniques. Do you understand?"

"I think some of it."

"Drop all religions, systems, techniques, impressions, and self-importance. Serving a god will lead you outward but true yoga will lead you back to yourself. Yoga loves you more than it loves itself! Do you understand? The real self has all the powers." He shakes my arm and raises his voice for emphasis. "Yoga loves *you* more than it loves itself." he says again, slowly. He didn't have to. The sentence is worth the trip alone. It counters Peter's accusation that I went to India to join a crazy cult and be brainwashed. This journey is for my true self first.

As he speaks, the wisdom of the East becomes clearer to me, and I realize it isn't necessarily "Eastern" at all. Wisdom, I realize, is really just common sense. It is not only whispered in exotic monasteries and printed in obscure, ancient texts; it is known to people from all walks of life. As they have discovered, a moral, unselfish life can lead to higher states of mind, while egotism and decadence lead to suffering and destruction. It may simply come down to how big an asshole you really are.

I stare into the dark flakes of my freeze-dried coffee, remembering a tow-truck driver in Boulder who once came to jump my battery. After talking awhile, he said, "Son, I meet a lot of people with nice cars, but most of them don't know their left from their right. When I come to their rescue, they're often rude or try to belittle me. Not doing the simple maintenance on their car because of a bloated ego is usually the problem." The tow truck driver looked at me and continued sagely, "If you become infected with self-importance, you are lost."

This sleepy, gray overcast day is the kind that makes most people want to crawl back into bed but not the Chapatti Baba. After a couple of sips of chai, he abruptly shouts to the dusty subcontinent:

I am the Chapatti Baba.
Every day I'm happy,
never any problems.
Happy, happy, happy.

Despite being probably in his mid-seventies, he climbs up on the table and begins dancing to his song:

Chapatti Baba, yes I am.
Happy, happy everyday 'cause
I'm the Baba,
the Chapatti Baba!
I'm the Baba,
the Chapatti Baba!

The Chapatti Baba is now flailing wildly, enveloped in a dancing fury. Laughing, I snort coffee out of my nose. Nobody cares; the coffee shop owner smiles serenely at the river as though some nut dances on his table every day.

After some time, I leave the Chapatti Baba to his unaffected happiness. I walk along the river alone, skipping stones on the surface where it is calm enough. Then, crossing the bridge, I follow a system of faint goat paths up a steep barren slope where I have never been. Locals invite me to warm myself by their fires.

I pass a shepherd, who puts his hands together in Namaste mudra and says gently, "All men are part of the mighty God, and I welcome you to my home as I do God himself."

His words affect me. I am nobody, a member of the savage West, the race of Winston Churchill and the Generals who ordered their troops to open fire on unarmed "colonials" time and again for centuries. Yet he considers my presence divine. I thank him, but continue upward. I wish I could kidnap racist people like Randy from summer camp and dump them in the middle of India without money. Would they continue to think they are so superior to these kind, hardworking inhabitants, the poor who see us all as part of God? It's hard to hold onto resentment in India because the Indians themselves have so little in their hardscrabble existence. Anger has no choice but to thaw in front of their beaming smiles, goodness, and impossible faith.

After wandering in the hills and reflecting on these thoughts for about an hour, I return to the river. As I sit resting on a bench in the shade, a large cow comes to inspect me. She stares at me intently through her big brown eyes. Back home, she is "McLunch." However, in India she is a privileged citizen with unalienable rights out for an afternoon constitutional. Reflecting in her sad brown eyes, I see my many burgers, dirty slaughterhouses, the cruelty of producing veal. All consumed by an insatiable, obese *beef: it's what's for dinner* crowd. I suddenly feel ill to think I ate an animal that could look me so penetratingly in the eyes. India is already making me soft, but a vegetarian? Back in Boulder, I couldn't stand the whiny "veggies." Yet this cow's moist brown eyes seem to be pleading with me. Pradeep says that to know someone well is to imagine their suffering. I never imagined he meant a cow. I can see the smokestacks of slaughterhouses in her shiny wet eyes again. Okay, I surrender. I will give up eating meat. Life forms are not widgets, and animals aren't things. Already, out of a new empathy, I have even begun to watch where I put my feet so as not to squash a bug. Surrounded by so many people, I feel as insignificant as an insect. I am beginning to feel compassion for this cow and for all life.

At a café, Pradeep sits sipping his coffee, absorbed in a newspaper with Hindi squiggles. He looks concerned, shakes his head and says, "Bad vibrations."

"What's in the news, Pradeep?"

"The assassins of our prime minister, Indira Ghandi, will be hanged today in Delhi."

"I guess there is violence in places other than America."

Pradeep brightens suddenly at the mention of America. "Do you think I will ever go to America?"

"Sure, but why?"

"To meet American girls," he replies, his eyes twinkling.

I shake my head slowly. "The U.S. is a different world than India."

Pradeep frowns. "What is the great difference?"

"Well, it seems like America is shiny on the outside, but our minds are often anxious, angry, and a lot are sick."

"Sick with ego?"

"Yes, that's what I've been trying to tell you. You want to drive on our freeways, but, despite nice cars and big houses, it isn't often a happy place. Americans strive to be the best, but no one seems to take time to enjoy life. There is always something to be done, and our appetite for drugs is colossal. Put it this way: America is the richest country on earth, but its jails are overflowing. Many people are so unhappy they see a doctor and take medicine."

Pradeep shrugs and a mischievous smile crosses his lips. "I would like to come to America and live in the jail."

"Live in jail?!" I stare at him in disbelief, trying to decide whether he's joking. "You want to come to America and be locked up? I don't think you'd be very happy."

"Happy?" Pradeep laughs. "Every day I'm happy! I chant Hare Krishna, Krishna Krishna, Krishna Krishna Hare Hare. Tum de dum. I need only food and a place for sleeping. What more could I require?"

"You want to come to American and live in prison?"

"Jail is in the mind! When chanting to Krishna and making yoga meditation there is no prison."

"There are angry men in jail," I remind him. "*Big* angry men."

Pradeep waves this image away dismissively. "Krishna meets a murderer on the road. The murderer's eyes are burning with hate, but he can feel the perfect love of Krishna. The murderer is weak against the power of love. Love, love, love. That is what men really want. Hatred and anger make people tired. The murderer becomes a great disciple of Krishna."

"What if the men in jail aren't impressed? What if they are so used to violence that they..."

"...kill me?" Pradeep finishes my question. "'Kill me then,' I will tell them." He is looking at me earnestly now, and I know he's serious. "When is the violence going to stop? When is hatred replaced by love? Sometimes one must be a martyr for love."

"Wow," I sigh, impressed and overwhelmed. "And I was afraid to come to India. I had heard it was *a beastly* place."

"Afraid of India?" he laughs. "India has caste systems and fighting, too. Our greeting '*Namaste*' is missing from our life."

"Namaste," I echo. "That word helped bring me here. I dreamed of a people living in a brotherhood of peace."

"'Namaste' is not only for Indian people. The divinity is alive within each person. That is where the sacred is, not in a temple." Pradeep looks up abruptly. "Her!" he shouts, pointing to a white woman standing by the river. "I want you to talk to that foreign girl and think of only speaking to the goddess that live inside her."

"What, now?" I hesitate, wondering what this new game is.

"Yes, go, *chota bhai*," Pradeep urges, pushing me toward the woman. "Like your music, 'Tear down the wall!'"

Suddenly, unexpectedly, I find myself talking warmly with this stranger about people and experiences. I find out that she is German, and, as we speak, she begins to smile. Perhaps she has been lonely. I feel a certain dignity for addressing her higher nature respectfully and wanting nothing in return, and the woman seems to sense it too. I realize that Pradeep is teaching me the power of charisma, to engage my fellow humans fearlessly in real and straight talk. It is a power amazing in its depth—namaste in action.

This morning is another cold, dark meditation, but now I can remain still for much longer without knee pain distracting me. Still, my mind wanders constantly like a restless monkey in the dark. I sit, craving my sleeping bag and struggling against anxieties and lonely thoughts.

"We go for a coffee, *chota bhai?*" asks Pradeep after class.

"No, this morning it's too cold."

"Love the cold, come on."

Reluctantly, I agree, though I am shivering in a long-sleeve shirt, mountain parka, and tennis shoes, while Pradeep has on only flip-flop sandals and a flimsy cotton robe.

"You will tell me more about American girls?" he asks again eagerly on the way down the path. "I would like to come to America and be yoga sex consultant."

"A yoga what?!"

"I will teach the secret of withholding the ejaculation using yoga concentration for satisfying sex experience. It is this way that you stop your ejaculation..." He makes a strained face, moaning, "hhhhhrrrrrrrrr." He smiles. "What you think?"

"As 'sex counselor' you will have all the sex," I laugh.

"Yes, that is also good plan. What is your job?"

"I'm a student right now," I say.

"Yes, but what do you want to do in your life?"

I pause and reflect. *What are you going to be when you grow up?* It was the most over-emphasized phrase in my world. I could have cared less for academics and ambition until my Constitutional Theory class. I'll never forget the professor, Glen Morris, a long-haired Native American with a Harvard Law degree. On the first day of class, he explained indignantly that the U.S. political system was based on the Iroquois' League of Nations, but our historians were too racist to acknowledge it. I had never heard such things. Morris protested or disrupted every Columbus Day parade our civic leaders tried to stage in downtown Denver. His Ivy League degree armed him as if he was movie character Billy Jack, the ass-whooping, ex-green beret, karate-expert Indian. The force of his conviction was mesmerizing. During lecture, I followed his every word. It was social justice through academic achievements that translate to political power.

In the following months, my grades soared until I was nearly on the Dean's list. I decided I was going to law school, not to be a lawyer like my father, but to be an activist like Professor Morris, a politician working to right so many wrongs.

Then one day Morris told us about the Rainbow Bridge case, one of his landmark legal experiences. Rainbow Bridge was a stone arch that had been a religious site for Native Americans. It was flooded by the Lake Powell water project and lost forever.

"Congress had drafted legislation," Morris began in a weary tone of voice, "stating they would protect religious sites for Native

Americans unless there was an over-riding national interest." He turned to the class. "Does anyone know what that over-riding interest was?" We were silent as his face turned red with indignation. "Waterskiing. Waterskiing was the over-riding national interest."

The dignity of the Law and its lofty pillars of justice fell to pieces before my eyes. Contrary to my formerly naïve ideals, the Law is actually whatever those in power want it to be, and what Congress wrote with a forked pen. The system is obviously rigged. Our democracy is a stroke of genius, but it's only as good as the quality of the citizenry from which it springs forth, and so often that's not very inspiring. Clearly, justice in politics is going to be a fight from day one.

I tell Pradeep about my daydream to be involved in politics: "Our politicians are awful so it would be great to have the ability to change things. I wish I could become someone powerful like a senator and work to protect the environment."

"If you were a senator, would you ask an older senator for his assistance?" Pradeep wonders.

"No, why would I do that?" I am taken aback by the direction of his questioning. "Asking for help means admitting you are stupid."

"A wise man admits he is stupid and will approach the older senators with humility to gain their knowledge and protection. You go to him like child," Pradeep says and makes a motion of supplication.

"That isn't the way it's done in Washington," I reply, shaking my head. "You should hear those in power carry on. They muscle to the top and humiliate the competition who are labelled 'losers.'"

"Yes, yes, you said they are awful people," he says impatiently, "but in war, earthquake and disaster a child is first protected because he is small, yes, but also because his heart is still pure, no ego."

"What does that have to do with politics?" I ask. I don't see how a submissive mind could accomplish anything in our chest-beating, back-stabbing Western world.

"Do you prefer to keep company with arrogant man, his mind full of his ego, or humble man with empty mind who can still learn?"

"The humble one, I guess."

"And so for your senators," Pradeep smiles. "This I promise: If you throw out ego you will be favorite one. You will know *true* power."

Bang, bang, bang! Pradeep is pounding on my door, disturbing a great nap. "Come out, *chota bhai*; there is fun today!"

The Icelandic woman, Uncle Joe, and some other foreigners are already gathered by the gate. Pradeep explains that a charity group is hosting a picnic for yogis, many of whom live wild in the surrounding woods, and we are invited to join them. The Western equivalent, a church picnic, would sound boring, but in India it probably won't be.

At a cafe by the river, a smiling long-haired man joins our troop. His bright woolen clothing sets him apart from the locals. I offer him peanuts. He bows gratefully and handles the peanuts carefully as if they're jewels. Perhaps the man has not eaten in a long time.

"Where are you from?" I ask.

"Nepal," he says and smiles brightly. His peaceful, radiant face seems to reflect the majesty of the high peaks of his birthplace.

Our group drifts down a dirt road on the other side of the river. I have never been this far up the Ganges deeper into the mountains before. Here, traffic is sparse, and the cool silence of the forest surrounds us. It is a joy to leave clanging Rishikesh behind. The Nepali man insists on holding my hand, for I am his new friend. Although I hope he does it out of gentle brotherhood, I still feel somewhat uncomfortable transgressing Western social norms by holding hands with some guy.

"The Himalayas are beautiful, yes?" I say.

"Hima ... leya?" he repeats, uncertainly.

"The mountains of Nepal."

"Ah, Hi-MAH-lia!" He nods, grinning widely. "Yes, very big mountains."

He tells me more about Nepal. It's fascinating to hear his perspective and the true pronunciation of his native range. Then he says he has malaria.

"Oh," I reply, shaking my hand free. In my ignorance, I wonder if his sweaty palm transferred the disease. My head spins with visions of inevitable sweats and death.

"I've got to wash my hands in the river. Western custom," I explain briskly, backing away. "See you later."

After scrubbing my hands for several minutes, I regain our group on the dirt road. Pradeep, in typical fashion, is bouncing incessantly between people, talking, gesturing and joking excitedly. We are now far up the Ganges from town. Above us, jagged hills clothed in rugged jungle rise steeply on both sides of the river. Just as the foothills behind Boulder mark the start of the great Rockies, it is here that the Himalayas begin.

Overhead, a band of monkeys appears. They are light gray with dark faces, giving them the wise aspect of ghostly, bearded holy men. Shy by nature, they are unlike the naughty, red-butted Rhesus monkeys that rampage through the town. On seeing us approach, they bound away gracefully without a sound.

Walking the unspoiled road, I begin to daydream about exotic travel adventures, such as riding a scooter from Delhi to Kathmandu. It may soon be the last *Indiana Jones* exploration frontier not marred by shopping malls and Burger Kings.

At a crossroads, our group slows to a stop to hear a man in orange robes speak.

"One must be careful not to get caught up in the material things..." he warns, but his voice seems worn-out and stale. It sounds like a stock speech.

Most of the Westerners seem captivated by this dreary sermon, but I am not. I notice a boy whipping a burro with a stick in a small corral nearby. The burro winces with every blow, unable to escape. As the little boy sings a song and whips him harder and harder, I can feel the poor beast's agony. I find myself drawn toward the tragic scene. Abruptly, I grab the stick and break it over my knee.

"Animals aren't things," I say, throwing the stick aside. The boy looks up at me in wonder, and I stand still for a moment, surprised by my own spontaneous action.

We arrive at the picnic and sit cross-legged on the ground. Some plainly dressed Indian men serve us colorful *subji* on giant green leaves woven into plates—completely disposable and biodegradable.

Wild looking men called *"sadhus"* begin to arrive. By tradition, these rough wanderers have renounced everything to live in the woods and pursue their higher being. I observe them keenly. Most are swaddled in grimy loincloths, sport unruly dreadlocks and don't seem to object to a little hashish.

As we eat, they scrape their throats frequently, spitting out mucous and coughing violently. If they are supposed to be my yoga role models, they don't exactly embody healthy living.

Renunciation to the point of drifting the land half-naked, half-starved and filthy doesn't seem right for me. Fortunately, I've just finished some of Uncle Joe's books on Buddhism which explain the Buddha's notion of the "middle way." The sadhus I see at the picnic remind me of the yogis among whom the Buddha initially lived. The Buddha eventually gave up his fellow yogis' regimen of self-deprivation, flagellation and starvation as an ineffective extreme. I agree this time with the Buddhist stories, silently rejecting the wandering sadhu model for my inspiration.

The man sitting next to me is a rock and roll drummer from Tokyo. As he tells me entrancing stories about Japan, I begin to believe that the secrets of meditation have moved on to more capable hands elsewhere. Yes – Japan! Forgetting about the Zen jerk I met the first day, I dream of going to Japan and *then* things will happen. With this resolution, I feel absolved for my failure and disillusionment with the Indian system of meditation. I am off the hook with crazy India.

As the picnic ends, Pradeep finds a fifty-rupee gift waiting under his plate. It is nice to see charity actually reach the poor, unlike so many fraudulent programs, that don't seem to change anything.

On our way back from the picnic, Pradeep catches up with me at a little market stall. Piles of sugar cane stalks sit ready to be ground into a sweet drink. The drink is supposed to be delicious, but the dark clouds of flies blanketing the crude machinery have deterred me from trying it.

Pradeep buys a stalk, but thankfully, he doesn't order a drink. "A gift for my little American brother," he says, proffering the sugar cane. "You must try. This is why Indian man has white teeth. Elephants come down from hills facing great dangers to pick the cane. All animals know its sweetness." He prepares the stalk by tearing away the outer layer to reveal a moist green sheath. I chew tentatively on this clean inner part. It is delicious.

Pradeep runs off, and I stroll unaccompanied across the footbridge, contentedly crunching on my stalk. Pradeep is right about the animals knowing the enchanting taste of sugar cane; moments later, a large rhesus monkey jumps down from his perch. The furry desperado confidently bares his fangs and extends a paw. Given the possibility of rabies, I don't delay in surrendering my loot. Mugged by a monkey!

However, it's impossible not to admire this hairy little bandito. He retreats with his prize to an airy perch on the bridge's suspension wire, where now he chomps away placidly, his fur caressed by the breeze rising off the Ganges. After being in India all this time, even if he is an unrepentant criminal from the mammalian underworld, I actually find the monkey's company a relief. He doesn't boast about his God or his superior method of meditation. I marvel at the monkey and realize my mind jumps to and fro more than his.

So why the sudden faith in going to Japan? And Zen instead of yoga? Did I not meet a snotty Zen monk the first week I was here? Not all the Japanese would be like the monk, but what am I thinking? Nothing calls the monkey away from the pleasure of eating the sugar cane he robbed off me. He isn't worried about a damned thing so long as his stomach is full. For Pradeep's sake, I only hope the monkey doesn't smoke.

KASHMIR JOHNNY

In one of the trinket stalls by the river, I buy some mantra beads like Uncle Joe's. Maybe they'll help me focus on counting each Om Mane Padme Hum that goes by and help me get into it. That is my hope anyway. Though the beads only costs the equivalent of 40 cents, my purchase makes me anxious about my money supply. The expense of getting to Delhi, a hotel, taxi fares to the airport and the airport tax hangs on my mind. I decide to inquire about selling some belongings.

A shopkeeper offers the equivalent of six dollars for my watch. It was a birthday gift worth $40, and it seems wrong to sell it. While we are still negotiating, the shopkeeper puts it in his pocket. My nerves are raw, and I boil over at him.

"Okay okay, here," he says in disgust handing it back.

I turn to leave, embarrassed by the tense exchange. Abruptly, I bump into a slight teenage Indian boy. He is wearing Western clothes and an especially bright grin.

"Which country are you from?" he says with a polished British accent.

The locals often ask this question as a hook before a sales pitch. The young man, however, seems genuinely interested.

"The United States."

"America? My favorite music is Michael Jackson and Madonna."

Bleah, I think to myself. Out loud, I say, "Really? You get that here? Are you visiting Rishikesh?"

"Yes my family is on pilgrimage. We come from Kashmir. What is your name, good sir?" His speech is full of out-of-date Britishisms, which sound particularly strange coming from him.

His tells me his name is Johnny, and he describes his northern home as an epic vista of mysterious mountains. Shining glaciers and crystal blue lakes surround his ancient village. "I love to climb the mountains most of all," he says, beaming.

After a few minutes, he politely excuses himself to return to his family. "Can I meet you tomorrow?" he asks hopefully.

"Okay," I respond with some hesitation.

"Two o'clock is possible at the bridge?"

"Two o' clock? Sure, why not?"

The next day, after a good post-lunch nap, I go to meet the kid. I am half an hour early, so I cross the bridge and continue onto a broad sandy beach strewn with large black boulders. One boulder is just high enough to present an interesting climb, but eons of polishing have made it desperately slippery. Pulling over the top, I find none other than Pradeep, sunning himself on the top. Somehow, he keeps turning up in the oddest places.

"You are climbing the rocks today, *chota bhai*?" he asks placidly, as if he expected me to appear.

I smile, settling down next to him. "Yes, I miss climbing a lot," I admit with a sigh, "and I must be getting weaker here."

"Your climbing is with ropes, yes? How high do you climb?"

"Sometimes 2,000 feet," I say.

"No!" his eyes widen.

"One summer my friends and I climbed Half Dome in California. It took us three days. We had to sleep on a ledge this wide." I hold out my arms.

"Sleeping on the mountain? Do you have pictures?"

"Yes, but at home. I'll send you one."

As casually as I can, I tell him that climbing helped bring me to India. "I always wanted to be a great climber, and I thought yoga might be the key. If I can learn more about the powers you describe, I could do the hardest climbs in the world."

"To conquer yourself is your hardest climb," Pradeep states philosophically.

Suddenly, I feel guilty boasting about a world Pradeep isn't privileged enough to know. He probably will never leave India.

"Can you do this?" asks Pradeep, effortlessly spinning a cartwheel in the sand.

Laughing, I tell him I'm not flexible enough.

"Ah yes, stiff muscle parts. Let us do yoga asana in the sand, *chota bhai.*"

Together, we stretch in the very sand where yogis perfected the discipline more than 6,000 years ago. To say the least, it is nicer here than in a stuffy, dank hall.

Time passes quickly as we bend and twist in the sun. Suddenly, I realize I have forgotten my meeting with Johnny. The time is almost three.

Noting my concern, Pradeep jokes, "You won't be late to my class today, *chota bhai*. You're already here."

"I was supposed to meet somebody at two o'clock," I explain.

We carry on climbing boulders, doing roly-polies, and inventing silly stunts on the rocks like Johnny Dawes would do.

Finally, we begin to make our way back to the ashram. As we approach the bridge, I see Johnny from Kashmir leaning against a pole. My heart sinks.

"Where have you been?" he asks.

"Oh, I came by around two, but I must have missed you," I lie for convenience. "I guess you weren't around."

"I am waiting here since two o'clock exactly."

"You waited almost two hours for me? Right here?"

"Yes, I gave my word!"

"Well, sorry, but now I've got to go back to my room."

"Can I come also?"

"Um, okay." I feel guilty. "If you've been waiting two hours, it's only fair."

We walk up the steep, tortuous path to the ashram. Though my mountaineer's pride inspires me to set a fast pace, the kid passes me easily.

"You are tired already?" he asks sportingly. Watching this skinny kid from Kashmir leave me in the dust, I realize I will never be a notable Himalayan climber.

Back in my room, Johnny pours over my few belongings with fascination. He seems a little too excited about them and meeting me for my comfort. The cheap lock on my door gives me no confidence, and selling my stuff is my ticket out of here. I become fidgety and make excuses to get him on his way.

"Okay," Johnny hangs his head. "Can you meet me tomorrow?"

"Um, I don't know..."

"Oh please. I meet you at two o'clock again in the same place. It will be jolly good fun."

"Okay," I agree reluctantly. "Tomorrow at two."

Tonight, I again have bad dreams. This time, they are based on occurrences where *I* was the victim. I remember the neighborhood kids' "ditching" game, where one pretends to befriend a victim, then rides off on a bike to hide from him.

One summer day in elementary school, I was playing tennis at the neighborhood club with a top class student.

"Can't you keep the ball in the court?" he whined after I had once again failed to return his serve.

"I'll try – I'm no good at tennis," I confessed. It was true. I was too uncoordinated, but most of all I didn't like it. I just couldn't get excited about a sport where you kill yourself to hit a fuzzy, little green ball.

"What *are* you good at? Certainly not school," he replied haughtily. "Try harder."

So I tried harder, but I only got worse. I smacked the ball out of bounds into the bushes.

"Stay here. I'll search for it," he said, trotting off the court. A minute later I saw him riding away on his bike. "Later, loser!" he yelled.

I had been ditched for not skillfully hitting a furry green ball. Apparently, that skill was where self-worth comes from.

Later in fifth grade, my former tennis partner and another guy were waiting for me in the playground after class to—using our colloquial American expression—"kick my ass" and "clean up that there town." I had become the hunted, just like the community misfit, Katie, and there were always two or three on the chase— never one alone. What had I done? I had been playing the class clown, and they didn't like it. But that very tension and peer disapproval compelled me to goof off more.

After a night rehashing a lifetime of suburban conflict and strife, I wait dutifully by the bridge. It is two o'clock, and that kid Johnny is nowhere to be seen. Last night's ditching dream now seems like a warning that I could fall victim to such nastiness all over again. I burn with anger and embarrassment, thinking how I, a worldly twenty-two-year-old Westerner, have been stood up by an Indian boy of sixteen. After waiting for thirty minutes, a hard-hearted satisfaction comes over me. There is no "Namaste," I realize; people are the same everywhere. My guilt over missing Johnny yesterday was pure folly. That kid, like the people I grew up with, was just playing the ditching game.

As I retrace my steps up the path to my room, I wonder whether Johnny is a thief who had planned to "turn me over," as the Brits say, or lure me out of my room for a while, but found an easier victim. It is the final straw. I want to lock my door and sit in my room for the rest of the trip. The path tires me out quickly, and that makes me mad too.

"I have something for you," calls my neighbor from his porch. He is dressed in his usual drab white robes and wool hat.

"I just want to take a nap, thank you," I say fumbling with my crappy Indian lock that never opens the first time.

"A young boy brought this for you." My neighbor comes over with a note in his hand. I take it reluctantly. The note reads:

Dear Thomas,
I am so sorry I could not meet you at two o'clock today.
I have a terrible headache from injury.
Please come to my hotel room 18 to see me.
Your friend,
Johnny Pershaw

"He seems to be a very nice boy," says my neighbor smiling. He has never smiled at me before.

Out of curiosity, I decide to visit the Kashmiri boy. Trudging wearily back across the bridge, I search for the hotel where Johnny's family is staying. I find it to be more of a religious retreat, much like a YMCA, with simple accommodations hosting Hindu pilgrim families.

I enter through a large orange colored doorway that leads into a compound of three or four stories of rooms facing a central courtyard decorated with flowers and huge statues of Siva, Vishnu and other Hindu gods. The square is surrounded by rooms painted in a festival of bright colors. It dawns on me that this place is the source of the horrendous bullhorn chanting parties that start up every morning at 5 a.m.

An Indian man comes up to me. "You are looking for Johnny?" he says. "I am his father. He is very sorry for missing you today. Today his headache comes. It is very severe from his climbing accident. Our Johnny loves to climb on the rocks and do very brave things, but last year he falls. Please, he is expecting you."

Inside a dark room, Johnny is sitting up in bed.

"Hello Thomas my friend!" he calls out cheerfully. "I am sorry for this afternoon, but my head has great pain."

His mother and sister greet me warmly—like a long lost friend of the family.

"This is my sister, Annapurna," Johnny tells me proudly.

"Like the mountain Annapurna?" It seems incredible that she should have the same name as the famous Himalayan peak.

Turning to Johnny, I notice a horrendous scar just beneath his hairline. Somehow I'd missed it before, wrapped up in my own idiotic world.

"You fell rock climbing?"

"Yes. Last summer, every day I climb. One day I climb very high and then darkness."

"I'm sorry to hear that."

"I wish to return to that place and climb that way without falling."

"I hope you'll use a rope."

"Oh, no!" he exclaims solemnly. "A rope would take away the adventure."

"You bash your head open and want to try again?" I tell him he reminds me of a famous British climber named Johnny Dawes. "Climbers named Johnny must all be crazy."

"Please, before you go you will have a picture taken with my family?" Johnny asks, hopping off the bed. His father is ready with a camera in the courtyard.

"Can I walk with you to the bridge?" Johnny asks.

"Sure. But is it okay with your headache?

"For now, yes ... Do you like Hindu religion?"

"Well I've nothing really against it, but look at that grisly statue." I point to a large, gaudily colored cement idol chopping off the heads of several victims. Blood is everywhere, and multiple skulls lie at the deity's feet. "I mean come *on*."

"Yes," replies Johnny, admiring the image. "That is Kali the ego slayer. Isn't it beautiful?"

I consider the statue in a new light. The gruesomeness is there for a reason—a symbol I didn't understand. "I didn't know that's what it meant. Then I guess it is beautiful, Johnny."

We walk further. "I wish I could slay *my* ego," I say with a sigh. "I used to be like you. I used to be full of joy. I don't know where it all went."

"You will visit me in Kashmir?"

"I'd like to, but I really have no money for traveling. I'm nearly out just staying at that yoga place, and it's pretty cheap."

"You need money?" Johnny asks with concern. "I will ask my father. How much do you need?"

"What? No, I can't."

"You are my friend, so it is my duty. Wait here please."

"No Johnny, please don't ask him." I feel ashamed. "I'll make it somehow. I'm mostly afraid of Delhi. It's such a horrible place."

"Oh, I *love* Delhi. All the hustle and bustle. One moment please, I must sit down." Sinking onto a nearby bench, Johnny closes his eyes, his head in his hands.

"You really are in pain. I'm sorry."

"Please forgive me," he moans. "In a moment, I will be fine."

I sit quietly next to my new friend, marveling at his selflessness. Though his head is killing him, he's worried about my money problems.

A few minutes later, Johnny springs up. "Ah, the pain is gone!" he rejoices. "Please forgive my problem."

Halfway across the main suspension bridge, we stop to say goodbye.

"I give you my necklace; it is silver," Johnny offers.

I refuse.

"Please take it. I have it since my birth."

"Then I definitely cannot."

"Then you take my bracelet, also from birth."

"I could never..."

"You must!" he insists.

"Johnny, no! It isn't right to accept that."

He looks hurt. The dirty children who sell fish food in the middle of the bridge to tourists stop to watch us converse.

"We have a saying in India that we pray for the peace and happiness of all mankind, for that will include ourselves." Johnny says and forces the silver bracelet into my hand. "Remember I will always be your friend."

I am speechless. His shining mind brings into relief my own psychological defilement. An hour before, I thought him a thief. My American youth has left me paranoid, faithless, fists ready to retaliate for any perceived insult. But standing here with this beaming kid, I feel a kind of healing I can't explain. Elation pours through me as I ponder the meaning of "Namaste" as if understanding it for the first time. Perhaps I never really believed people had *any* divinity in them until now.

"Thanks Johnny. I will try to slay my ego."

"There my good friend. I wish you luck with your yoga practice." He gives a noble bow and turns to leave.

I stand in the middle of the bridge holding a bracelet that is too small for my wrist. I feel awful taking it, but to refuse seemed even worse.

A few moments later, there is a tiny white splash in the river below. Now I can never lose Johnny's bracelet. It rests in the currents of Mother Gunga, who will remind me of the true meaning of *Namaste* taught to me by a sixteen-year old Kashmiri boy.

"Plop! It goes in," says a voice behind me.

I turn to see a blond European man watching me with interest. *What does he want?* He looks like any other hippy traveler bouncing around the East. I am tempted to ignore him, but then I remember the lessons Johnny taught me. There *is* a divine presence in people, and I have to try harder to find it.

"A friend gave me a bracelet," I explain. "I didn't know what to do with it, so I made an offering to mother Gunga." I laugh.

"He was a good friend, yes?"

"Yes, yes he was.

The blonde man is a German named Karl. As we talk, he seems to understand my awe and share my past. Karl is well-travelled in Asia, so he has experienced both sides of India: her hardscrabble living and disarming generosity.

"Yes, like you said, the people here are incredible," he agrees. "In my country, people will trip you walking past to start violence. My German people love to begin a fight—all for nothing."

"In the States, we love to use guns. What a waste, like you said—all for nothing."

"Ja," he agrees. "Our countries look prosperous on the outside with fine BMWs, but the life inside is diseased. We cannot talk as a people anymore."

"You are right. I can't remember when I've enjoyed myself like I did today."

We arrive at a little doorway not far from the main road. Karl knocks, and some Indian teenagers appear, graciously inviting us into their home. I recognize them from a nearby chai shop where they work. They serve us chai and revere us foreigners like gods. Their smiles are catching.

"Have you seen the Beatles Ashram?" asks Karl as we sip chai.

"No, I haven't."

"Tomorrow I can take you there. And then I would like to visit a German woman who lives in a cave. Would you like to go?"

"Why not? Every adventure leads to another one here."

Back in my room, I sit on the bed, feeling wonderful. This Indian world is not so desolate anymore. The quality of even my short friendship with the kid, Johnny, has changed me profoundly. A thousand people may say "good morning," but when one really means it, everything is different; it transforms my whole outlook. I view so many people in America, Europe, and currently Asia, as vermin, but one Johnny with his shining mind challenges my cynical generalizations. It isn't who we really are. I have to stay aware but give people another chance.

Before afternoon yoga class I play Led Zeppelin's *Tangerine.* As the song starts, its lyrics surprise me by triggering powerful emotions.

The words "slips away to gray," hit me hard, as did Ray Bradbury's "suddenly summer was over"—a reminder that time is passing quickly. This impermanence is what makes everything sacred. The music seems to jump out of my headphones. The breeze quivers in the trees overhead, and I gasp at its beauty. *What is happening to me?* Maybe the yoga practice *is* working, and remarkable people like Pradeep and Kashmir Johnny are doing the rest. I've got nowhere to go, so I guess I'll find out.

Suddenly I realize I am late for afternoon Hatha Yoga. Hurriedly, I scramble into my routine of carefully hiding my cassette player, locking my door, and making the trek across the garden. Arriving breathless at the yoga hall, I am surprised to see Pradeep sitting outside smoking a bidi. It's already several minutes past the hour.

"Hey Pradeep!" I hail him, beaming. "What a great day this is. Man, I love this place."

"Good *chota bhai*. I feel good vibrations from you."

"Everything here is changing: me, you, Uncle Joe and the everyday people. Let's do some advanced postures today. I really want to go hard at yoga now."

"Hard?" Pradeep frowns. "You can't do yoga hard."

"But…"

"Look at the students in there expecting *me* to teach them."

Through the screened door I see a mix of Europeans and Asians, the latter mostly Japanese, warming up. They check their watches and peer out at Pradeep with irritated faces.

"I guess I don't mean hard, just *well*."

"Ah yes," he teases, "so you become a great yogi but with great yogi ego." He looks at me intently. "Little brother, don't become like so many of the foreign people. They think yoga is stretching and exercises, something to show and own. This practice is not something to hold in your hand. Yoga is for change on the inside."

"Okay, but I can hardly touch my toes."

"A yoga master is a free man who is alive in the now. It is fifteen past four, and the people inside are unhappy. Their life is a train schedule. They are dead people."

His words seem to describe the Western mind to a 'T.'

"I want another bidi," says Pradeep, settling onto a bench. "You want bidi?"

"Sure," I giggle.

"Good vibrations," he says and leans forward to light it.

The smoke wafts into the air and I laugh to myself at how the world is turned upside down in India. In the States, we are expected to compete, to succeed and certainly to be punctual. Here, these concepts hardly exist. Instead, the meaning of life is not to be the best, but rather to destroy the ego.

I muse on these thoughts as Pradeep dances and hums in the sun. At last, his final ashes fall to the ground.

"Are you ready now, *chota bhai*?" he says, as though he has been waiting for me.

"Yes, I'm ready for yoga class," I reply, smiling. "And I will never do it well enough to get a big ego. It seems to come naturally."

"You are luckier than you will ever realize, little brother."

Strangely, after Pradeep's lecture I am able to go much deeper into the stretches than ever before. Without consciously trying, I can now touch my toes and am dramatically shifting towards flexibility without really trying. To say the least, the experience is vastly different than my previous experience of feeling stiff and frustrated, straining and cursing my muscles, to no avail.

In the evening, I sit in my room smoking a bidi from a pack Pradeep insisted on giving me. Because it burns my throat, I can only tolerate puffing on it lightly like a cigar, hardly inhaling. Soon I begin to feel a mild, relaxing buzz. I decide I am still against smoking overall, but, as Pradeep claims, life is no fun without a few mild vices.

Because there is nothing else to do, I practice a little meditation, helped by the buzz from the bidi. I find I can sit completely still for nearly thirty minutes in the half lotus.

After some time, I unfold my legs and play Pink Floyd's album *Wish You Were Here* in my cassette player. "Shine on You Crazy Diamond" starts with an arching, cascading guitar over sustained, haunting organ chords. Normally, this intro seems painfully slow, but in my relaxed state of mind this part becomes a piece of soaring beauty. Every note stirs deep emotions. I am entranced, fascinated, and incredibly moved. This song, so familiar, has become an epiphany. The mesmerizing sound effects and dignified but sad tone of the track continue into "Welcome to the Machine," a terrifying song that conjures up a devastating loss of soul joining the workforce in a place as such London or New York City. During the synthesizer solo, I feel like I am flying. The music's power astounds me, and yet I have heard the album many times before. I left Pink Floyd's epic *Dark Side of the Moon* cassette at Mark's flat. What would *that* album be like in this state of mind? I feel keenly and thrillingly awake, and I am starting to rediscover that unique state called happiness. It is a strange thing to realize that a little music and a few laughs with good people can bring such great pleasure.

In Ray Bradbury's *Dandelion Wine* there is a character, an old man, named Colonel Freilegh who is very ill and attended by a strict home nurse who will not allow him to excite himself by using the telephone. Against her orders, the colonel calls a contact in Mexico City where he was stationed as a young soldier. He asks his far away friend to hold the receiver out the window so he can relive the sounds of the clanking, lively city and his youth. Will I call some contact person when I am ninety and ask them to hold the phone out the window in Delhi to remind me of this trip? Of my departed youth? The concept has a grip on me; it is inevitable, holy passage of time.

Time has a sweetness to it like it did when I was a child. The rushing, the craving for my time in India to be over has diminished greatly; a craving for the end, which is, of course, the coming of death. Now my days are starting to feel full and "lived."

As I sit here, I think of the Kashmiri boy Johnny and the nightmares of the past lose their hold. The bitterness melts away from my mind like a glacier under the bright Himalayan sun. Now I feel a rising pity for the *uberjungen*, for despite their privileges they seem to subsist emotionally in lower realms. They certainly don't emanate the goodness of the cosmos of a guy like Johnny. And I laugh to myself, thinking that somewhere in Kashmir an Indian family will have a vacation photo with a silly white guy towering over them.

MOST UNUSUAL MEN

In the morning, I find Karl waiting patiently by the bridge. It's a fresh, sunny day in the village. We buy sugar cane stalks at a stand by the river. This time, I am alert for monkey ambushes, so we cross the bridge at a brisk pace.

Karl leads me to the right, past Johnny's hotel. We dodge meandering cows, stepping carefully over their piles of dung, and skirt rows of run-down little shacks. Karl grows more energized with every step. He claims he is the world's biggest Beatles fan.

After we have gone about a mile past the first bridge on the east side of the river, Karl shouts, "There it is! The Beatle's Ashram!" He slows down to point, then changes his mind and takes off in a hurry. I have to run to keep up.

"Do you know the history?" he asks, panting and nearly out of breath. "It is here they make the *White Album*."

Clearly, Karl's enthusiasm for the Beatles outweighs my own. I always preferred the Rolling Stones with their reputation as the bandmates "that no one wants their daughter to date," but no one can discount the Beatle's pioneering influence on rock music. I catch up with Karl in front of a reddish cement building with a strange beehive design. There seems to be no explanation for departure in architectural style, and the Maharishi Yogi's outlandish cylindrical windows stare at us menacingly. Like the mysterious ruins of Angkor Wat, the jungle has reclaimed it.

High cement walls surround the abandoned compound, making me feel like a pre-teen tiptoeing around a haunted house. Karl explains how the Beatles parted ways with their guru here amid accusations of dishonesty, inspiring John Lennon's bitingly sarcastic song, "Sexy Sadie." The sinister mood of the building seems an echo of the band's disenchantment with Indian spirituality.

"That is the hut where their groupie friend refused to come out," Karl says pointing through the locked gate to a small stone hut. She preferred to meditate non-stop and became a bit crazy. Do you know her name?"

I shrug.

"Prudence."

"Yes, 'Dear Prudence,' of course," I say smiling.

It is delightful to stand in the shadow of the beautiful song, "Dear Prudence." I feel closer to rock history here, but the place also has a cultish vibe. The compound is a monument to the end of the Beatles and Sixties idealism.

Karl seems oblivious to these darker implications. "Now let us visit the German woman," he says brightly.

He starts down a faint trail into the jungle, motioning me to follow. The trail goes on for some time, winding up a steep hillside. Karl stops at a strange tree that's not like the others around it.

"Her banana tree. We are close," he says. "Show no fear or aggression, for she has guard dogs to keep monkeys from her banana tree and to discourage tigers. Last week, she saw two large males from thirty meters."

A few yards past the tree, we come to a makeshift fence of sticks and twine. Suddenly, three enormous German Shepherds appear, stopping us in our tracks. The flimsy fence barely restrains their ferocious lunges.

"Halt meine Lieblinge!" calls a little white-haired European woman. She emerges calmly from a cave, dressed like Robin Hood in the colors of the forest. At the sound of her voice, the dogs tranquilly lie back down on the grass. They look remarkably well cared for, a stark contrast to the scabby dogs foraging for scraps in town.

The woman beckons to us. "Willkommen! I vill prepare tea."

Her "cave" is not a wet, miserable hole in a rock. It is a luxurious fortress with articulate carvings of Hindu gods and goddesses hewn into the rock walls. The figures are entrancing—a high art.

"Those took me a long time," she says moving a candle affectionately beneath her art work.

"Do you miss Germany?" I ask.

"Ach, Deutschland. Ve lost our vay long before Hitler."

After a delightful tea, she goes out to feed her goats. Karl and I wander along a path into a sunny meadow nearby and sit.

"You are familiar with Carlos Castaneda books, yes?" he asks. "Hold this rock and feel the power of it. Notice its texture and qualities."

I roll a pink pebble in my hand. Like the rock of *Supremacy Crack* in Eldorado, it is quartzite, much denser than limestone, maybe more than some granite. I feel its qualities, its friction, its smoothness, and I imagine what it would be like to climb on. In my mind, a new realm opens in the observation of a pebble.

Suddenly, I become aware of a German shepherd inches from my face, barking and baring his fangs. Following Pradeep's advice about the red-butted monkeys, I calmly look away and begin humming, careful not to make eye contact or show fear. The dog soon gives up barking and licks my face.

Running toward me, Karl calls out, "Be careful. It has escaped the fence!" He looks concerned, but as he sees me, his expression relaxes. "Ah, I see you have made friends with Helmut. How is your pebble?"

"The pebble is quite interesting," I reply, petting the dog. "I like rock climbing. You must understand a rock's qualities to climb it well."

"It is wonderful to increase awareness," Karl says.

As the afternoon progresses, I explore the hillside as Karl chats with the woman in German. I am careful not to stray too far in case of tigers. The sun has ignited the flora and fauna with gold. I stand under big Yosemite-like trees marveling at the German woman's chosen life. Except for the chapatti flour she buys in the village, she is completely self-sufficient. Her garden produce, banana tree, goat's milk, and the company of the dogs are enough. Most Westerners would believe she had lost her mind to live this way. What would Freud say about her analysis? As she put it, her people lost their way long before Hitler. I suspect we all have a long time ago.

After another hour, Karl and I return by a different path that passes a five-story white temple. Karl tells me it belongs to the Indian mafia. "They take donations from the pious but keep the proceeds for themselves."

"Isn't that what all churches do?"

"Mafia temple!" Karl shouts defiantly up the steps.

We shake hands on the bridge. In the two days I've known Karl, he has been great company, with a remarkable sense of justice and decency. I realize that if it hadn't been for Johnny Pershaw opening my eyes, I would have dismissed Karl as another stupid Kraut. Karl is on a journey around the world that has no end or beginning, so I doubt I will ever see him again. It doesn't matter. I am just glad to know such people are out there.

After Karl has gone, I stand alone on the bridge, lost in thought. Time passes slowly and sweetly, and I savor the memories of the day. Gradually, I become aware of an old Indian man watching me. He wears glasses and the orange robes of a monk.

"Namaste," I bow respectfully.

The man scans me up and down with deep, intelligent eyes. "Would you join me tomorrow for tea at my home?" he asks in impeccable, scholarly English. "Come to number thirteen along that side of the river." He points. "An auspicious number, don't you think?"

I have only a little more than a week remaining. So much didn't happen for the first two weeks and now, it is non-stop. I can only wonder what will come in these final days.

This morning, at the gate of number thirteen, I find the man sitting in a chair on his porch. His lap is full of papers.

He opens the gate and invites me into his sanctuary, a small, charming cottage on the sandy part of the Ganges. We sit together in his garden in silence for a moment. Then, the man closes his eyes curiously as if to gather the energy to speak.

At last he says, "I would like to talk to you about God."

The words fill me with dread. Now I feel like I've been tricked into coming. I steel myself for another dull, incomprehensible speech about India's complicated religious systems. But the man's next words surprise me.

"What are the markings of an enlightened man?" he asks philosophically. "A cow moos, and a dog barks, but how do you know an enlightened man?"

I sit silently, turning his question over in my mind.

"In Rishikesh, many wear the monk's robes," he explains. "I do not condemn others when it is the only way they receive food, but they are truly not interested in a spiritual life. Also, many foreigners come to this sacred place, but they remain tourists. Some take a class here, speak to a yogi there, and are then ready to open a money-making center in their country.

"A serious man in the spiritual quest is rare," he continues. "He is like a fish swimming upstream. Jesus said: 'Let the dead bury the dead.' These are the spiritually dead, who eat, sleep, procreate and die in the current of the stream." He turns to me intently. "You must fight against this current, though society will say you are crazy. All progress will depend on your sincerity and your capacity."

The man's words resonate with me, but I remain suspicious. "Are *you* enlightened?" I ask.

"There is no *is* and there is no *is not*."

I pause to contemplate this statement. The books I have read, especially ones about Buddhism, are filled with stories of desperate longing for enlightenment. This end goal becomes their only goal, inspiring all kinds of misery for the monks—and for me, reading their books. Yet, they don't seem to know what *it* is. With this man, the objective appears less exotic and distant; enlightenment seems attainable.

"There were some workmen here today," he says. "How I dislike their clattering about. When it is quiet, I can sit back and feel God." He sits back comfortably at that moment, as if demonstrating his point.

"You feel God yourself?"

"Yes, when all is still I feel God quite strongly," he says, a blissful look spreading across his face. "Enlightenment means you are free of bondage, free of fear. Nothing is holding you!"

His words entrance me. I admire his simple, confident, down-to-earth demeanor. A deep instinct tells me he is not another fraud. His persona seems strangely familiar. As we sit in silence, I am reminded of the chance encounter with Layton Kor in Boulder.

Now, as I sit with another unusual man, I wonder why he reminds me so keenly of Kor. I decide that this Indian recluse exudes the same strength of character, the same indefinable qualities of an archetypal hero-guide but most of all that same down-to-earth humility. However, I have to test him more.

"Is it necessary that I become a monk and wear the white robes?" I ask the hermit, dreading his response.

"No," he tells me firmly. "All is dependent on the quality of the mind. External symbolism means nothing. The monk has a psychological makeup that vows and robes alone cannot change. In some cases they make things worse; they become an ego barrier."

I feel a great sense of relief.

"Do you have these feelings of God, young man?"

I hesitate. "Sometimes, when I'm mountain climbing."

The hermit smiles. "Someday you will quit climbing," he says with an odd certainty. "I read the story of a young Englishman who became fascinated with climbing Mount Everest. He read everything possible, and one day he tried to climb the great mountain alone."

"What happened?"

"He died, but his spirit was unconquerable! What is this life compared with the spirit?"

"It was dangerous to go alone."

"Alone!" the hermit exclaims. "I live alone with nobody to look after me. Is that safe for an old man? No, it is not, but I love it. My spirits are high always. Would you like tea?"

I nod and he pours creamy brown chai into the standard issue Indian aluminum cup. As I sip my tea, the hermit recites a poem:

Oh to be a wild flower,
Plain and standing in the corner,
Untrampled by the masses,
While they rush to pick the roses,
To place in the temple of their vanities.

"I wrote this poem for the New Year," he explains. "It is very special to me." He looks at me expectantly, and I can tell he sees my incomprehension but does not judge me for it.

"Let me explain," he continues. "The man who wishes to be the wild flower, plain and unknown, is wise. To wish to be the radiant rose of riches and fame is for the fool who will be trampled by the excited masses and picked for his beauty." He looks around cautiously like he has a great secret. "Live a simple life, and stay close to nature. Man must be close to nature, or he will lose his feeling of God and his heart."

I nod appreciatively. "Are you Hindu then?" I ask.

"I have renounced this world. Do you know what that means?"

I tell him that, in the literature I have read, it means to renounce all material possessions.

"Possessions are only the superficial start, and some possessions are necessary," the hermit warns. "I must have clothing and food and shelter. I own this house, but it is a simple one. Your possessions must fulfill their basic purpose and not arouse your pride or the jealousies of others. Keep life simple or it becomes artificial. True freedom is beyond possessions. True freedom is to have renounced worldly life! To have renounced everything!"

"*Everything?*" I repeat uncertainly.

"I have no need for all the ideas that come from society, religion, or philosophy. Enlightenment means you are free of bondage, free of yearning, free of fear!" He closes his eyes and his face retreats into ecstasy once more.

His silence feels more comfortable now than it did at first. Presently, the hermit breaks the silence, pointing out a sign on his cottage, written in Hindi. "It says: *Hermit's Cottage of Peace,*" he explains. "I accept few visitors and do not like to be disturbed. Would you like to chat with a silly old man again?"

"Yes, of course," I reply with warm enthusiasm. "When would you like me to return? I don't want to be a bother."

"Come in two days. For now, sit by the river and clear your mind completely to silence. The Indian people will understand and not disturb you. You never know when something remarkable might happen. Goodbye."

I return the greeting and, thanking him for his time, gently close his gate behind me.

As I stroll toward the sandy beach, I reflect on my chance meeting, barely able to believe my luck. I am certain I have met a teacher with a nonconformist temperament, who knows something priceless. I find it reassuring that he wants so little in return; nothing beyond some fruit and perhaps other small gifts for his well-being. The Beatles gave the Guru Maharishi piles of money, even a helicopter, but something went wrong. This hermit just wishes to be left alone. Above all, there is no religion to join, no dues to pay, no complicated explanation of the universe, and no suspiciously easy path to enlightenment. I am still required to achieve something myself—the hermit merely is a living example of someone who has attained a pure state of ecstasy and freedom. There are no free rides.

Around the globe, there must be millions of senior citizens dying for companionship. Yet this hermit is never lonely. On the contrary, he defends his solitude; it brings him joy. Like Layton Kor, he is the real thing.

Back in my room I am reading Jack Kerouac's *On the Road* for the third time, but something new is happening as it did with Pink *Floyd's Shine on You Crazy Diamond*. Now every sentence reveals unspeakable beauty. I marvel at Kerouac's description of how he and Dean "dug life" as they travelled pell-mell through 1950s America. He held "hobos" in holy regard and placed life experience before financial security. His unconditional brotherhood and life-affirming travels, the humor and the counterculture lifestyle, are the exact opposite of contemporary American values. Though much of the story takes place in Colorado, it is an American world that is foreign to me: vast and wild, yet kind and ready to blossom.

Dean Moriarty, the main character and focus of the book, is a larger-than-life 1950s Wild West outlaw with a car and a taciturn craziness that reminds me of Johnny Dawes. Dean was big, like America, thundering his enormous cars, whether stolen or bought on credit, through America's open road taking the role of the outlaw, while Johnny gets his high-speed kicks on the *Routes de Provence* in his Rally car. I had thought English people were quiet and mousy, but even his name—Dawes—sounds like an old-time gunslinger. His dangerous climbing parallels Dean's criminal daring—Dean stole five hundred cars during one year, but most similar are their prophetic reflections mixed with triumphant joy, sadness, and isolation.

The book's influence started the Beatnik trend, which in turn inspired the 1960s counterculture, but not everyone gets the same thing out of it. According to Ray Manzerek of The Doors, *On the Road* helped inspire them to start the band, but they were most attracted to its description of a Mexican whorehouse. Red had summed up the book as "guys partying their way across the country." But to me, the book's sex-and-drug references aren't important compared with Kerouac and Dean's saga of searching for IT. What is IT? In Dean's words: "Now you are asking me impon-derables—ahem!" Unlike God or enlightenment, 'IT' is a perfect word, unencumbered by the baggage of a religion. IT is free to describe the truth it means.

Jack Kerouac concludes his first chapter with the words: "Somewhere along the line I knew there'd be girls, visions, everything; somewhere along the line the pearl would be handed to me." The Pearl. What a beautiful way to symbolize that time in your life when all promises and ecstasies converge. As I put down the book, the red setting sun on its cover beckons me. Every day here in India, my mind is becoming more aware and more open, eager for the next adventure around the bend. More and more, I want to "dig" everything like Jack and Dean. I can see myself and my own Moriarity—Johnny Dawes—"on the road" in Provence. That sun on the book's cover promises to shine on me through a beautiful spring in Europe, fulfilling a part of the dream I've held since my first chimney rappel. Now I feel like the pearl will be handed to me. The pearl will be handed to me.

IT

Pradeep bangs on the door, startling me out of another great afternoon nap. "Come *chota bhai*! We go for coffee on the river."
I left the door open to let in the warm air so Pradeep enters
and pulls me, still in my sleeping bag, onto the porch. He giggles,
dumping me upside down with my legs tangled in the railings. Of
course, I am coming. Like Jack Kerouac and his character friend
Dean we are going to "dig" Rishikesh.

"What is most difficult about change to a yoga life, *chota bhai*?"
Pradeep asks as we start down the path.

"I don't know. I think being a goody-goody. Most 'good' people
I've known are more difficult to stomach than the bad."

"Yes, many do 'good' with ego," Pradeep agrees. "So, do good
without ego."

"That seems different somehow." I am moved by his simple but
powerful words. I think back to high school Sociology class when
Mr. Foxwood made us read *When Bad Things Happen to Good People*.
The very idea of the book, clearly stated in the title, is the vain
idea that if you are one of the "good people" you should be above

anything bad happening to you and the author is there to console you, if the inexplicable happens. The memory of that self-righteous, puritanical label makes me realize how closely intertwined the concepts of goodness and egotism are in the West. "Good," a label too often used with ironic undertones. A "good" American supports our multi-billion dollar a year arms industry.

"Yes, yes ego," Pradeep continues as we walk along the sand. "Krishna was very naughty as a child. One day he take his mother's sugar bowl and break it. He says an elephant take it."

"Wait, I thought Krishna was your *god*, not a lying thief."

"Why do you think he did this? Because it was her favorite!" Pradeep laughs. "Krishna is not 'bad' like society say bad. Krishna is outside of good or bad. He clears the way to enlightenment like Ganesha who has the strength of an elephant."

"Why did he break her bowl then?"

"His mother was conceited about her fine bowl. Krishna breaks her bowl and attachment to earthly things. Krishna is only naughty to serious people. He did many things that were very funny."

Pradeep tells more stories about the wild blue jester that I haven't heard. Oddly, in the exotic Krishna, I now see a delightful parallel to the spirit of all humor. I imagine the mischievous Hindu god, along with the Three Stooges, Monty Python and other bearers of bananas, pies, and buckets of paint, on a divine mission to make people let go and not take everything so seriously.

Our conversation drifts to other subjects, and I tell Pradeep about the elderly hermit I met.

"You are not afraid he is liar?"

"No, I don't think so. He lives alone as a hermit and dislikes having his peace disturbed. He tires quickly of visitors, not the type to trap Westerners. It doesn't matter. Everyone has been my guru in a way, even some awful people back home I can think of. Some of them were the best teachers of all."

"Yes, I told you. You are a lucky one, for you are here now to experience this and meet this man, and they are not. When do you visit him again?"

"Not until tomorrow. He is in no hurry to be disturbed."

The next afternoon I was back at the gate of number thirteen.

The old man welcomes me into his garden. "Have you thought about my poem? A scientist's mind cannot grasp these concepts, but a poet's can."

As we sit, I ask him about his faith. "How can you feel God without being Hindu or practicing some other religion? The Christians say it's impossible without going through Jesus Christ."

"Look to yourself," he replies softly. "No one can take the spiritual path for you. If Jesus came to visit, I would welcome him and be a most respectful host. But after some time, I would ask him to please go. You see, he cannot do for me what I must do myself. I have renounced religions, including my native Hinduism, to experience what they promise directly."

"You don't need religion?"

"As I said before, to find your way, *look to yourself.* A Christian man came to visit me one day. He had been a monk in a European order. For twenty years, his life was designed to rise in rank to someday preside in the large chair in the middle of the large, ornate monastery, while a beggar outside remains hungry. It is all power and politics. What do they know in their great monastery building that a humble, good man does not?"

"Is this true in all religions?"

"Of course. There was another man who lived in an Indian-style Ashram near Los Angeles. One day he realized it was only for money. The founders are bloodsuckers, he told me. All churches, organizations and cults want to indoctrinate you, control you. They have many mouths to feed. The man who goes alone, no one wants."

The hermit exhales and looks sideways to signal our meeting is over.

"Before I go, is there anything else to know?" I ask, standing up.

"There is more to experience but not more to be explained. You came looking for the secrets of the Orient, and now you have heard them. They say the Pope is the messenger from God. All life, all men are messengers from God, even a beggar." He repeats this last phrase with a fierce, menacing grimace: *"Even a beggar."*

As I wander back to the Ashram, the hermit's final words seem to echo off the walls of gaudy temples and in the eyes of the poor. My mind reels with the strength and conviction of this simple man. I feel my own ideas reinforced and given new life, new meaning. Like me, he sees established religion as a deception, but his rejection of convention contains the absolute confidence that mine has not yet blossomed into, and it holds the promise of something greater, something good, pure and personal. George Orwell conceived of *Animal Farm* when he observed "a little boy, perhaps ten years old, driving a huge cart-horse along a narrow path, whipping it whenever it tried to turn." Orwell explained, "It struck me that if only such animals became aware of their strength we should have no power over them, and that men exploit animals in much the same way as the rich exploit the proletariat." Mark Twain parallels these thoughts when he claimed the royal family was an insult to humanity. The arrogance of the church or a religion to tell the public their institutions are indispensable to find god is outrageous. Inspired by his conviction and his rage, I can clearly see how supposedly needing the "experts" within the Church to guide us—any Church—is the ultimate insult to humanity. All men and animals are messengers from God. Even a beggar.

After morning meditation, Pradeep says: "Come on American brother, there is life outside. Uncle Joe parts from us."

"Okay, I'm coming," I mutter.

My eyes are still half shut as I shuffle down the cement path with Pradeep and Joe. As we walk, Uncle Joe shows me a picture of a young Tibetan monk whom he is sponsoring.

"*Om Mane Padme Hum.* Say fast, say slow," he beams, his great smile making him appear more Indian than a proper Italian gentleman.

At the road, he turns to look back at the ashram, nodding his head appreciatively as though thanking the simple cement buildings for a meaningful experience.

"Ciao, Uncle Joe!" I say warmly, shaking his hand.

He looks at us meaningfully one more time and bows, still smiling. Then his silver head ducks into a rickshaw, and he disappears for good. I can't help but wonder how I will feel when I leave.

"The great Uncle Joe is gone," comments Pradeep. "Come, American brother, for coffee."

We stroll across the bridge and into a dingy cafe. A waiter proudly brings our drinks, two filthy cups of dark, lukewarm liquid, charging me four times the Indian amount as usual. A wave of annoyance washes over me.

"Pradeep..." I begin, spilling coffee over the cup's rim in my established sanitation ritual, "I heard that guru friend of yours is in trouble with the police for exploiting young girls at his place."

"Really?" Pradeep fakes the sounds of surprise.

"Why are so many gurus corrupt?"

Pradeep sighs. "Everything is corrupt: Indian society, American society, and Europe people. All politics, all religion is corrupt, so I dance and chant Krishna."

"But that doesn't change society," I counter.

"Change society? Fuck this fucking society!" Pradeep suddenly yells at the top of his lungs, pushing his coffee away like he never wanted it. Jumping from his chair, he runs out into the street, shouting, "Fuck this fucking society! Fuck this fucking society!"

He begins to dance, spinning wildly like a dervish. As he whirls, he begins to chant his Krishna mantra, his voice exploding with energy and madness:

Hare Krishna, Hare Krishna,
Krishna, Krishna, Hare, Hare.
Hare Rama, Hare Rama
Rama Rama, Hare Hare

Around and around he goes, a funnel cloud tearing up everything in his path. He spins out of the café, still shouting and chanting, and dances like someone out of a Bollywood movie across the footbridge to the other side of the river. I follow, laughing sheepishly.

"Come on *chota bhai*, it is *your* turn to dance," Pradeep beckons, still spinning.

My laughter stops. "What? Why? I'm not a Hare Krishna."

"Am I a Krishna, a Jew, a Moslem, a Christian, or am I a man?" Pradeep challenges.

"Well ... you do have that funny haircut," I point out, refusing to take him seriously.

"I am a man first!" Pradeep rages. "Like you are a man before you are American. We are both human and divine before the ego mind divides us."

Defiantly, he twirls and dances faster than ever before. On and on he goes, oblivious to onlookers. He maintains his impossible pace for several minutes, until at last he staggers and falls to one knee, gasping for breath. Sweat soaks his face and madness gleams in his eyes.

I go to his side with an arm out. "Pradeep! Are you all right?"

"You dance!" he shoots back.

"How about later? I'll do it later. Let's go."

He eyes me with disappointment. "You are not a serious people. What do you fear?"

"I don't want to right now," I tell him firmly, sitting down on a bench.

The sun touches the Ganges in a silver spark while Pradeep dances on. Turning away, I am struck by the staunch, serious faces of even the humble Indians around us. A man pushing a cart stocked high with rice bags wears an expression as cold as a Wall Street banker's. *Why am I so reluctant to join Pradeep?* Suddenly, I am reminded of my camp experience.

By my last summer, Cheley seemed increasingly businesslike and bureaucratic. In keeping with the Go America! trend sweeping the nation, the camp also went a more conservative direction.

The camp director gave a speech in the open-air chapel about how wilderness inspires greatness, using the example of a former Cheley camper whose fast food franchise went global. We were supposed to laud the entrepreneur as though his success equaled a spiritual redemption. Apparently, greatness in the 1980s meant creating minimum wage jobs and drive-thru meal deals, and sending a few million chickens a day to the deep fat fryer.

That, plus the camp leadership's distain for my "Jumping Jack Flash" cover at the campfire music program talent show, meant the end of my camp experience. The directors had expected a wholesome song like "The Gambler," by Dan Fogelberg, but I morphed into a wild Mick Jagger while my camp mate played guitar. The director was furious and wanted to see me immediately. I didn't care about making a fool of myself when I was sixteen, so why do I now?

I come back from my memories to see that Pradeep has stopped spinning and is watching me closely. "When do you break with the world and society?" he says. "Death comes so quickly. What do you fear from joy, *chota bhai?* Tear down the wall!"

I am startled by his words, which so perfectly parallel my own thoughts. Reluctantly shaking off the last traces of hesitation, I get up and dance with Pradeep. In an instant, the heavy self-conscious fear of embarrassment and shame, that ever-present fear and shame instilled throughout western life, is replaced by lightness. The weight of the oppressive human world dissipates, and I feel as though I'm walking on a cloud. Together, Pradeep and I laugh, dance, and make fools of ourselves as Indians stop and point. Many disapprove, but Mother Gunga smiles.

A few days later, I decide to pay the hermit another visit. He stops me at the gate, warning that he is not feeling well. We greet each other across his fence, and I tell him I am taking more responsibility for my meditation.

He looks pleased. "Yes, look within and trust yourself. The best way is to be alone. Avoid contact with society and its many troubles. Depend on yourself, as most monasteries and ashrams are 'bloodsuckers,' as the American man before you said."

At the end of our brief exchange, the hermit excuses himself, asking me to return in two days.

After the allotted time, I am glad to find the hermit looking better, sunning himself on his small porch. He asks me to enter and sit. Although Indian tradition dictates that a disciple should touch his guru's feet, this hermit does not seem to expect it, and I have no desire. He is humble, down to earth, and I imagine that the gesture would embarrass him, much like when I told Layton Kor he was my hero. Instead, I present some ointment for his health, which cost about 30 cents, and a small package of dates. These gifts are my only form of payment for his advice. Indeed, what greater honor can you pay a genuine teacher than to listen?

"If every person signed a book," he begins, "no two signatures would be the same. So it is with spiritual matters. There are many ways to proceed depending on your temperament. However, the man who goes alone, who follows a direct route, is the most likely to succeed."

I nod, thinking of free solo climbing and Derek Hersey moving directly and confidently up the *Naked Edge,* unencumbered by ropes, equipment, or fear.

"You will swim upstream without the sympathy of others," he warns, "for no one likes the man who can go alone. To not join their team is a great insult. To shun a church or temple, you are as good as robbing them." He chuckles.

"How should I go about meditation?" I inquire, "There are so many techniques."

"The best technique is the most natural: Go to silence." He exhales, the familiar look of deep, blissful peace returning to his face. "Things may arise, but do not be afraid. Some people think they hear the voice of God speaking, but that is irrelevant. Continue in silence until nothing is holding you, and you will become free of all bondage."

I press him further. "What about within yoga practices? I saw a sign for Kundalini yoga lessons. Would that be a good mediation technique to learn?"

"There are many mouths to feed," he replies. "The temples are filled with gods and people paying their tributes. But something is lost when man serves religion instead of religion serving man."

He pauses. Then, as if divining my earlier thoughts, he continues, "How do you climb a mountain? Do you wander for miles to each side? No, the most direct and simple path is the best, is it not? Go direct to the top. Go direct to God. Go back to your original silence, but don't expect to find many friends."

"What do I look for? What am I trying to accomplish?"

"Accomplish?" he echoes. "Alexander the Great was buried upon his shield with his hands outstretched, as he had instructed. The greatest conqueror of the world was born holding nothing, and he died holding nothing. There is nothing that even the mightiest of us can grasp and take with us. Be like Alexander the Great and let go of accomplishments!"

THE MOUNTAIN LAKE REFLECTS

Leaving the hermit's cottage, I am drawn to the banks of the Ganges. I sit in the sand and watch the mighty river lazing by in front of my crossed legs before the currents break into a rush downstream. I try to forget my anxieties by absorbing the sounds of the water and the birds squawking above. Just as my mind begins to still, an Indian woman sits down next to me. I can't help but resent the intrusion. I find myself thinking that the hermit was wrong about Indian people respecting the peace of foreigners. Our presence seems to advertise commercial opportunity.

"Helwo," the woman says. Her smile reveals the brown, stubby remains of her teeth.

"Hello," I reply reluctantly. Her harsh, beat appearance makes me unable to look at her for long.

"You wish to see picture of my friend?"

"I would just like to be alone."

She ignores the comment. "This is my friend," she tells me, lovingly caressing a snapshot of a homely, sickly, pale blonde-haired girl, and humming contentedly.

Impatiently, I wonder how this photograph will figure into her demand for money. Though I have only a couple of rupees, I impulsively reach for a coin to speed her on her way.

At that moment, her humming stops. She turns to me, still smiling, and says matter-of-factly, "I die soon. I have malaria sickness." She laughs and continues rubbing the picture of her friend.

This is not what I expected. I look more closely at the woman's pockmarked face, and I believe her story. She radiates the nobility of someone who won't be on this earth much longer.

I am stunned by her nonchalance. "Do you need some money?" I volunteer. "You can have two rupees. It's all I have with me. I'm sorry."

"Oh no, thank you! I need only the sunshine." She hums some more and laughs again, a hoarse laugh that is unmistakably fearless.

Each year, Hollywood presents a thousand manly heroes covered in the latest weapons blasting round after round of ammunition across the silver screen, and Americans themselves frequently horde arsenals of guns. This woman's smile reminds me that such weapons aren't developed from courage, but fear. A sword can't slay fear. True mettle is in a subtle shrug of the shoulders, a resigning breath. Death is everywhere in India; thousands die every day from minor disasters or third-world illnesses, whole Indian cities built so slipshod they are more vulnerable than a trailer park in Oklahoma. This woman is tiny, haggard and sickly, but she laughs. My body is young, fit and healthy, but I am afraid; my spirit is a beggar impoverished by my own anxiety. I gaze at her in wonder.

"You laugh at death, don't you? How do you do it?"

The little woman shrugs and laughs again. In my mind, the sound resonates with memories of Derek Hersey's fearless laugh echoing through Eldorado Canyon as he climbed just about everything without a rope.

Unexpectedly, the hermit's story about Alexander the Great comes to mind. At the time, it seems no more than a good anecdote, mere words. Now I see its significance in this woman, who laughs at her impending death with her arms outstretched. She is not grasping at any worldly thing. She is nobody's fool. Her impending demise means she is free.

In a flash, everything has changed, and I sit awestruck. All my fear is gone! I have experienced Lao Tzu's paradox, the drunken man who "let go" under the influence of alcohol. *I am not the doer,* I think to myself. To climb or do anything well, I must simply let go with the help of meditation. If there is no "I," then there is no ego to do the grasping that makes one miserable. "There is no mirror to collect the dust," as a Zen Buddhist master wrote. Whether I die here in India and am thrown into the Ganges, or seventy years from now dumped into the ground of a Colorado cemetery, I can take nothing with me. I realize that for myself as for all humans, young and old, death is not a question of *if* but *when.*

My mind can grow silent now. It is no longer tortured by endless chatter, refrains of pop songs, fears or desires. These distractions only arise when I am grasping for something, especially enlightenment, reinforcing the concept of myself as separate from the world and enlightenment itself. How embarrassing to think I came to India to learn the secret powers of yoga in order to triumph over climbing. Yoga is letting go of *both* the Yin and the Yang. The hermit was trying to tell me that to be one's own master means to one's arms out and grasp nothing. Now, this woman has illustrated his point with a laugh.

After some beautifully silent moments, she gets up to leave.

"Goodbye and thank you," I say meaningfully, putting my hands in the prayer mudra as she departs. She waves and walks off in the sand towards the sun.

As I watch her disappear, I believe that I can see beyond her tattered clothes, her diseased skin. Death had smiled at me, an angel visiting in the body of a haggard old woman. When they torch her body and dump the remains in the river, she will become part of the lazy Ganges, laughing all the way to the ocean.

The evening meditation brings strange new sensations. For the first time, I find I can sit effortlessly and still in an upright half-lotus posture for the entire period. Even more remarkably, my mind has become completely quiet. I can feel my breath patterns and hear my heartbeat. The sound of my breath seems loud, but only to me. I listen placidly to the subtle whistling from my nose as air enters and exits—"Krishna's flute," Pradeep calls it. It is a sound I never noticed with such awareness before.

I realize that this sensation is what my Denver yoga teacher once described. The *vrittis,* or thoughts, are like ripples on a mountain lake. Now they have ceased, and the reflection shines. In the absence of disturbing thoughts, my emotions and energy flow unhindered. I am stunned, ecstatic, and utterly calm; I have found what I have been looking for. They say that to gain knowledge or strength, one must add something everyday, but to find the Tao, one must lose something. I have let go and have forgiven all the rest. The sense of peace and bliss has swallowed me whole.

The rain tonight is unrelenting, so I hurry back to my room after meditation class. Everyone must be running for shelter in town. The electricity flickers eerily several times, then shuts off for good. Fighting with a handful of shoddy, Indian-made matches, I finally manage to light one of the cheap Indian candles I bought for such outages. It sputters and spits fitfully.

As I watch the flame struggle, I light up one of the *bidis* Pradeep left behind. I slide softly to the floor, my back resting against the bed frame. Like a campfire, the lone candle flame naturally attracts my eyes.

Becoming absorbed in the fizzle and flicker of the flame, a sensation of sheer ecstasy comes over me. I am riveted by a strange, beautiful familiarity, as if I'm waking up from a long sleep.

Powerful, warm emotions pour through my chest in a flow of bliss. With a force of its own, "The Joker" by Steve Miller begins to play in my head. The bluesy bass lines tap my heartstrings: *Some people call me the space cowboy.*

In my mind's eye, I see an image of myself skiing in Steamboat Springs, ten years-old, after having ditched my ski school class. The instructor had ordered us to be "reindeer" by putting our poles on our heads like antlers. When they took the right-hand trail, I had discreetly chosen the left, which was a tranquil road. The sun poured through the bare winter aspen trees as I snow-plowed along, and that song came into my head, filling me with the greatest joy. Hearing it now, the music is not a memory but something *precious* returning to me, something lost through the disenchantment of early adulthood.

As I continue to watch the flame, more dreamlike visions arise, possessing a mysterious connection to my newfound emotions. These images aren't fact, just the feeling of the Seventies of my youth. Oddly, they all revolve around happy days skiing when I was very young. One occurs in a bar in Vail, the bartender is a brawny but gentle fellow with long blonde hair and a handlebar moustache. He smokes a cigarette in long, ecstatic draws, just as I am smoking this *bidi*. There is a blonde woman in a cowboy hat who looks like Stevie Nicks. I feel a unique closeness to everyone in the bar and further melt into a warm happiness.

These Vail visions are more than just daydreams; the richness of emotion springing from them astounds me. I am returning to myself after a long journey away. I discover, dumbstruck, that underneath my silly anxieties, quarrelsome thoughts and absurd desires breathes a paradise. The journey is different than I imagined though—like sinking into a wonderful, warm pool away from the turbulent surface. I can breathe just fine at the bottom and feel more bliss the deeper I go. Surrender, surrender, surrender-so delicious. Most importantly, this ecstasy is *familiar*, and that is how

I know I am truly returning to myself! The true journey goes in a loop so now I can understand how religion mistakenly, or deceptively, sends one outward on a linear path. I feel the unbelievable personalized bliss of return while joining a religion I would be obliged to serve the outward god. There are many mouths to feed. "Yoga loves you more than it loves itself!" said the Chapatti Baba. Beginning to experience and understand that concept alone is worth the cost of the flight, the craziness of traveling, the risk—everything.

Just as the hermit described, there is no isolation, no fear, nothing is holding me. The experience in Sanskrit is a *moksha*, but, whatever the term, it is a liberation from mental slavery. IT is there. The dark veil of the nightmarish night has been pierced, lifted to see what is beyond! Love is all pervasive, not a wussy Hallmark greeting card love, but a timeless bliss has come. Everything is okay and I realize it always has been.

My body goes completely limp. I am spreading onto the floor like a liquid. There is no hurry and yet never enough time. The universe has been flowing with a perfect ecstatic love all this time, but tonight I can finally feel it. I am no longer separated from the cosmic joy.

From parts of my childhood the warmth, love and awe of everything has returned. Apparently, *I* had changed, becoming educated, sophisticated, arrogant, sarcastic, self-conscious, and cynical. Every passing year added "bricks in the wall."

In the books I read about enlightenment from the both the library and on loan from Uncle Joe, the authors reported experiences involving bright lights and the face of a god dancing with his flute. I do not see Krishna or Mother Mary floating in the air. I suppose such visions belong to the followers of those traditions. My gods are rock climbing and rock and roll, so *I* experience *The Steve Miller Band*. It makes sense, really, returning to my own nostalgia: the 1970's of my youth, when my heart was most alive.

301

Remarkably, I had been so close to quitting, and I certainly would have left this place weeks ago if I had the money. Now, magically, Mother India has let me in the back door. I know that, despite this breakthrough, I have far to go, but a glass of champagne is to know the vineyard. In perfect contentment and utter disbelief, I lie collapsed on my yoga mat near the candle, now burning to its base. Soon, the candle goes out, spreading thick darkness throughout the room.

In the morning, I feel alive and awake and eager for meditation class. Five a.m. *is* a very good time for meditation. The sensations of last night are still a little bit present, and now I can remain still and quiet with a subtle bliss flowing through me. The hour ends too quickly, and I don't want to go back to sleep. There will be time for that when I am dead. Whether or not I can transcend time, there is not enough, there is never enough time! I look for Pradeep, not wanting to miss any of his joking around. I also want to better understand my experiences last night.

"Pradeep, the most incredible thing happened last night!"

"Yes, little brother?"

"Well, I was pretty bored last night and sat in my room smoking a bidi."

"Ah, bidi very good."

"I smoked the bidi and stared at a candle flame."

"Yes, that is called *tratka* meditation. You must put the candle at your eye level, three feet away."

"But the candle was on the floor. Hey, I didn't even do it correctly."

"Yes, yes stare at the flame without blink and your mind will be driven deep into meditation. Become free from like or not like and all become candle flame. After deep concentration, the *Siddhis* come!"

I tell him about the emotions that surged through me and the song that filled my head, as though I were part of it. Impatient to communicate the full depth of my experience, I repeat the lyrics breathlessly, like an over-stimulated child.

"'*I am joker, I am smoker I am...?*'" Pradeep asks bewildered.

"Midnight toker."

"*I am joker, I am smoker I am midnight toker?*" He looks at me for confirmation.

"Yes, that's it! Things happened last night I can't believe, Pradeep! No more anxieties, like I was whole again. I didn't try to do anything. It just happened."

"How is it?" he asks. "*I am joker, I am smoker, I am toker?*"

"No, *midnight* toker," I correct. "My favorite part may be: '*Cause I'm a picker, I'm a grinner, I'm a lover and I'm a sinner playing my music in the sun...*'"

Pradeep grins. "Did I not say you may be the luckiest of all? Through these dreams and songs, you are finding liberation."

I can think of no better words to describe it. One thing is for sure: almost everything I have been taught in the West about happiness is wrong. There we look ever-outward for fulfillment. But what is down is up. At home, humility is a disgrace; in the spiritual world it is a boon. Here the phrase, "to enter the Kingdom of Heaven one must be like a child" finally becomes clear. If I had what I *thought* I wanted, I would never have achieved this tremendous realization.

In the Christianity of my youth, however, such experiences are not supposed to happen. Big stone churches full of even well-educated, accomplished citizens are told that heaven is in another realm reachable only by death. Dutifully, they become passive spectators regurgitating dry Bible stories. What about us sitting in the pews? What answer can you give us, Preacher? Someone must stand and shout "My soul comes first!" Then the whole dusty structure, misleading to so many, will come tumbling down. And it's not about the selfish ego but the true self and the self-empowerment of coming back home to yourself. It's that blissfulness liberating you that must reign supreme.

Buddhism seems little better. Their leaders would tell me I need many lifetimes before I could be fortunate enough to take refuge in the Buddha. Indeed, no single world faith seems able or willing to help me find my way. At this moment, it seems to me that a tragedy is played out around the globe, as murder in the name of dogma and tradition continues without end.

I play "The Joker" through my cassette player for Pradeep. I'm not sure what he sees—probably not skiing in Steamboat—but his closed eyes radiate with ecstasy. I don't know if he fully understands or appreciates what I was trying to explain, but it doesn't matter. People in India have strange spiritual experiences all the time. After all, this is the land where Krishna played his flute, and, of course, that's why I am here.

In Pradeep's afternoon yoga class, I apply myself to the postures wholeheartedly, and the effect is amazing. Though I suddenly can touch far beyond my toes, the accomplishment doesn't seem to matter. There is no stopping at a reached goal. The Hatha yoga asanas calm my mind further and drive me deep into meditation. Pradeep guides us through the plough position, a routine that starts with a shoulder-stand, feet over the head, followed by the feet touching behind the head straight-legged, then bridge pose and fish pose. Every breath is rhythmic, harmonious, the postures balanced and removing blockages. It is delicious, pure ecstasy.

In evening meditation, I once again sit effortlessly with crossed legs and straight back. Most importantly, my mind is quiet. Thoughts still come, but I don't hang on to any of them; I don't take them too seriously. They are like the gang of Rhesus monkeys that surrounded me and Pradeep a month ago. Don't look them in the eye, pretend to be busy, and they will grow tired and leave. I feel like I am penetrating layers of my psyche that even drugs could never mimic; they might relax a person or take them on some trip, but it isn't the same, and it certainly isn't as pure. Meditation is an earned experience and, as such, it is more permanent and real.

As I sit in meditation, however, nothing demands my presence in this world, so I let it fall away. The mud of the lotus pond is settling and the water above shines with clear, sheer beauty.

THE RED FORT OF DELHI

My roughly four-week stay is over, and today is my last morning in Rishikesh. I pack my bags in disbelief. The trip has been beyond transformative. My shoulders hang low, my jaw muscles don't clench, my flexibility has opened my muscles like never before, and present is an overall deep feeling of health and well-being. Mentally, of course, it has been a complete change.

One of the American "lifers" hears I don't have any money to get back into England. "Just wrap a twenty-dollar bill around a bunch of ones and, whatever you do, don't say you are a damn Hare Krishna." he laughs hoarsely.

"I don't have a twenty or any one dollar bills either."

"Oh. Then you had better not say anything at all."

I go to see the hermit one last time. At his gate, I describe my extraordinary night after our last visit. He looks pleased, but his knowing smile makes it is obvious that my experience doesn't compare to the bliss he exists in every day.

"Rishikesh is changing," he offers. "Not just materially but also in spirit. People come now looking for recreation. Jesus said 'the

Kingdom of Heaven is within' and this is so. Contentment cannot be bought."

In his last sentence, the hermit destroys the entire myth that American civilization is based upon—the concept ingrained so deeply in our national psyche that entire lives are devoted to it.

He looks up into his tree thoughtfully. "What can the leaves from this tree tell me? Being alone and still, I can feel the gifts of nature." He recites a poem about moonlight streaming through his window.

Too soon it is time for me to go. I tell him I don't want to leave, but that I'll be lucky to get home with hardly any money. I confess my dread of Delhi.

"When the microcosm is in order so will be the macrocosm," the hermit says. "In other words, when all is right on the inside, all will be right on the outside. Goodbye, young friend."

"Goodbye," I say to one of the most remarkable men I have ever met.

An hour later, Pradeep stands at my door.

"I can't believe it's time to go," I say.

"You wanted to leave very much before."

"When I first got here, I was terrified I'd end up with my head shaved like yours," I admit.

Pradeep studies me. "Since you go, can I have money for socks?"

I laugh. "I don't have a rupee to spare, Pradeep, I swear. I still don't know how I'm going to get through Delhi."

"Please, they are very fine quality."

Pradeep falls to his knees in supplication, the most dramatic begging gesture next to cutting off a limb. I find myself promising to send him something when I get settled at the French school in Aix.

"Oh, yes, yes, yes. Please send money, yes!"

Pradeep accompanies me as I struggle down to the road with my overstuffed backpack. The sun reflects off the Ganges. Realizing that I may never see it again, I suddenly feel choked up.

"Come, little brother, this is not life," says Pradeep, noticing my emotion.

"I did nothing but complain most of the time, and now I don't want to leave."

"You are much improved, *chota bhai*."

I dutifully recite the dirty phrase Pradeep once taught me: "*Maya tamara chuta marunga*."

"Perfect," he nods approvingly. "I am joker, I am smoker, I am midnight toker."

We settle into silence. After weeks of taxi drivers pestering me, there are none to be found. Finally, a little rickshaw putts around the corner with three guys up front. Pradeep knows them of course and negotiates a non-tourist fare for me.

"This is it, Pradeep. Take care of Rishikesh for me," I say, promptly hitting my head with a thud on the taxi's low metal roof. Pradeep laughs hysterically, and I feel dizziness and the beginnings of a lump, but no hot anger. I have changed.

I settle back into my cramped metal seat holding my aching head, and putt, putt, putt, we are on our way. Behind me, Pradeep recedes into the distance, laughing and waving. What a character—I miss him already.

My bus ride to Delhi feels completely different than my trip in the opposite direction five weeks before. No longer intimidated by the staring natives, I give them a head bobble and smile, only to have them return one even brighter. We pass alongside a truck carrying sugar cane, and stalks poke through the windows on the other side of the bus. I watch passengers break them off and suck happily at the sweet cane, laughing like excited school children. *I'm going to live life to the fullest*, I promise myself. It's a promise that becomes fulfilled from hardship—life bursting forward.

We pass the ominous sight of a smashed-up bus, similar to ours, being towed out of a pond on the side of the road. The likelihood of many survivors is slim. All the passengers look stunned as they gape at the wreckage with a "that could have been us" silence.

After many dreamy hours, the bus arrives in a dark Delhi bus station that is mad with activity. I gasp at the big-city rush as if it's my first time off the farm. Unsteadily, I descend the steps into a flurry of offers and taxi drivers trying to grab my pack. In an instant, my contentment is lost.

Shouldering my backpack, I walk deliberately into the night, through an obstacle course of holes in the road, confused cows, piles of garbage, and sleeping citizens wrapped in blankets on the sidewalk. After several miles, I arrive at Connaught Place in the city center. I have just enough cash left for a dingy hotel room and a cheap dinner.

I find myself back at the restaurant Robert took us to when I first arrived in India. Quickly scanning the menu for something I can afford, I point to what I think is a hot meal. A few moments later, the waiter brings a small bowl of doughnut balls in syrup. I haven't eaten all day, and my heart sinks as I realize what I mistakenly ordered for my last supper. The dessert costs the same as a complete dinner in Rishikesh, and it takes my last rupee. I am left with no more than a few tiny coins.

No sooner have I finished my meager platter than the waiter returns to shoo me away. "We are closed," he says sharply.

Now I am broke and hungry. I remember how my parents scolded me as a child to finish my dinner because "people are starving in India." I never dreamed I would be one of them. But as I make my way to my hotel, I realize that many have even less than doughnut balls. I don't know how they do it.

In my room, I lie awake, anxious about traveling with absolutely no money at all. I close my eyes and focus on my breath. Soon the worries melt away and everything seems all right. Something will work out. After all, I still have my calculator and cassette player to sell.

The next morning, I awake early to pack. My flight leaves late at night, and I plan to spend most of the day at the Red Fort. Besides being a magnificent refuge, the bazaar is rumored to be the place to sell possessions for cash. From Connaught Place, I make the long walk to Old Delhi through bright, crazy markets with their goods strewn all over the sidewalk. During the walk, thousands hit me up for financial aid and stare bewildered at my response of having no money, unable to believe this claim from a foreigner.

The Red Fort has an entrance fee of 5 paisley—hardly a penny—but enough for the majority of the populace not to bother going inside. I hand over the sum, and I am not disappointed. It is heaven on earth. Today the stone monuments seem as stunning as I remembered, but they now have a deeper, more special charm. The red sandstone blocks of one temple remind me of the warm rocks of Eldorado Canyon, while the white stone of a mosque is as sublime as El Capitan. Out of habit, my eyes scan the blocks for holds to climb.

On the walls of the inner palace, magnificent carvings of flowers are hewn into the marble. As the hermit's poem described, they are not loud and overbearing, but subtle, like the secrets of the Orient. Their simple beauty is easily overlooked by hurried minds. For those who slow down, masterpieces are everywhere. Mesmerized, I stand admiring them.

"Hello," says a soft voice behind me.

I turn to see a small boy. "Hello. What's your name, little friend?"

"Thirty rupees. You give me."

"Um, you're too late. I am all out of money."

"Thirty rupees!" he snarls, jolting me out of my happy daze.

"My, you are a big city boy," I say soberly.

The boy glares with discontent. "Give me jacket!" His eyes flame with desire for my dirty, worn, red Patagonia jacket, from which I had removed the logo tag to not be a billboard ad.

"It's the only coat I've got, and it wouldn't fit you."

"Give me."

"I would never wish the curse of materialism on you," I reply, hefting my heavy pack and walking briskly away. Out of the corner of my eye, I see the boy make signs to a friend and they give chase. For the next hour, I hear the mantra "thirty rupees you give me" in front, behind, and to the side.

I try being polite, then rude, anything to convince the boy that this slot machine is not paying out. Nothing works. Finally, I find a far corner and sit down, concentrating into the void. Tired of being ignored, the boy hits me over the head with a small stick.

"Listen partner," I tell him sternly, "I'm sorry for your poverty, but you'd best get lost. Namaste."

"Thirty rupees."

A museum near the gate costs literally my last coin to get in, but, at this point, I would trade a gold mine just to lose that aggressive kid. On display are curved Arabian swords engraved with fascinating sayings of the Prophet Mohammed.

When the coast is clear, I slip into the bazaar of shops surrounding the Red Fort to conduct some business. I find a shopkeeper who shows interest in my calculator, but he makes a low bid that won't cover a taxi ride and airport tax.

Following the custom Pradeep taught me, I walk away. Sure enough, the man runs after me proposing a price that is just enough to get me out of here.

"We also change U.S. Dollars at good rate," he offers, laughing gruffly like a comic book villain. It's funny how corrupt people in India are so easy to spot.

"I thought changing currency outside a bank was illegal," I say audibly.

"Don't say so loud!" he cringes, disappearing into the crowd.

Exhaustion suddenly overcomes me, and I have to sit down. Feeling weak and woozy with enough money to escape but not a rupee for food, I decide the best plan is to stay in the Red Fort and not to wander around getting hungrier.

There are few foreigners among the throngs of tourists in the Fort, so I am surprised to see a white woman coming toward me, sweating and looking worried. Her male counterpart sits nearby guarding their luggage as a large gaggle of Indians stares in an unsympathetic standoff.

With an Australian accent, she asks humbly, "Do they always stare at foreigners so? What should we do?"

"They are normally gentle, but very curious," I explain. "Just smile and say 'Namaste.'"

She does this and the thirty or so Indians gawkers break into sheepish smiles and disperse. The Australian couple looks at me in amazement, just as Simon and I had viewed Robert on arrival. I am now a veteran of India.

"Cheers mate, I thought they were going to attack." The boy-friend wipes beads of sweat from his face.

It is somehow refreshing to see this tough-looking, beer-swilling Aussie unnerved. We are outnumbered ten billion to one after all.

The afternoon is advancing, and it's time to say farewell to the magnificent Red Fort. Outside, I barter for my last Indian taxi. Hundreds of drivers pitch expensive fares: "Airport very long way. Many rupees."

Finally, I choose a young man about my age, who has been the least aggressive. As he kick starts his go-cart, great plumes of black exhaust spew out. There are few private cars in India, but most all engines on the road are in terrible condition, triggering the world's air pollution crisis with relatively few vehicles. As we speed away, I wonder vaguely who will fix this threat before the Third World chokes the earth.

The afternoon air feels good flowing through the cart. I watch the driver for any monkey business, but he is very relaxed. I offer him a bidi, speak some Hindi, and we are soon friends of sorts.

"You want to stop for coffee or chai?" I offer, mimicking Pradeep.

Though he isn't interested in stopping, we spend the trip to Gandhi International laughing and joking. As the city disappears behind us, I contentedly inhale the last sights and sweet air of a more rural India. The late-day sun illuminates the golden fields. Rounding a bend, I watch a long magical ray of the sun touch a green field and am overcome with emotion. On my arrival here, I kept wishing for time to pass, and now it has, all too quickly.

At the airport, a cranky turbaned guard with a shotgun on his shoulder can't make sense of my ticket. He reads it over and over again before finally losing interest and letting me into the airport lobby. I pause to savor one last ray of the Indian sun before crossing the threshold of international linoleum floors. It is only four p.m. and my flight doesn't leave until 11:30, so I have plenty of time.

I collapse into a plastic seat, utterly relaxed, and amuse myself with the spectacle of a Western man frantically running from desk to desk covered in sweat and in a fury to get information on his flight. His anxiety reminds me of the manic pace of the world I come from and how different it is from this last five weeks.

Later, a couple of friendly French guys sit near me and show off an enormous wooden trunk, which is brimming with beautiful weathered bracelets and relics.

"Zis one is over 200 years-old," one of them brags, proffering a silver-lined skull.

"Isn't it illegal to take out artifacts?"

"Yes, but zere is nothing 'baksheesh' cannot take care of."

"What did you buy to take back?" the other Frenchman asks.

"These beads," I reply, pulling my 40-cent mantra bead necklace out from around my neck.

The two Frenchmen study me closely. "That is all you take from a journey to India? You could have made a great profit!"

"I did make a great profit."

Slowly, understanding spreads across their faces. "Yes," observes one. "We lived with a man in Nepal. He has nothing but wakes up happy every day."

"They have a hard life," his mate adds, "but they don't have…"

"Depression," fills in the first one as if on cue. Their enthusiasm over their booty has faded, and their heavy faces suggest that both are thinking of the world to which they are returning. They are from the gloomy north of France.

As the plane shoots down the runway I'm surprised it's not honking to get the other planes out of the way. The runway is also inexplicably clear of cows and other traffic that seems everywhere. Maybe we will make it off the ground.

I find myself sitting next to a pleasant British couple. At last the stewardess serves dinner, my first meal since the measly dough balls of the previous evening. I devour mine in seconds, and my neighbors generously surrender their leftovers, probably in horror. The plane shoots into the night. Goodbye, Mother India.

BOOK THREE

Return with the Elixir

"If you didn't care what happened to me,
And I didn't care for you,
We would zig zag our way through the boredom and pain
Occasionally glancing up through the rain.
Wondering which of the buggars to blame
And watching for pigs on the wing." Pink Floyd *Animals*

A PRISONER OF THE QUEEN!

After hours of floating across dark continents, our plane arrives in the blue skies above England. I say goodbye to the sun as we descend into the gloom.

The British woman next to me tells me about the beautiful wedding she and her boyfriend attended in Delhi. "The men certainly love their women in India," she says, looking accusingly at her boyfriend as though he is devoid of emotion. He seems oblivious to the jab.

As the plane drops into the inevitable drizzle blanketing Heathrow, the couple shares with me their phone number. I am tempted to ask them to loan me money, but decide against it.

I feel a certain dread as I exit the plane and queue to get my baggage. An Indian looking man cuts the line and the British gasp and tut with indignation. Queuing up is their sacred tradition, the symbol of civilization, all that separates man from the red-butted apes.

Now I que up behind the other undesirable, non-British passports.

"Next please," calls an attractive but businesslike brunette. "Coming from…?"

"India."

She looks up suspiciously. "And where are you going to be staying in London? Do you have hotel reservations or have you made other arrangements?"

"Oh, I'll be staying with friends. I have to give them a call, so I'd better be off."

"Hold on mate. I've got to ask you a few more questions. How much money do you have with you?"

"Counting rupees?"

"*Not* counting rupees," she replies stiffly.

My dread grows, but I reply honestly. "Three pence."

She gasps. "*Three pence* is all you have to enter Great Britain? You had better step over here." She leads me into a little cubicle and pulls out a form. "Right. What were you doing in India?"

"I did some yoga and meditation."

After fixing me with a horrified stare, the woman starts writing vigorously.

"Well, I never joined the Hare Krishnas," I explain.

She appears relieved. "This is for you, mate," she says handing me a paper.

"Thank you very much for your kindness," I tell her in my best impression of a sane, innocent, upstanding citizen, tucking the document away. "Well, I'd better go call my friends and see who's going to pick me up."

She stops me. "Perhaps you had better read that first."

The form is decorated by the coat of arms for the House of Windsor with a lion and unicorn. In flowery language, it explains that I am to be withheld by the customs agents of Her Majesty Queen Elizabeth II.

Playing my last card, I scan it with seeming incomprehension. "Wow, thanks. That's kind of cool. Can I keep it?"

"It means you're under arrest, mate."

The ignorance ploy didn't work. She ushers me into a room where two hard-boiled agents, Charlie and Bill, begin scrutinizing me and my belongings. I'm a prisoner of the Queen!

"You needn't bother; I was frisked every ten minutes flying Iraqi Air," I joke. The officials are not amused.

They dump my pack out on a large metal table. My laundry is embarrassingly smelly, and they poke at some cheap books on yoga as though they are incriminating evidence. They also confiscate my address book, and the brunette starts calling the British numbers at random.

"Come on, lad. Let's have a look at you," says Charlie. I have the pleasure of stripping down to my underwear in a private room.

"Ah ha! We've got you nicked!" exclaims a new man as he rushes into the room. "Picked up a little hashish, did we?" He holds up a pair of tweezers encasing some green gunk he scraped from my rain jacket pocket, his face flushed red with excitement. This is the chase the man lives for. I realize I am once again surrounded by a gang of dangerous monkeys. I focus and choose my words carefully.

"I have no interest in drugs," I say in a firm but non-argumentative tone that comes from my higher self. The man is crestfallen. The power of true and correct speech dissolves his accusation.

The brunette is still busy with my address book, so to pass the seeming hours in solitude I listen to the Rolling Stones' *Tattoo You* on my cassette player and try to pretend I'm not in such hot water. It's a long jamming album, and I feel better with each passing song. After an eternity, she returns wearily to my cell. I am becoming an all-night project.

"This chap's parents said he went into the army, and they aren't going to have any part of you," she says pointing to Peter's number.

My heart sinks to think of Peter's mum leaving me to die, but, after all, I did put ketchup on her roast beef.

"This Janice isn't about either," the lady continues. "She is visiting a boyfriend in 'ospital who's been stabbed, and her parents want nothing to do with you either. Worst of all is this "Zippy." When I identified myself as a British customs agent, he called me a 'fascist' and hung up." She pauses, overcome with exasperation. "What kind of friends do you have? It's very possible we will send you on back to India!"

"Back to India?" I echo, incredulous. "You can't…"

"We bloody well can. Nobody can enter the U.K. on three pence!"

In horror, I imagine myself begging at Gandhi International Airport, dirty and lost among the throngs of ragged people.

Thanks, Zips! I say to myself. "Zippy" is one of the Sheffield gang I met during my previous time in Buoux. His nickname comes from a cruel resemblance to the comic book character "Zippy the Pinhead." He's one of the best climbers in the world just behind Jerry Moffat and Ben Moon. He is also an anarchist who hates the police, on principal. Well, he would be very polite to them as people; in fact, he would probably invite them in for tea, but he would also curse their totalitarian existence on theoretical principal. Of course, Zippy didn't explain such nuances to the customs agent, so his lofty ideals are about to send me back to "Gandhi-land" to die on the sidewalk.

Miraculously, or maybe because I am cheerful and polite, the customs crew gradually loses its enthusiasm for pinning a felony on me. My pack is unceremoniously returned with the contents tossed separately in a heap. The brunette apologetically helps me pack, and I catch her glancing at my yoga books, which lie on the steel, formerly sterile, sorting shelf.

"Have you ever been to India?" I ask softly.

"No, I haven't made it over."

"There are monkeys everywhere, and the people are wonderful," I say shamelessly romanticizing India. "I tried yoga and meditation. It's a little strange for us Westerners, but I think there really is something to it. I feel like yoga can save the world."

The brunette gives me a less disdainful look than expected. Perhaps she seldom hears words of hope in her gloomy cubicle. Suddenly, she cracks.

"Look I'm sorry about all this, but if you had some money we could let you go," she gushes in a motherly tone. "I'm going to ring this Janice again. Do you want something to drink?"

In all the fuss, I feel a strange detachment and dignity. My detainment in Heathrow is a mere trifle compared to Indian travelling. Though I'm under arrest, I'm still alive. Most importantly, Pradeep was right. I went to her like a child with humility, addressing her higher nature. Now she is working to free me.

"I've gotten ahold of Janice," she announces triumphantly. "It's clear you can't stay at her parents' house, but she has arranged for a mutual friend to wire you a train ticket to Kent and stay with him. A chap named Roger."

"All right, Roger!" I say enthusiastically, not knowing who in the world he is. I met a lot of people at the Fox and Hounds.

"You are free to go."

Those delightful words echo in my ears. After thanking my new friends, I bound down the linoleum tiles to freedom. I call my mother collect to reassure her before boarding the train with Roger's ticket in hand.

On the train, I feel like I have pulled off the bank robbery of the century. I laugh uncontrollably, chuckles ripping out of my mouth. I want to shake a mother chatting with her son on the next seat and make them understand what I have been through, how beautiful life really is. However, I decide to leave the dozy Londoners be. I've been arrested once today already.

Though I arrived at Heathrow in the early afternoon, my ordeal with customs detained me for hours, and it's getting dark by the time the train gets to Victoria. Sitting on the ground at a junction of the underground tunnels, I pass a red-haired woman begging dejectedly, her dog slumped over nearby. My heart sinks in pity.

"I've got three pence for you," I smile, handing her the last of my change. "I guess that's not very much in a place like London, but here you go."

She looks as miserable as ever.

"I'm sorry I don't have more."

It is awkward pausing in my rush to get to Roger's and safety, but I want to see if I can feel "Namaste" in a place like London.

To talk to her goddess, I have to imagine her suffering. I do so, and suddenly, I am lost in the hells of a big, cold, expensive city, destitute, maybe running from some nightmarish home life or relationship, with a dog as my only friend.

And this is the point of all the chanting, the sitting cross-legged for hours, the postures; the point of yoga: to become a better human being. Even the most austere, macho yoga means nothing if it cannot pass this test. The siddhi, or super-power, that has come to me now is the ability to see the "invisible people" that others look past every day. I also sincerely believe I have no more, or less, importance than the woman. She is divine and a messenger from God. Behind all these illusions there is only the heart.

"Everything is all right," I say petting her dog gently. She hangs her head like she is going to cry. "The sky above Britain is blue. The clouds might hide it, but the sun is there and always has been." My highest point in yoga is reached, I can finally think of someone's plight besides my own. Feeling true empathy is now real and I'm not embracing the greatest enemy: a yoga ego trip. I'm so sure I'll stake my life on it and I owe it all to D'Anne's untimely passing and even Red who awoke my outrage.

"Thanks," she says smiling weakly. A tear runs down her cheek as she nods.

"Namaste," I whisper and bow before continuing down the escalators into the commuter crowds.

As the train pulls into the Kent station, I try to pick Roger's face out of the crowd. I had chatted with him for all of five minutes in the Fox and Hounds. Now he is putting me up and is legally responsible for sponsoring my stay for up to three thousand pounds.

A fellow with thick glasses calls out my name.

I wave, coming toward him. "Whew, thanks for saving my life."

"Did they let you out of the stockade? I hate customs," Roger says.

It is a short walk through the rainy night to the little flat that Roger self-consciously calls a dump. I can't believe I am free to walk on the sidewalk without a rickshaw running me over or stopping to ask where I am going or recommending a good hotel. After all that, Roger's flat looks like a penthouse suite.

After making a pot of tea and turning on a cricket match, Roger narrates his adventures with customs: "I was working in L.A. for a family and earning good dosh. One day the beach was deserted being a bit overcast, so I sat down next to the only bird there. She's all friendly like she's chatting me up." The woman was an immigration officer and Roger was deported within the week. "The tart!" Roger continues ranting. "So when customs rings up and says will I sponsor you for three thousand pounds—I say sure. Ha! I'm on the bleedin' dole, you know, haven't worked in ages."

Roger's cricket match extends on into the night, but I pass out in minutes. I sleep like a rock, well into the next afternoon, unaffected by the murmurs of a cricket match on Roger's telly. Watching cricket is about all Roger does besides going to the pub. Apparently, he has quite a winning streak doing pub quiz nights.

The next day, I decide to be a good lodger by making dinner, so I borrow some cash from Roger, who I promise to reimburse once my mother wires some money, and brave a partly clearing sky to wander down to, oddly enough, the local Safeway. The aisles seem shockingly clean, with no noticeable smell of urine, or monkeys about to pounce from above. I marvel at the brightly colored packaging and ridiculous arrays of food, and I have to remind myself they are not likely to harbor botulism. Silly though it is, the sterility of the Safeway is proof I'm not delirious from malaria or dysentery and lying half-conscious in a dirty Indian hospital. I couldn't be more grateful.

Back at Roger's flat, a copy of *The Sun* newspaper lies on the breakfast table. "Sarah Shamed," reads the headline of an article about a tennis player who lost her match. "Shamed?" It is a vicious, overly-competitive world far removed from the philosophy of "I am not the doer." The nasty, mud-slinging tones of the tabloid story startle my naïve frame of mind, reminding me of the aggression on all fronts I grew up with.

There is "balance" in the tabloid's coverage, however. Page three contains a full-page picture of a scantily clad "bird with her huge knockers flopped out," as Roger described it, so the working lads will buy the paper. There is nothing lower than a British tabloid masquerading as a newspaper. I am back in the West all right.

In the afternoon, I set to work cleaning Roger's kitchen—normally not my cup of tea—but this incredible gratitude to make it out of India alive makes me want to be of some kind of service. While rescuing Roger's neglected stovetop from a layer of grime, I listen to Led Zeppelin's "That's the Way" in my cassette player. Powerful emotions hit me as the acoustic guitar strums through, what is arguably one of Led Zeppelin's most soulful numbers, forcing me to lean against the counter for support. I am still cheerfully scrubbing away half an hour later, when, Peter's friend who works at the Fox and Hounds, Janice, comes round to visit.

"'Ow's India then?" she asks.

"Incredible," I say solemnly. I want her to really understand what has happened, for the answer to stop time. It is not another holiday to put in the scrapbook, but I don't know how to describe it.

"I can tell you are a different person already," Janice observes.

Stories pour out of me, sweetened by the charm I learned from Pradeep. I describe monkeys, elephants eating sugar cane, the mysterious subcontinent and, of course, yoga and bliss. Like I did for the Heathrow agent, I paint a picture of a far-off sunny world. Gradually, Janice forgets she is in miserable, rainy England.

"Would a child be okay to travel with?" she asks cautiously.

"Well sure," I stammer. Bringing a small child into the madness of India? I picture Janice holding Anna close on a bus ride through the Indian chaos and filth. However, after the current rash of stabbings around London and shootings in L.A., maybe travelling with a baby isn't so bad.

"I don't think I could raise the dosh worki' the pub," she reflects with disappointment.

"I know. But you *have* to see India someday," I tell her. "You must. The yoga practices there have something. Anyway, practice here all you can. It's important."

"Right, I'll try to get over there someday."

Roger comes in and out of the room as I relate more stories. My excitement embarrasses him. He fidgets uncomfortably with his thick glasses as I describe to Janice a pranayama breathing exercise that Uncle Joe taught me. Roger is too English for all this.

"What time is pub tonight, Roger?" Janice asks, breaking the spell.

"Janice," I call, bringing her back, "promise me you will go to India someday."

"No worries. I promise."

Half-seven rolls around, and Roger is collecting his friends in a taxi for the pub quiz championship. Though he is on the dole, it is his proudest moment to get all smartened up and go down to the pub in style. We are all there to watch him win his round. The Fox and Hound is a different universe from the ashram, but I enjoy myself before falling asleep from the time difference.

Today, I'm taking the train into London to join Peter's brother, James, for his lunch break from Harrod's. After a couple of days in England, I'm starting to feel back in an ordinary existence, granted an English one, what with cricket matches on the telly and quiz nights at the pub, and now sharing a cabin with sour-faced commuters.

Oddly, when I play Pink Floyd's *Animals* through my cassette player, a magical change elevates me. The train's methodical rolling in time with the music becomes hypnotic. I drift into another world. Outside my window, the bleak, red-brick, post-industrial landscape of outer London reminds me of George Orwell's novels. I am struck by the similarity between Orwell's *Animal Farm* and this album. This very scene may well have inspired Roger Waters to write the lyrics to the album *Animals* that bring to mind the horrors of the Industrial Revolution, and coincidentally, I look up to see the Battersea Power Station, the memorable cover photo of the *Animals* album. The looming smokestacks and gray façade of this Victorian-era complex stare blankly back like they are trying to tell me a revolting tale. This is where it all began: from these bleak brick factory chimneys, the modern industrial world had risen.

I feel, as an intense physical sensation, the loss of so many souls to the graveyard of capitalism. The experience is a curious mixture of pleasure and pain. I am in an otherworldly ecstasy, but also perturbed by the eerie scene. It is remarkable that these strange feelings are not confined to a faraway mystical India but also flow through London's desperate factory ruins. I'm having an ecstatic *moksha* on the train, while, the other passengers don't look past their crossword puzzle.

We arrive in Victoria Station, and I get out with the masses. Unlike last December, London's crowded streets feel like a glorious homecoming parade. The hermit's words are true. When all is right in the microcosm, all *is* right in the macrocosm. The Londoners look divine like knights and ladies of court, and I love them all.

Perhaps sensing this openness, people approach me with ease. By the frozen lake in Hyde Park, a young girl stops to tell me her story. She comes from Iraq, where she lived with her family across the river from Iran. One night, her father was murdered in his sleep by Iranian guerrillas. All she wants is someone to talk to, and I listen with a newfound patience and compassion, happy to do something for her. Instant generosity—foolish or otherwise—pours out of me just as it did from the kind people of India, and I give her my favorite Led Zeppelin tape.

At the end of the park lies Kensington Palace and I can't resist being a tourist. Inside, dark wood-paneled walls rise majestically above me. I feel torn between disgust for royal family—the greatest insult to mankind as Mark Twain put it—and a touristy admiration for the beautiful panache of the palace. I marvel at Victoria's bedroom, the night chamber of the woman who ruled the world. She had some pretty nice lodgings. Too bad she could not be amused.

Seated in a little Thai restaurant, a stuffy well-dressed middle-aged man being led by the hostess gives me a disgusted look and asks to be seated elsewhere with his party. "Sorry," says the hostess repeatedly to him for her "mistake" of attempting to seat his party near me. I am in the Royal Borough of Chelsea, a snotty neighborhood by the palace for a quick lunch. I'm not used to experiencing that kind of hatred after India. And the thing is, it isn't a very formal restaurant and I look like a pretty normal American tourist in his early twenties. No incriminating evidence of Indian sympathies. I never did "go Indian" with the white or orange robes and shaved head because the external identity change is only superficial. The gentleman seems to have an immediate distain for me, but as the Buddha said, "enlightenment does not come from the side of me." The incident does not affect me deeply like it might have before.

At a bank on Bond Street, I withdraw the money my mother wired me from my college account. I accept it gratefully, knowing that, even in London, many people have much less. I make a point to stop and talk to each destitute person I meet, hopefully cheer them, suffer with them, and offer a small donation.

On the bus I ride across town, a quintessential red double-decker, three musicians start playing and passing the hat.

A portly, middle-aged-woman protests to the conductor, "Stop this bloody racket, and throw these beggars off the bus!"

Even after only a five-week trip, I am not used to such British fussiness. In India, there was always music blaring and of course, plenty of beggars. It's time for a revolution of joy, the kind Pradeep would support, and that entails the very un-English blaring music and frantic dancing. As the hermit said, "Even a beggar is the messenger of god."

"Forget her," I tell the musicians, tossing a couple of pound coins in their hat. They smile and enthusiastically resume their song.

I find Peter's brother, James, behind the camera counter at his department store job looking smart in his suit and tie. We step outside on a short break.

"Bloody 'ell, you made it back alive!" he exclaims. Just then a troop of Hare Krishnas appears around the corner, chanting and banging their drum. A few of them aren't even properly shaven. Instead, they have rubber, bald head theater costume pieces, like devotees on their lunch hour. James's face twists into a suspicious grimace. "Bloody Krishnas!"

"Yes, a beastly religion!" I say jokingly. James doesn't get the reference. "Naw," I say with a shrug. "I met some in India; they're all right. Everything is all right."

"So, is that what you are now—a Hare Krishna or a Buddhist?" James accuses. He spits out the words distastefully.

"Me? No."

"Hindu, Jain?"

"Nope."

"Well, what *do* you believe then?" James continues. "You can't go all the way to India and not come back without some fanciful religion. You've got to believe something."

I laugh, remembering my horror at Peter's proclamation that I would return in orange robes chanting Om. Though it was helpful to keep my perspective, the comment was, of course, degrading and arrogant. I don't have a new costume or strange philosophy, I muse to myself. My favorite saying: "Yoga loves you more than it loves itself," comes to the forefront. I am not a follower; yoga brought me back to myself. I merely try to decipher what the ancient chronicler and saint, Patanjali, meant with his prescribed method of slowing down the mind. I don't know what Patanjali looked like or care to celebrate his birthday, but I am grateful he documented and organized what the ancient yogis were on to.

"Well?" James presses further. "What do you believe after your big trip to India?"

"I believe..." I pause dramatically, signaling him closer to whisper it privately. James smiles, satisfied he's conjured up the confession he wanted. "...I believe your lunch hour is over."

On my last morning in England, I square up with Roger, adding in a bit extra since he is unemployed and did save my life. He looks pleased, and his suspicions wash away. Roger accompanies me to the bus stop which connects to the motorway south. My plan is to hitchhike all the way to Provence.

The northern sun shines bleakly on the dark, mossy stone of the wall in front of the bus stop. It is unusually sunny for January in England. Apparently, a drought is ruining the ski areas in Europe. Soon, a red double-decker bus arrives, and Roger says goodbye. I look around one last time, taking in the pleasant sounds and sights of suburban England.

The conductor grudgingly makes a special stop to let me out at the motorway. I step off amid his protests and the annoyed tut-tuts of passengers. After wandering to the wrong side of the motorway, I take up my post on the M1 South with a cardboard sign for Aix-en-Provence. The unusually cheerful January sun warms me, and I feel like Jack Kerouac in *On the Road.*

"I can give you a lift towards Dover." A voice surprises me from behind. It belongs to a middle-aged man with a showy sports car and a smart blue Italian wool business suit. I walk to the right-hand side of his car and see a steering wheel.

"Yank, eh?"

"Afraid so."

The man opens the other door half-heartedly, with the air of someone earning karma points, giving this lift as payment of a debt. I do my best to entertain him with polite conversation.

"What did you do in India?" he asks after hearing where I've been.

"I went to learn about yoga."

At this news, his reluctant tone changes entirely. He considers me closely. "In the '60s I went to India to chant Om and stuff the West," he says, adding in a somber tone, "Had some bad times with heroin. Now I sell car phones ... Did you learn to meditate?"

"Yes. I had some wonderful experiences."

"Did you meditate on Om? I have Om tattooed on my hand." He pulls back his sleeve to reveal a blue-ish symbol. It is the last thing I would imagine concealed under his stylish suit. I smile, surprised by this secret world hidden beneath his clean-cut posh exterior.

"Everything is beautiful," I say earnestly, and he can sense my contentment. "I'm sorry you got into heroin."

"Aye, me too. Me too," he sighs, looking thoughtful. "I should meditate again."

We ride on, engaged in deep conversation, past white sheep grazing in the nearby fields like wispy clouds on the shining green grass

Then the man pulls over. "Sorry to say it, mate, but you've gotta get off here." He exhales with genuine disappointment at our parting. "I haven't thought of India in years ... Maybe I *can* do it!" he whispers mysteriously. "God bless you, young friend, God bless you," he says with great sincerity, putting his hand out one last time.

A slow cloud drifts across the sun, turning the day immediately back to winter. I am still far from the coast, and I begin to wonder whether anyone will ever pick me up. Will I have to spend the night freezing by the side of the road? I'm surveying some nearby shrubs for potential bedding when a small-black coupe screeches to a halt beside me.

The driver hops out. "Zis number is Paris!" he exclaims, gesturing to his license plate. "You understand? I take you zere. Zis is your lucky day."

I love hitchhiking here. This Frenchman seems genuinely pleased to help me, and I feel as if I've made yet another friend. Remembering my mistake last time, I confidently step around to the left side of the vehicle. Of course, this one time I remember to get in on the proper English passenger side it is a French car that drives on the right side of the road.

"Thank you ... um ... *merci*." I struggle awkwardly with my failed French. Fortunately, the driver speaks English well and without a grudge—almost.

"Ze English, zey sink I am a little froggy, a little insect." He laughs. "Zey look down zeir fine noses at me."

I nod in sympathy. "The British treat everyone like dirt. We Americans kicked them out years ago, with *your* country's help, of course."

Soon the rolling green hills of the southern English countryside funnel into the white cliffs of Dover. As we speed toward the dock, I study the massive castle above town where the D-Day assault launched. My uncle, who died in that battle, possibly spent his last free hours here.

The Frenchman has timed his journey well: the ferry loads almost immediately after our arrival. I am surprised by the unexpected obligation of a hefty passenger fare. Then the French driver settles in the bar, and, in an effort to provide good company, I buy a round. Suddenly, the idea of drifting south without money or complications becomes a distant fantasy, yet I feel calm, happy, almost incapable of worry.

The ferry crossing to Calais takes three hours, and, in the lounge, pretty English girls chat excitedly about adventures ahead, creating a festive holiday atmosphere. On deck, seagulls escape the chilly afternoon air by diving in the warm exhaust of the ship's chimney. Watching the birds play in the exhaust plume, I think of Janice, Roger, Peter, and the stifling rainy island they call home. *Goodbye, England.* I look forward to sunny Provence, climbing and good times ahead.

French customs consists of a man waiving everyone along while rolling a Gitanes cigarette with his free hand. After nearly being shackled in Heathrow, I greet this experience as a pleasant French joke.

I drift asleep as my driver takes us ripping out of Calais on the toll highway they call the *péage*. When I awake an hour later, his speedometer hovers at the equivalent of 100 miles an hour.

"Shhhhh! I must concentrate," he cries, stifling my effort at polite conversation, which is fine with me at this speed.

Dusk has an enchanted purple softness. We speed past brown signs indicating mysterious castles and historical sites. I dream of myths and legends, with knights jousting and troubadours playing.

Paris is an hour away, then half an hour. All roads lead to the glamorous capital. At last, the city's glow of lights engulfs us.

Beaming with patriotism, the Frenchman takes me far out of his way to sightsee. "Zat is ze Statue of Liberty," he exclaims, pointing toward a smaller version of the one in Staten Island.

I had no idea there were two. "Wow, you must be proud."

Eventually, the tour ends, and this stranger, now my friend, deposits me at the Gare du Lyon, disappearing back into the rush of traffic.

Paris's central train station warms me with a romantic air. As in a classic film, everyone looks like they are in love and ready to dance under the soft happy lights. I am almost reluctant to leave, but the thought of sunny crags draws me on. I deliberately book a slow sleeper-train to save a hotel bill and avoid arriving in Marseille in the middle of the night. Once on board, however, the duck-billed conductor informs me that I paid only for a seat, not a cabin bed. Now I have to sleep sitting up all night.

The Marseille station appears so grim in the early pale hours it's hard to believe that I'm in Provence. However, on the short train ride to Aix, the sight of farms and open fields refreshes me. Provence, even in January, is like summer after the sleepy drizzle of the North. The sun shines strongly, and a white morning moon hovers regally over Mount St. Victoire on the horizon. I feel close to nature again, and it seems tragic, shameful that so many people live out of touch with her.

THE PEARL

Just in time, I reach the apartment of the British guy Mark, where I'd stayed with Red. He is moving to a new flat, and this is his last load. If I had missed him, I'd have nowhere to stay for a week until our school started.

"My new place is a right shithole," he says bluntly. True, his flat is in a dreary-tan semi-high-rise covered in grime. However, it's warm and clean inside, and the beautiful Aix fountains and cafes are just down the *rue*. Besides, everything seems luxurious and easy after India. In the evening, I offer to make dinner to pay for the doss. Mark thus becomes an innocent victim of my experimental interest in cooking. I knead flour into Chapatti pancakes, just as I saw street vendors do in India. Then I chop vegetables and sauté them in oil, covering them with curry powder. Soon, we sit down to eat and both realize I have no idea how to cook Indian food, and especially how to make chapattis. Mark opens a can of ravioli.

Later, my attempt to do some yoga in the corner elicits sarcastic jabs from the Londoner. It seems there is no privacy for weird and unmanly exercises in his tiny studio. The yoga poses feel exhilarating despite the unwanted scrutiny. The only thing Mark appreciates about India is the buzz off the strange bidis cigarettes I give him. When he sees me in the upside-down plough pose, however, Mark grows competitive and mimics me. He is annoyed to find that I am more flexible. "I wonder why one side of my body is stiffer than the other?" he asks, straining.

"My yoga teacher in Denver said it was because one side is your spiritual side and the other more material."

"Right, well, I think when you're dead, that's it, end of story," he snaps. "Bloody bunch of freaks those yoga people."

This flood of Western cynicism sours my mood. I wish I had some privacy, but at least I'm off the street. Mark thinks he's a hard lad, so I decide not to mention '*ahimsa,*' or non-violence. I also avoid the subject of my new-found happiness and respect for all living things. He would think I was a pufter for not wanting to step on a bug. Yet I feel a remarkable amount of *prana,* or in Chinese philosophy *chi,* surging through me. Renouncing the temptation of violence, I receive more energy in the process should I need to fight. It's the world upside down again.

The next day, we are off to climb in the fabled Buoux. Mark's silver Metro roars out of Aix, blaring George Michael's *I Want Your Sex,* testing me, it would seem, with the most dire and superficial song imaginable.

Finally, I convince Mark to change the cassette to U2, whose songs are instantly entrancing.

Though I have seen them before, the Provençal sights are mesmerizing. Endless vineyards, picturesque villages, and the stately chateau of Lourmarin drift by as in a dream. The drive is immensely enjoyable topped off by descending into Buoux's carefree paradise of blue-white cliffs bathed in golden southern French sunshine.

As soon as I step onto the rock, I realize that something has changed. I haven't climbed in almost two months, but I feel in tune with every edge, pocket, and slope. My movements absorb me, concentration is effortless, and, perhaps for the first time on a climb, I feel no fear. The classic "mind over matter" challenge of *The Inner Game of Tennis* comes back to me; my mind's eye clearly sees the difference between a rope and a snake in a darkened room. Intuitively, I understand that, as long as I do the safety stuff correctly, there is nothing to be afraid of. Maybe for the first time in my life there is no fear of failure. It is only a game in which I am voluntarily participating. I can now move with great accuracy, using the holds like a master painter plans his brush strokes and choses his brushes. It is the most beautiful of sensations. My faith is justified; the trip has paid off in this way too.

On the trip back to Aix, I feel extremely hungry. My paltry Indian diet of munching on peanuts doesn't hold up against the rigorous climbing. "Tonight is pizza," I announce, planning aloud my second meal as resident vegetarian chef.

Mark says nothing.

An hour later, the uneaten so-called pizza lands in Mark's metal rubbish bin with a ringing bang.

"Didn't you let the yeast rise?" he asks.

"Yeast?"

"Yeah, yeast. It saves on trips to the bloody dentist. Don't tell me there's none in here."

"Um, what's the French word for yeast?"

Mark throws a dictionary at me and opens a can of soup.

French supermarkets don't sell pre-made meals, as the French consider frozen meals and junk food an abomination of one of the great pleasures of life. This means I have to make everything from scratch. While not convenient, I accept it as a welcome consequence of living in paradise. Fresh tastes better, and when it comes to food the French are the experts.

Suddenly, there is a knock at the door and everything changes. The "lads" have arrived from a long journey down from north England and in strolls Johnny Dawes.

Johnny is at his crazy best. The very night he arrived we went out to the Bistro. Johnny slumps in his chair dejectedly, until he manages to make eye contact with a French girl sitting "across a crowded room" as the song goes. She smiles, and he's off to the races.

"I'll see you all later," he says, and disappears with his new companion.

At three in the morning, Johnny bursts into Mark's small apartment, and stumbles over snoring climbers and piles of gear. He turns on all the lights and wakes everyone up to tell us about making love to the French girl on the bonnet of his Peugeot. Then, suddenly, he recoils in horror at the thought that he and the girl might have scratched the paint on his car. He rushes back outside, slamming the door and clambered down the hall. Mark moans and holds his head in his hands. It is only the first night.

In the morning, Johnny's Peugeot sped toward Buoux loaded with climbers. I sit next to the manic driver, eager to share stories from my trip to India. "Yes, yes I want to hear about it," he says earnestly. "Meditation, I need that. God, I feel awful this morning, really fucking awful. *It* just comes over me and I become a monster."

"It? A monster?" I echo trying to decode his unique speech.

"I don't know why I did that last night," he tells me as a sincere tear fills his eye. "Desire, lust, it all goes dark. I must be in the triples, you know. Must be over a hundred birds I've had it off with now."

At Buoux, Johnny's mental aggravation pours onto the rock. He attacks hard routes with furious leaps of boundless energy. "Here's the best meditation going, mate," he crows, flashing a 5.12c. His guilt is forgotten, and he is on fire.

The next day finds us hiking along the bleached limestone cliffs of Paul Cezanne's beloved Mount St. Victoire where, like a yogi, Cezanne rejected the material comforts of Aix to live here alone for a period in a cave, developing his art and vision. I had never made the connection between art and yoga before; French painting is a pretentious affair at home. But here we are in Cezanne's cave, a mysterious recess in the rock, witnessing his austere quarters.

Not far from the cave, there is a naturally-formed limestone bowl surrounded by steep walls, and Johnny begins a frenzied run up and down the rock in his trainers—what we Yanks call tennis shoes—in a one-man show. He sprints back and forth across the craggy bowl as if it were an empty swimming pool using the centrifugal force to propel him higher and higher up the vertical walls, to heights where most climbers would want a rope. One mistake would break his neck. He then slides down the rock, skidding on the soles of his feet as if he were skiing.

Johnny flies through the air to attempt a two-handed dyno and misses and skids past us like an out-of-control car. Johnny pushes down with all his might on his soles and regains control. Fully present, with one hundred percent concentration, he returns to run up the slab and leaps an incredible distance through the air to make his unbelievable dyno.

Johnny had me sliding down the slab on my shoes. In all this play there is a lesson to be learned—another chapter from the *Inner Game of Tennis.* I skid out of control but with practice and awareness, using varying degrees of friction, I regain some control—all in minute degrees, like Johnny's racing hero Senna listening for just when to shift.

Back at Buoux, Johnny coaches me on *No Man's Land.* I find that playing on the Mont Saint Victoire slabs has enhanced my awareness to the degree of pressure necessary for friction and balance. This new understanding counters my normally poor balance on the sloping footholds.

Isolated in the woods with my mantra beads, I chant *Om Mane Padme Hum.*

Many top athletes use a technique of mental preparation called "visualization" in which one imagines achieving one's goal, such as climbing a route perfectly. I go deeper, pairing visualization with the mantra the way Uncle Joe would walk, synchronizing each step with each word. I close my eyes and picture how it would feel to move in tune with the chanting. *Om* and up with my right hand to a pocket, *Mane,* to an edge with my left hand, *Padme,* my right foot up on a high hold, and *Hum,* reach over to another pocket. Over and over, I rehearse the moves in my mind, accompanied by this ancient mantra.

I tie in and started across the traverse. *Om Mane Padme Hum.* The brilliant sun streams down, and time melts as I float past hard sections, a witness to a dream. The crux comes and I instinctively use a little edge I had not tried before. It works, and I find myself clipping the top anchors having just climbed my first 5.12. I lower to the ground, still feeling detached and peaceful, as though waking up from a nap. I have broken through, what was for me, a mythical grade barrier.

Evenings bring us face to face with Aix's intriguing night life. At the Bistro Johnny and I meet super model-esque Swedish girls. They invite us for dinner, then they cancelled it last minute all in a whirl.

"It doesn't matter," I say. I am entranced by the distant sunset. The great symbol of Provençal warmth slowly sinks behind the distant hillside. Unlike my rebuff by the blonde in high school, the Swedish girls' snub doesn't bother me. India has put a protective layer around me; I am beginning to feel the strength in stepping back from life—even from its most attractive aspects.

"Let's go have a meal anyway and down this wine," suggests Johnny.

He treats me to a fancy Asian restaurant with a minimalist neon Zen décor. We feel out of place among the prim, polished patrons representing Aix's "haute couture des cuisine." In the middle of our meal, the waiter reluctantly stops by and forces himself to inquire on our well-being.

"It's quite good food actually," replies Johnny brightly. "Here, try some." He holds up a bite on his fork toward the waiter's mouth.

Shuddering, the waiter scurried off, too traumatized even to give us the finger wag.

Back in his Peugeot, Johnny races us around Aix, circling the main fountain again and again while milling crowds, café patrons and the apathetic police force cheer us on. Round and round we go, till I begin to feel sick. Dawes is out of his mind like a true rock and roll star—wild and gallant—but also a kind big brother.

A few days later, I say goodbye to Mark's overstuffed apartment when my dorm room at the French school became available. I shoulder a heavy pack for the trek across town and stop to rest in a lonely church with high dark ceilings and huge gloomy paintings. Everything is ancient and dusty. Despite the winter chill in the high vaulted ceiling and stone walls, I savor these first moments alone. The burning question is *can I resurrect my concentration practice, or will I succumb to the West's negativity and distractions?* I close my eyes, and a warm feeling spreads through me. It is still possible; I just need solitude and quiet.

After thirty minutes of stillness, I feel reconnected. Looking around, I suddenly see the little, forgotten church in a new light. The great archways and the imagery of the large paintings fascinate me. The images seem to present the universal experience of transcendence with a language of symbols that not unique. For example, the mysterious connections with other world religions, such as the halos of Christian saints, which also appear as halos on the

Buddha and *his* twelve disciples thousands of years and thousands of miles apart.

I sit in the church for a long time, this quiet sanctuary. Christianity is taking on a new light, but remains an overbearing religion with an incredibly violent history. Even our precious Buoux valley was a Protestant stronghold until the Pope's armies captured the "heretics" and burned them—men, women and children—alive at the stake. The wars of religion unfolded right beneath my favorite climbs. With a shiver, I recall the horror I felt as a young boy in Sunday school hearing such cruelty unfolding through the Bible stories.

Before negativity can engulf me, I remember the word monk comes from the Greek "mono," which means alone. Indeed, many Christian saints also have a formidable history of withdrawing from the world, performing miracles similar to the *siddhis,* or powers, attributed to yogis. But my soul comes before the history class. I shut my eyes and look inward, as the hermit instructed, and become aware of each breath. It brings back the boundless joy of the eternal present. I become grateful for the opportunity the church offered in this quiet, inspiring place of worship bringing me back to myself.

I resume my stroll through Aix's medieval streets, and the harsh tones of three female American students echo across the cobblestones: "So then she turns into the queen bitch..." It was a brutal awakening. Our gods have deserted us—driven away by our hardened minds. I'd grown accustomed to the quieter dispositions of the English and Europeans, and those sharp, familiar tongues pulled at my innocence, a reminder of a brash and unsympathetic world I've tried to forget. An American world.

My dorm room is located right next to the kitchen and a Canadian student, Katherine, engages me in conversation to boast of her proficiency in five foreign languages. Within five minutes,

Katherine makes it clear she is a mover and shaker and pauses to inform me my accent was too *Provençal.*"

"But this *is* Provence."

"Yes, but it is not a proper French accent. You aren't going to get very far sounding like that. Why are *you* here?"

She won't understand Buoux and all, so I shrug my shoulders as she launches into a do-as-the-French-do lecture, oblivious to my indifference. It is like my first day of grade school, when a girl kept asking if we were on the "primary" playground, just to show off she knew the word "primary." I had been warned that the institute is overrun with over-achievers and begin to sorely miss the toothy grins of Indians and the earthy climbing-bum Brits.

Class doesn't meet every day, so naturally I spend my free time at Buoux. The laboratory has become like home, and the small contingent of Brits are like family. We rarely see someone we don't know, and my new friends seem as interested in my success as their own. Negativity and criticism is replaced by "Come on, Tom … See it through!" All from the best climbers in the world, who have an amazingly mature attitude towards climbing.

After several huge falls at the crux, I redpoint a 5.12c, nearly as hard as *Genesis.* Johnny belayed and coached me, but our unequal body weight pulled him up several feet in the air each time I fell. Before my successful attempt, I wandered off to rest in the woods. Amid the cool, shady trees, I gradually regained my focus, rehearsing the moves in my mind again and again.

After about an hour, I launched myself upward through a sea of small, painful holes, continuing to the top. I stared at the lower-off chain anchor in disbelief.

"5.10 to 5.13+ in a season. That's what you're going to do," Zippy tells me. I am astounded. Would *I* really be climbing 5.13+? At first, it makes my head spin, but after some reflection, sieging routes just for their difficulty seems stupid. As Pradeep had said, about not trying too hard in yoga, I wanted to enjoy Buoux without pressure. From then on, I spend more time flashing easier climbs, taking walks in the woods, stopping to watch lizards dart in and out of the rocks, and enjoying the wonderful Provençal sun setting over the Luberon range.

However, after such a long struggle for success, ambition didn't let go that easily. On an overhanging climb I practice the hard moves with little enthusiasm while my belayer, Zippy, watches in disgust. Then I pause for a session of *Om Mane Padme Hm* and fly up the rock to complete the climb in a whirlwind.

"Bloody hell, Tom! You went from zero to hero!" Zippy says. "That yoga works. Sign me up with your bloody guru!"

The same thing success happens with the German Dahvid on a 5.12b where he hesitates on the run-out top slab moves and grabs a bolt. Lowering off, he curses his fearfulness and nearly breaks down in tears.

On my attempt, I start off climbing rather poorly to internalize the moves, how it feels to use every edge and hold. Then I hide again to chant *Om Mane Padme Hm.*

The sun is bright against the white stone as I lead above the shady tree line, and her warmth sends me upward, detached from notions of success and failure. I make the 5.12b moves and spicy top section on my first redpoint attempt and second try overall.

Dahvid is shocked. "You did ze whole tour! I can't believe!" he sputters. "You looked zo veak and incapable the first time, and I believed you vere, and then you return a different climber."

His comments amaze me. As I get to know the European mind better, I can appreciate that Dahvid is almost incapable of lying. When he says that you were a terrible climber, you are. But if he praises you, you're climbing well. Contrary to the vacant American "let's be positive" cheerleading, compliments from Europeans really mean something.

But Dahvid isn't finished. "Wiz this mind-training, you are a better climber zan Red," he adds.

I am stunned. His sentence breaks a decade-old spell. I spent my whole life wanting to beat Red and climb *Genesis*. For the first time, I fully realize the mental illness I suffer from in my rivalry with Red.

But India's magic and poverty has changed me. Childish competition has become petty. Perhaps at this very moment I am better than Red, who, rumor has it, is gorging himself on takeout pizza back in the States, but what does it matter? Besides, my secret is mentally opting-out—and I can hardly take credit for what I do in a trance. Like the Chapatti Baba said, "I am not the doer."

I have gained a reputation among the climbers for having a balanced, relaxed, mental fortitude, come what may. Johnny becomes curious as to what I am doing to my mind.

We go for a drive and park in a deserted farmer's field. I play my "Eternal OM" cassette tape, and instruct Johnny to let the strange sounds slow and calm his mind. Johnny relaxes a little at first, but then becomes restless.

He tries again, but after a few minutes I sense Johnny fidgeting. His eyes are closed, but his mind bounces everywhere. If he is not climbing an on-the-edge route or driving like a madman, Johnny feels tortured with no danger to silence his mind. I wish he could find some peace.

I also feel an enormous gratitude as Pradeep's words—"Yoga can bring you anything"—sound in my mind. Through "good vibrations" I have won many new friends, including the infamous Johnny Dawes. Best of all, yoga had brought me a quieter, happier mind. I certainly am lucky.

"What I've got to do is get away from all this and really focus," he tells me excitedly. "We should go to India together and spend the whole time doing this Om lot. I would be a new person. It would be brill. I feel better already. Let's keep at it."

To his credit, Johnny is opened-minded enough to try meditation. The other English, though they cling all day to rock faces, brand yoga as weird.

"Those lot are crimson!" Johnny exclaims offering an insightful adjective to describe his fellow Brits and a lot of other people. Yes, crimson: the color of a funeral home or the lining of a coffin. Let the dead bury the dead.

As the sun sets, it becomes a large, bright disk reminding me of the sun gracing my edition of *On the Road*. I watch its golden tentacles spread across the bountiful hills above rural Provence. It is the last day of an unusually warm February, and gifts have been bestowed on me that I never would have imagined. The pearl *has* been handed to me.

THE SHIMMERING LIGHT

As March begins, the English climbers vacate Aix for the campsite in Apt, leaving Mark behind. When not attending French lessons, Mark keeps himself busy shoplifting in the local Aix climbing shop, even though he had plenty of money coming from home. Giving the finger to the Frogs by stealing them blind apparently proves his British superiority.

Before long, Mark tires of Aix and decided Germany is the place to be. He interrogates Dahvid about Freiberg, the Black Forest, and Dahvid's favorite climbing areas.

Since Mark left I have no transportation to Buoux. I try hitch-hiking, or *autostop*, on the tiny, rural roads but it is hard going. One trip has me stuck for hours at a Lourmarin gas station while the daylight fades, but a beautiful Led Zeppelin song called *Out on the Tiles* plays through my head, lulling me into a blissful daze as I walk with my thumb out. Finally, I am picked up by a man dressed in the familiar orange robes, a picture of his guru wearing garlands of flowers sits on his tiny dashboard. I realize with a pang that this nut is who people think I am if I mention yoga. The man is happy and I am grateful for his generosity and free French lessons. I arrive at the main fountain in Aix five hours after leaving Buoux, normally a one-hour drive.

I am pressed to find a more reliable form of transportation and look into buying a Vespa scooter. They are rumored to be as cheap and plentiful in Italy as pasta—and putting around Provence like Cary Grant in *Roman Holiday* sounds too cool to pass up. A classmate, Ed, a Scottish earl or whatever he is, wants to come along and buy a Motto Guzi motorcycle. We just have to get across the nearby Italian border.

After a frustrating and confusing trip, we make it to Genoa, the first decent sized city from the border, but as we tour the streets, we see an abundance of prostitutes in fishnet stockings instead of motorbikes for sale. Ed's travel guide is insightful: *"Italy may be a boot, but Genoa is the armpit. There is nothing here of charm or interest."*

Not speaking Italian, answering a newspaper ad for used scooters by telephone is impossible and the local scooter store is closed for the season.

The day wanes and it's hard to find a cheap hotel. The novelty of Italy and buying scooters is wearing off. After walking futile miles, we settle on a dingy hotel well over budget.

Ed is a blue blood aristocrat who comes from a world of fox hunting, quail shooting and horse riding on the grounds of his father's estate in Scotland and, unfortunately, is all too eager to share his viewpoints that mostly mirror Winston Churchill's—especially about India.

"So if India's so great why don't you teach me this meditation business?" Ed says in the hotel room.

"I don't know what to say, Ed. Why would you want to do that?"

"Because I'm dead miserable!"

Surprised and touched by his honesty, I give him the instructions I had learned. He squirms and struggles to concentrate. Ed boasted that his father could get a table without a reservation at any five-star restaurant in Europe, and the staff would line up to lick his feet.

"I have been told that to meditate one must lose one's self-importance," I said.

"Easy enough for you, cowboy, but do you know who I *am*?"

Ed closes his eyes to try again. His character seems so far from the selflessness that the Chapatti Baba said was necessary: sin, arrogance, selfish behavior will keep one attached to the surface, unable to sink downwards into oneself. The Western notion of domination and tyranny over the spirit doesn't work either. Ed soon gives up the effort.

I remember a passage in the Bible that said: "it is easier for a camel to go through the eye of a needle than it is for a rich man to get into heaven." Ed's attempt seems to affirm that the ability to mediate is a gift born out of hardship and humility. While people like Ed and Mr. Olafson are the envy of the world with their hunting trips and yachts, *this* door might be shut to them. It's not for me to say; none of it is, but perhaps the spiritual barrier is justice.

Back at school on Monday, there is a desperate letter from Pradeep waiting for me. He got the £20 note I sent him a month earlier but writes he has been fired for sleeping on the rooftop when he was supposed to be teaching yoga class. Pradeep lived by the river for several weeks, nearly starving. Then he finally gave in and called his mother, who came to pick him up and took him back to his wife and two children! He had never mentioned having a family. I realize he was on the lamb in Rishikesh from a stifling arranged marriage that may have fueled his, "Fuck this fucking society!" mantra. His letter has no forwarding address so, sadly, there is nothing I can do for him. It is the end of an era with him gone, and I feel the loss.

I continue my quest to acquire transportation and finally settle on a car instead of a scooter. It is no ordinary car, but a Citroen 2CV, the silliest, most haphazard vehicle ever built with only a two-cylinder engine.

"Zis car eez France. Zee 2CV is a classic like Bridgeet Bardot, you know!" says the hippy who sold it to me from a nearby town. After paying the equivalent of $450 USD, I sputter off into the dusk trying to make sense the car's crazy gear lever and bizarre gauges. The 2CV has a top speed of about 50 m.p.h. The hideous, bright-green exterior will need a paint-over, perhaps some artwork from Pink Floyd's *The Wall* album. It wobbles a lot and the brakes seem ready to fail, but at least I am on the Provençal road.

Driving to Buoux in my own car is a wonderful luxury, but I am too late to join the British. Unable to stand weather over 60 degrees, they went home, including Johnny. To me, the weather is perfect. I miss them and good, competent partners are hard to find.

The semester has ended and I prepare to move north to the Verdon Gorge. On my last evening in Aix, I stroll through the streets, reminiscing, saying goodbye to friends both foreign and French. The Canadian overachiever from the dorm, Katherine, was wrong about French society. They largely didn't sneer at my accent but were amused and flattered—mostly amused—when I tried to speak their language at all.

In the Verdon, the climbs typically start from the top of the cliff, and there is nothing quite like the excitement of being jerkily lowered over the rim, bouncing and spinning with an instant two thousand feet of exposure under one's feet. The difference to Buoux is immediate as there is an "out there" adventure feeling to the Verdon by the sheer enormous drop.

In these rural hills, I enjoy most authentic Provençal lifestyle yet. Little had changed in centuries. Petite old ladies in blue-flowered dresses wander down to the market from their farmhouses. Many don't speak a word of French but only know the local dialect. Mysterious abandoned villages lay just across the lavender fields. Time comes to a pleasant halt under the southern French sun.

In a café nearby to the Verdon, I spot the legendary Patrick Edlinger. "Patreek" and I chat in French about our meeting in Colorado and how he inspired me to come here. He seems pleased and, complimenting my French skills, doesn't revert to English. When we walk outside, and I see him off in his large, black BMW M4—that his sponsorship money paid for—I feel ill at ease. It was shocking enough when he did *Genesis* first try during his visit to Colorado in 1985, but he recently took first place on a plastic competition wall for the Snowbird World Cup. His easy win makes it clear how far Americans are behind the French. To me, his fancy BMW—symbolic of the coming commercialization—is a hearse, carrying the golden age of rock climbing to the cemetery.

By the middle of July, the cliffs are baking hot, and the Verdon is overrun with tourists from the sun starved north. It is reportedly nothing like in August, when all of Italy goes on vacation. The crowds and heat have me calling Mark and Dahvid to join them in Germany, and I set off for Freiburg.

With the 2CV's top down, I pass hauntingly beautiful villages such as Sisteron, the northern guardian of Provence and up winding alpine passes to the breathtaking sight of the distant Ecrin Mountains. As darkness falls, I use a field for an economical bivouac. Awaking in a drizzle, I have second thoughts about leaving sunny Provence.

Mark and Dahvid are keen to visit Germany's best sport climbing area, the Frankenjura, surrounded by dense green woods and fantasy-like half-timbered gingerbread houses. The campground serves beer in large ornate steins, and men sit at the bar wearing the traditional lederhosen, smoking long, twisted wooden pipes.

I strike up a conversation with an American guy, who has stockpiles of Bibles in his station wagon. There are rumors the Communist border is getting ready to open just a few miles to the east, and he plans to be first in to convert the former communists.

"I know I'm right!" he exclaims fiercely as though he is trying to convince himself. His aggressive tone reminds me of the voices Roger Waters recorded for special effects on Pink Floyd's *Dark Side of the Moon*. Reportedly, Waters questioned roadies, studio employees, and fellow musicians who weren't used to being interviewed. He began by asking them what their favorite color was, etc., building up to: "When was the last time you were violent?" Their responses add chilling effects to the tracks:

I certainly was in the right!
He was cruising for a bruising!
Yeah, I was really drunk at the time and there was all this yelling and screaming-why? Why?
Gave 'em a short, sharp shove as I let him off easy. Manners don't cost nothing, eh?

The Bible guy's tense, self-righteousness brings back the concept of the arc from yoga. The direct path will lead you back to yourself in an arc, a circular loop returning home. The saying "yoga loves you more than it loves itself" leaves no room for Evangelical proselytizing as a soldier for the cause.

After a couple good days, the rain comes down in buckets flooding our sad tents. We return to Freiberg and while it has been fun seeing crazy Dahvid, Mark is so serious. I think Germany's gloom makes him worse than in Provence. I call Sheffield and make plans to go north and visit Johnny and the gang in England.

As soon as I cross into France, the sun comes out. I am filled with joy to be on the charming French roads again. However, often when I am just getting entranced by a medieval stone French village, I inevitably drive into the brightly colored, strip mall, "McDrive" side. The intrusion of largely American fast-food restaurant chains is an unpleasant shock. There are also frequent ads for the newly opening Euro Disney. My country's greatest ambassador is not its Founding Fathers, Thoreau, Twain, Hemingway, Keroac or the music of *The Doors*, but Ronald McDonald. The world may soon believe Colonel Sanders was a Founding Father.

On a deserted road, the 2CV ran out of gas. A Frenchman picks me up and goes many kilometers out of his way to a station where he cheerfully pays for the gas and remains at my car until it starts. I think of the many French people in Provence and Paris I have met and now this man. Aside from their brutal use of the finger wag, they are rarely the stereotype assholes described at home; in fact the majority are just the opposite.

Continuing through Normandy, I look for the small village of Saint Croix, where my uncle was killed in World War II. Without a map, I fail to find it but, instead, arrive at Giverny, where Monet did his greatest work. The Japanese bridge and ponds remain, and the light on water shimmers just as it did for Monet's epic water lily collection. It seems Monet painted the lilies like the lotus flower rising above the muck and mire of existence. That sparkling light on water, like a bright pearl, is proof positive above the surface, everything is all right. There may be tragedies like babies dying in India and stabbings in London, but above it all shines the mysterious light of goodness and peace. Almost half a century ago, my uncle gave his life to liberate France. This year, she has tried to repay me by sharing this beautiful world where the light still shimmers on water just the way Monet painted it.

CLIMBING FOR THE QUEEN

It's late July and after Normandy, there is no more France. The English Channel glimmers in the late afternoon sun. I park my 2-CV in Calais wondering if I will ever see it again. It is too expensive to take on the ferry and in too poor of condition to be allowed on the British roads. I poke around the pier waiting for the discounted late-night ferry. I feel wary about England, but I do want to see the climber's Britain, and I miss the energy, inspiration, and wit of my British mates.

The English morning is typically gloomy as we chug towards the white cliffs of Dover. In the customs line, two young punk rockers start to fight. One threatens to come back with a knife and finish it "properly." *That* word again—I haven't missed it. A silver-haired bobby appears, as in a slapstick vaudeville act, and chases one punk down a corridor while the other smashes a window with a brick and yells "Fook off ya coonts!!" at our queue. From the movies we watch at home, most of us think the English sit around in large country manors by roaring fires dressed in tweed, quipping witticisms and sipping cognac.

At customs, I am detained because of the special entry stamp on my passport indicating my arrest last February complete with a trip down memory lane of interrogation and luggage searches. I am worried they will ring up Zippy again, but they finally let me through. Apparently, they want the tourist dollars.

It is strange to be back in London after all that happened last winter. However, it is now summer and the sights and sounds of the capital mesmerize me: great leafy green trees blooming on the avenues, the stately architecture of historic inner London, and gorgeous women appear everywhere.

Peter is long gone to the army, so I hop a red coach north to Sheffield. Four hours later I am dossing on the floor of Ben Moon's flat with Johnny, and Zippy sprawled out next to me. The best climbers in the world camp on a stained carpet as trains blast by every few minutes, shaking the block of red brick flats.

Perhaps the most impressive thing about these British climbers is their sheer drive and motivation. Everyone goes climbing almost every day whether it's raining or not, especially Zippy, who regularly walks the several miles out to the Peak District—for the ethical reasons such as boycotting the petroleum industry—but also because he failed his driver's test.

The "Peak" has hardly any peaks in it, but is a beautiful green checkerboard of farms and stone villages in a charming Jane Austen countryside and Little John, of Robin Hood fame, is allegedly buried at a small, picturesque church near Haversage. It is also home to the unique rock called gritstone. "Grit" is a dark sandstone with an incredibly rough exterior that calls for all sorts of strange techniques to adhere one to it. It is also the most "ethical" of climbing venues, as it is traditional climbing only—no bolts allowed. Stanage is arguably the most formidable Gritstone outcrop, but after time in Yosemite I have to laugh at its non-offending size.

It is an idyllic scene where there is always someone to climb with and English humor reigns supreme, with fast wit and moan-inducing puns. I am happily living a second childhood outside of corporate America, though its' hand can be felt in the many products stocked on shelves, and among a great group of mostly "lefties." They have a robust Labour Party and I can appreciate their intelligence as they know the ultra-rich are their enemies and don't fall for their "you need to work harder" blather.

During rare non-climbing moments, we visit the game arcade in the gritty city center of Sheffield. Johnny hunches over a Grand Prix video game for hours making "vroom, vroom" noises. His video race car screeches in and out of control, banking on bends with the tires smoking. I wondered why he wasted his money and time on the game when it was no different from how he really drives. Occasionally we go drinking at the pub, but no one can afford more than a couple of pints since they are "climbing for the Queen," meaning that they'd signed onto the dole.

Some of the less-famous climbers in the scene made as big or bigger of an impression on me. One "scouser," slang for a person from Liverpool, was not content with the stipend he received from his benefactor in Buckingham palace. This scouser was quite a thief and even stole a full suit and tie from one of the local shops. He needed it for facing his shoplifting charges the following afternoon in court. "It would be disrespectful to show up scruffy," he stated in all seriousness. His actions perfectly fit a British joke: what do you call a scouser in a suit? Answer: the defendant.

I walk out to Stanage with a climber called "Mad Mick" to witness Johnny Dawes in a mad frenzy soloing everything, especially the strange, obscure routes. Not one to follow the beaten track, Johnny attempts a route called *Breakdancing*, which requires him to rotate his body upside down and swivel his legs over his head in a horizontal chimney.

Johnny then flies, no hands, up hard boulder problems—rocks small enough to normally be climbed without a rope and retain a degree of safety—balancing effortlessly across traverses most people would be glad to have both hands for. Whether it's eliminating limbs, holds, or whatever the crazy stunt, it's all just another game for Dawes, a true individualist with the greatest kinesthetic awareness on the rock I'd ever seen.

A typical torrential rainstorm soon chases us into the nearest pub, where Johnny talks enthusiastically about a trip to India. Pradeep is gone from the ashram, and summer isn't an ideal time to go, as the weather is alternately unbearably hot or pounded by monsoon rains. Still, I am moved by his interest and the idea. In the months since my return to the West, the beautiful feeling I brought back has slowly dissipated. I've found it hard to keep up with meditation, and I've given up on yoga stretching completely. It's not easy to do asanas when your personal space consists of a small patch of someone's dirty floor. I long for the chance to renew myself again. As we discussed plans over our pints, my excitement builds. If Johnny will go with me to India, anything seems possible.

Jerry Moffat invites me to Wales, and picks me up in his shiny new red Italian sports car, no less fancy than Edlinger's BMW. It is a new era where the best rock climbers drive expensive racing cars, not old rusting Volkswagen buses. Jerry Moffat was once one of the world's top climbers. On his first trip to the States in 1982, he had made the second ascent of our hardest climb, *Genesis*, which he then top roped in his tennis shoes. When asked what he liked most about climbing, Moffat once replied, "Burning the other climbers off." After overtraining for years, Jerry is just recovering from the near complete destruction his elbows and making a comeback to nearly rival Moon for pure difficulty with his hard routes and Dawes for talent and daring.

As we speed across the British countryside, our joking makes me appreciate how even the top climbers enjoy goading each other on by having a good slagging in jest, and their positive attitudes propel them to the top.

In a flashy hi-fi shop back in Sheffield, I join Ben and Jerry as they shop for top-end stereo speakers. Symbolic of their new sponsorship wealth, this is hard for me to witness. Ben and Jerry have worked very hard at the sport, suffering extreme poverty, malnutrition, dossing under rainy bridges and in smelly cold caves but the sudden influx of money climbing saddens me. Every pence of sponsorship is an investment by companies anticipating a big return. That means convincing the mainstream public that climbing is "cool" so it can be put up for sale. Besides, having the right state of mind to appreciate music is more important than an over-the-top sound system. However, that point is surely lost among the £1,000 high-fidelity enhanced super woofer speaker towers. Ben and Jerry, with their new speakers spewing trendy new bands like Wham!, suggest that climbing is merging with the flashy hollowness of the MTV age.

Jerry Moffatt and Johnny Dawes drive me towards Black Rocks, a distant Gritstone crag, and like a partner in crime, Jerry goads Johnny's wild driving to its' maximum. We go howling along the green pastures and dark stone walls of the Peak District, passing everyone on the road, taking bends at insane speeds and doing all the stock fancy rally tricks: four wheel drifts, emergency brake assisted turns. It is hard to remember that the English drive on the left with Johnny swerving all over the tiny road. Often a muffled "Slow down you bastard!" floats back from an outraged victim as we scream by.

While he drives, Johnny pops in a cassette tape with the voice of a female passenger protesting her male counterpart's driving style. "Oh my, do slow down, please!" she complains again and again in a prissy upper-class English accent, between the sounds of reckless engine revving and gear-shifting. "This just isn't *sensible!*"

"Stupid Bird!" Johnny yells. "Everything has to be validated by having a bird along to comment." Yet it is *his* cassette. The morning's country drive with the high speeds and background cassette is absolutely surreal.

On arrival, Johnny leaps out of the car and powers up the steepest boulder problem at the area, getting quite high above the ground.

"Bloody hell, Johnny—you did that without even a warm up!" Jerry shouts up at him.

Johnny returns to earth, and on a whim, I pick him up with a comical bear hug. The gesture infuriates him claiming I was insinuating he was short. As long as he was engaged in a death-defying activity he was ecstatic, but if he stopped to reflect, Johnny was wound tight and miserable.

Confused and saddened by his behavior, I bring up what a great time we'll have in India.

"I can't go to India," Johnny says flatly.

He had talked about it with such enthusiasm before, yet gives no reason for his change of mind. What will he do with himself? Play video games? Of course, one doesn't have to go to India to recreate themselves, especially such a unique person like Johnny, but if you want to learn to speak French, I think it's best to visit France. Johnny's wild antics once seemed like they could lead to his liberation, perhaps they'll lead to his destruction instead. Everything he does has to be on his own unfettered, whimsical terms, or he'd rather be in the arcade.

I can't shake the feeling that I have to go back but with Johnny out I am on my own for India, and just as strapped for cash as last winter. After phoning several dodgy bucket shops in London, I reserve a ticket on Afghan Airlines. Ben and Johnny dropped me off at the Sheffield train station.

"Sorry about India," Johnny says in parting. "It's hard to be friends with an Englishman, isn't it?"

In order to get my Indian visa, I have to spend a few days in London before my flight, and the only accommodation I can afford is a huge tent city in Acton. For ten quid a night, I spread out my sleeping bag on a piece of grass under a massive circus tent. My fellow boarders are mostly desperate immigrant workers from the Eastern Bloc, one step above the homeless. Once again, London shows me her squalid Dickens side.

That wasn't all London was up to. There were riots to protest Thatcher's Pole Tax plan, where she planned to levy each inhabitant of a household. The working people were understandably upset, and there was unrest all throughout the city. In Trafalgar Square, a big fight flared, which the tabloids dubbed the "Battle of Trafalgar." The town erupted with crazy mobs of Anarchists and Trotskyite Communists on the march. The scene was as tense as the tone of the Rolling Stone's *Street Fightin' Man*. But no matter how rowdy the riots get, everyone stops for tea at four o'clock. Police and protesters chat about the day's events and even joke with each other. Then it is back to work with clubs and riot shields. They are British, after all.

At the Indian Embassy, I find my visa has been refused. A distinguished-looking Indian gentleman, perhaps an ambassador, guides me back to his lush office to explain over chai. His hospitality brings back warm memories, but his words are not encouraging.

"You cannot conduct yoga in India without permission of the government," he begins. "This is a special cultural activity, and such permission is rarely bestowed."

Not allowed to do yoga? I can't believe it. "What about my first visa?" I ask. "I put 'yoga' as my reason for visiting that time, and it was granted."

"That was a mistake on our part. It should not have been approved."

I wonder what would have become of me if I hadn't been allowed to go last winter. I find myself silently thanking the Indian

Embassy for its mistake. Aloud, I say, "But I've already bought my ticket for this trip."

"I am sorry, but you had better go ask for a refund," he replies calmly, ushering me out and turning off the lights in the massive, wood-paneled bureau. We are the last ones to leave the building.

Dejected, I hunt down my travel agency. It is sketchy indeed. Claiming that my paper ticket has already been issued, they tell me that my refund will take six weeks to process. I suspect that they are stalling until I leave the country. I don't expect ever to get my money for the flight back, and with the unexpected costs of running all around London for several days, I am nearly broke again.

With hardly a pence left in one of the most expensive cities in the world, I buy some bread, mustard, and cheese for dinner and phone my mother, who generously books me a flight home departing early in the next morning. The tent city is too far out for my early-morning flight and out of my price range. I spot a clump of bushes in front of the bus stop across from Victoria Station where I can conceal myself just enough to bed down for the night.

The city noises keep me awake, so I reflect on what Europe has meant to me. I discovered the beauty of Provence and the warmth of its people. I feel lucky to have stumbled into such a fun, friendly community of British climbers. Spurred on by their positive support, my technical abilities have blossomed. I am red-pointing 5.12d pretty consistently, on-sighting 5.12a or b every once in a while, and have successfully top-roped sections of 5.13. I am happy and proud of my progress.

At the same time, this sport-climbing has led me away from the dreams from the day I saw the Diamond of Long's Peak. Zippy says my fingers are getting strong enough to do desperate routes anywhere, but I was happy enough climbing 5.8's on Lumpy Ridge with Larry Moffett. For me, all the training, training, training, descending into Ben Moon's wooden torture chamber day after day, got old quickly. Hanging from a piece of wood in someone's damp cellar is a long way from the sparkling white granite of Yosemite. These sport climbs give me little buzz or deep emotion. They are merely hard. I want to keep moving, and get up a real mountain.

After all I'd experienced climbing in Europe, it is plain that the mountains belong not to those who can pull on their smallest holds but to those who receive their grandest visions. However, there is one hard route I must do before I regress into doing 5.8's on Lumpy Ridge forever.

GENESIS AT LAST

A light dusting of snow coats the shadows of Eldorado Canyon on this February afternoon. I am worried if I have completed my German homework for class at C.U. as we weave our way through boulders to the base of *Genesis*.

"On belay," says Jochen as I finish tying into the rope.

Jochen is a visiting German climber I met in France. He derisively calls the tiny holds on the overhanging wall above "slab climbing." True, it is different from the steep, pocketed climbs of Buoux, but that doesn't make it easy. Jochen can be cynical and superior, but I'm glad one of the Buoux gang is here. It is hard to find a belayer with the skill and patience to lend me the confidence I need to attempt *Genesis*.

The rock is dry and the friction is "top," as the British climbers put it. I lead up some strenuous lay-backing protected by traditional gear. It is tiring, but nothing like what is to come.

At a little roof, I step around to the left to rest. A glance across the canyon takes me back to my first climb here when I was twelve-years old. The memory is bittersweet, and it brings back echoes of childish taunts:

"*You* climb *Genesis?* What a JOKE!"

Even a decade later, I still feel the hot sting of insult, and it saps my confidence as it was designed to do. The weight of misgiving and skepticism is nearly enough to pull me off.

Now I face some harder climbing on small 5.11 edges, and I'm concerned to feel a little forearm fatigue already building. If I can't shake off the burning in my muscles, the moves above will be impossible. Failure so low becomes a real possibility.

Derek Hersey is climbing nearby with Annie Whitehouse. His merry Manchester laugh reverberates through the cool afternoon of the canyon. It is the fearless laugh of a man who has mastered himself. The sound helps me to chase away the "bad vibrations" pestering me from the past.

At a tiny ledge that normally marks the end of the first pitch, the climbing I've come for begins. I take a last deep breath and pull upwards. Clipping the bolt above, I shift my left side pulling hard into the wild layback necessary for the crux sequence. As the moves come together, memories of my childhood failures are replaced by more recent ones of my Sheffield friends, Johnny Dawes in particular. I discard the calm, cool, even bored "Boulder" poise and try to replicate Johnny's ferocious energy, yanking on holds less than the width of a pencil. Suddenly, good holds are in sight just above me. *After waiting ten years to prove Red wrong, doing the hardest climb in the world is inches away!* My body twists left as my right hand reaches toward a high edge. It is a sequence I didn't try on my previous attempt, and it works. Still, the crux isn't over. Adjusting my Ninja climbing slippers on their tiny smears, I stretch up with my left hand, reaching toward the winter sky, reaching up and up and up...

Abruptly, my foot pops off its miniscule hold, and I am gliding backward into space. It is a long but painless fall, as Jochen instinctively provides a soft, skillful catch.

As I rest on the rope, I wonder at the journey that has brought me full circle, back to this iconic climb, over ten years after I first set eyes on it.

I think about my time in Aix after I returned from India. All I see are colors: colors bright like a Cezanne painting, bright like Provence itself. I saw a bright 'new Europe' emerging, progressive and to be led in part by my fellow students, whom I got to like quite well. The days passed in a whirlwind of enchantment and happiness that I can only attribute to what the hermit and Pradeep taught me. The pearl *was* handed to me. I was so content that my German classmate, Uwe, compared me to the Greek philosopher Diogenes. As the story goes, Alexander the Great was willing to grant Diogenes anything he desired. Diogenes, who lived a life of simplicity and leisure, replied: "Okay, move out of my sunlight."

After a short rest, I launch into another attempt on the climb, this time trying a sequence that came to me in a dream last night. Strange dreams seem to be a common experience for those attempting *Genesis*. While working on the first free ascent, Jim Collins once dreamed that he had passed the crux only to find himself climbing on loose blocks.

In that dream, "The only thing that saved me," Collins recalled, "Layton Kor was there clutching a block between his knees so I could pull around the corner."

I have been throwing my left hand up first without success, but in the dream, I used my right. I put my faith in this tip from the world beyond, hoping it is the key to unlock *Genesis*.

But I am too excited, too energized, trying too hard, and I hastily grab the hidden hold in the wrong place. My hand skates off, and once again I find myself airborne. The rope comes tight on my harness after another painless, long fall. I could pull back onto the rock and start again where I am, but that would be considered cheating. The rules of fair redpointing dictate that I must lower to the ground and pull my rope for every attempt to free climb the route.

I am still struggling to adjust to American life—the land of the used car salesman. As George Harrison once said, "India was color and excitement, while the U.S. was like: 'Stop! What's your Social Security number?'" Zippy also left me with a prophetic statement to ponder on my return to the States: "America rewards all the wrong behaviours." Even the flight home was strange, with a melancholy steward constantly calling me "sir" though I had slept in the bushes outside Victoria the night before. As if the plastic respect weren't disturbing enough, the consumerism of American culture hit me like a hammer on my arrival at La Guardia Airport, with advertisements and action figures from the latest Batman flick.

My family certainly didn't help me overcome my reverse culture shock.

"I'll bet you're glad to be home from that goddamned Europe," exclaimed my father when he picked me up at the airport. "You're lucky you're young and healthy what with their socialized healthcare nonsense."

Though he has never visited the continent, my father knows all about Europe's Socialist evils, thanks to the right-wing talk shows he listens to.

"Actually, I did get an ear infection from the damp weather and saw a British doctor. He gave me a $3 prescription for antibiotics, and I was fine."

"Lucky to be alive," was his only reply, as though the British National Health Service practiced cannibalism.

Dad initially paid for part of my trip out of my college fund, which I will have to pay back in to graduate, and yet he doesn't want to face the truth of what I learned: socialists have more fun. He and my step-mother were outraged to hear that I had lived among England's unemployed. Of course, there was mass unemployment by the end of Thatcher's reign, so it was unavoidable. I didn't dare tell them about the scouser. Their shared Rush Limbaugh ideology supports a hatred of the poor and working class. They are desperate to keep the system in place. "Who's going to pick up the trash?" is their best argument against socialism.

Dad's an attorney for a leading savings and loan in Denver. At a rival savings and loan called Silverado, Neil Bush, George H.W. Bush's son, was put under investigation for fraudulent loan practices on the board. Now the Feds have shut down all the savings and loans in Colorado, and subsequently, my dad is low on clientele and his savings ruined. Neil Bush got off with a slap on the wrist because his daddy is president.

"You just don't get it," my father says. He can't find any fault with the Bushes or the ruinous Republican Party.

So now I'm trying to finish my last year at CU-Boulder, a year after Ronald Reagan has left a crippling deficit and destroyed the economy. It's hard to find work after the "economic miracle" the elephant party ignited. I am still waiting for some dollars to trickle down to me.

Driving to Boulder past the industrial wasteland called Commerce City north of Denver, chills my soul just as London's Battersea Power Station did in England. And in the year I've been gone, a sterile wasteland of sprawling high-tech office parks has appeared along the rolling prairies outside of Boulder. They gobble up the open spaces, replacing green with drab grey-metallic steel and concrete. Chartres Cathedral was built over one thousand years ago, and now we've "advanced"… to this.

The isolation of American society is perhaps the hardest to bear. In Aix, there was always someone willing to go get coffee, or, in Sheffield, to laugh over curry or a pint. Here, I hardly see my American friends, many of whom work manically at strip-mall chain restaurants and have no time to spare. After living abroad among people who are, on the whole, much happier, it is a shock to witness Americans' daily mental strain. Humanity loves to imprison itself. There is no sense of *Namaste*, that is, little realization of the value in fellow human beings and an electronic video game or mindless T.V. is often preferred to human interaction. Time accelerates into a miserable cycle of overwork, debt and burning out. Pradeep's description of people working only for ego and becoming robotic has a deep and devastating truth to it. So many lives are unsatisfied, unfulfilled, and wasted in the accumulation of needless wealth, so much "cancer of the soul," as Reinhold Messner put it.

In Europe, people have short work weeks and lounge in cafes chatting for hours. Few own cars or need to. My memories of the universal camaraderie in India and relaxed living in France are becoming a far-off, idealistic fantasy.

Even America's counterculture offers little consolation.

"I know Om, man. I mean *I know* Om," a guy in the Penny Lane coffeehouse confided one day from a nearby table, without any provocation or introduction. "When I was little I could lie in bed," he continued, "and heard the Om signals being transmitted through the electrical lines outside my parents' house. I'm not one of these mainstream people. I *know* Om."

I find myself wondering: *Do people think I'm a nut like this guy?*

But perhaps the most unsettling part about coming home is war. I always thought some sunny day I would climb *Genesis,* and there would be trumpets blowing, but instead bombs are being dropped. The United States and its allies have attacked Iraq. It all sounds above board: an international police action against a tyrant like Saddam and his massive army. But where did he get that military force? Reagan. Hussein is a Cold War puppet gone bad. To me, it all reeks of *Animal Farm*'s dark political intrigues with Rush Limbaugh as the propaganda pig "Squealer."

Back at CU, my roommates gather to watch the attacks on television. The majority of my fellow students have never travelled anywhere beyond their comfort zone, unless you count Acapulco or the *Let's Go* hostel circuit in Europe. So many of them look at the darker-skinned inhabitants of the world as a threat, and they are ready to strike.

A few days ago, it was announced that the Bagdhad airport had been bombed to pieces. My roommates roared with delight, while I felt sick remembering the line of gentle goat herders in the terminal.

"Have you ever met anyone from Iraq?" I asked a roommate's boyfriend, Jeff.

"We've got to get those guys," Jeff replied. "They all pray to the wrong god."

A year before I had seen such nobility in humanity. American T.V. seems designed to show that mankind is not divine, that man is in fact so evil he must be controlled, ideally with a gun. During my travels, I began to believe that an era had begun when we could put hostility behind us, when I could put all hostility behind me. Then, despite all the optimism with the fall of the Berlin wall, the Gulf War came.

The great philosopher Roger Waters wrote of this war:

From bars 3,000 miles away
We play the game
With the bravery of being out of range.

Most people want a fancy car to turn heads, but is killing some goat herders worth it? Too many say "yes." These Ameri-Nazis who claim to love our country so much and wish to relieve their frustrations through vicarious military action will be the cause of its premature downfall.

Lowering down *Genesis*, I hear Derek Hersey's throaty laugh again. I wave. Derek wishes me good luck and returns to climb with Annie. It is a great comfort to have Anne and Derek here. Jimi

Hendrix wrote, "It's not the music, it's the notes in between." After a lifetime of climbing, the routes and movements themselves don't hold the strongest images—people do. Between the climbs were unforgettable characters.

I pull the rope and start back up *Genesis* a few minutes later. The bottom section still feels tiring, but I pull through it to the rest before the crux. As I clip my rope into the crux bolt, Red's jeers and Johnny's encouragement again vie for supremacy in my head. This time, however, I shut off all the *vrittis*, be they negative or positive. They are opposite sides of the same coin, and I need to choose only the edge of the coin and make an "effortless effort." *I am not the doer. I am not the doer. I am not the body. I am not the mind. Om Mane Padme Hum. Om Mane Padme Hum.*

I relax amidst the strenuous layback and reach up powerfully but more calmly than before. With a sigh of detachment, my left hand finds the best part of the hold and this time remains. A decade of commitment to the "absurd sport of rock climbing," as Jim Collins described it. If I can climb it, would I have finally proved myself to Red? Red has mostly quit climbing to take up water sports, but he would mention that the mythical realms of difficulty in 1979 are not so in 1990. True, *Genesis* is no longer the hardest climb in the world by a long shot and modern climbers warm up on climbs of this grade. But do I have to climb a 5.17, ascend Everest in under an hour or saw my limbs off in the wilderness to be worth something? I no longer care.

In the light of day, royal families, popes, tyrants, snobs, elitists, list-makers, racists, Social Darwinists aren't real; they disappear in a puff of smoke if you don't believe in their nonsense. Humans aren't things to be valued only according to their abilities. When one has been released from the bondage of ego, even temporarily, you realize that all life—from the tiniest of bugs to us poor copies of apes—has great yet equal value. One knows that the universe is flowing with love, and all living things shine with dignity and understand what *Namaste* really means: *I am another you. I am adequate as I am.*

So the ultimate realization is that I don't have to do *Genesis*. My worth is not external, but rather a force within. For the last ten years, Red, and people like him, convinced me that I was inadequate, but it was *my* fault to believe them. I now know that I am worthy from birth, as is every living being. Attempting to free climb *Genesis* was an exhilarating challenge, but what I have really learned from attempting *Genesis* is that if my self-worth was something I already had, then enlightenment is also already a part of me.

The satisfaction of completing *Genesis* would be fulfilling, but compared to the *journey* I took to be able to free climb 20 feet of rock it is nothing. It doesn't compare with the exhilaration of my revelations in the ashram, or listening to Pink Floyd's *Animals* on the English commuter train. I think back to Pradeep's concept about thanking those who have belittled and humiliated me. I am certainly grateful to all I mentioned who inspired me, but for a trip like that to India; I must even thank Red.

Sure, I have a long way to go to perfection. I have not crossed the "river of birth and death" nor experienced all my "lives past and present," as those silly Buddhist books describe the process. Also, I have lost much since my return, through the necessary pull of a worldly life along with the foolishness of parties, beer, and a failed relationship with a girl I met at school in Aix. Our relationship made me struggle, I was being pulled back up to the surface by attachment from my deep pool of self-contentment. We quarreled, and I was jolted back into the world of pain and desire, my Indian experience a distant memory all but gone, a door slowly closing.

But it *did* happen; for a while I *was* centered as an axle instead of subjected to the merciless spinning wheel. I was free of bondage and fear, and nothing was holding me. My future challenges may not be met so easily; some liken the path to walking a razor's edge.

The winter evening darkness descends fast over Eldorado Canyon. I look up at the red-tinted clouds, just as I did after my first rappel off the Parkers' chimney. I stand below *Genesis* in the waning light with my arms outstretched. I cannot tell you if I completed this climb or hold on to the accomplishment if I did, so, like the dying Alexander the Great, I let it go. Gone is my lust for mention in a guidebook. I am content to be a plain wildflower passed over by the masses looking to pick a rose. According to an ancient Hindu saying, "In war one may defeat a million invincible enemies, but to conquer one's own self is the greatest victory." The hardest climb in the world is within.

YOSEMITE DECIMAL RATING

SYSTEM GUIDE
(how hard a "free" climb is-supposedly)

5.0	
5.1	
5.2	Easy but rope still a good idea
5.3-5.6	
5.7	
5.8	Easy except in Eldorado, Yosemite or the Gunks
5.9	
5.10a	
5.10b	
5.10c	Getting respectable
5.10d	
5.11a	
5.11b	
5.11c	Getting difficult
5.11d	
5.12a	
5.12b	

5.12c	
5.12d	The outer limits in the 1970's
5.13a	
5.13b	
5.13c	
5.13d	Ridiculously hard
5.14a	
5.14b	
5.14c	
5.14d	
5.15 and so on	Reaching top levels of today's climbing

GLOSSARY OF STRANGE TERMS

Big Walls-the huge rock faces found throughout the world but especially in Yosemite, California. These are giant routes that may take several days to complete—a vertical camping trip. Bring a poop tube for good reason.

Bolts-a type of protection or anchor used in rock climbing that is permanent. A hole is drilled into the rock by either hand drills or cordless power drills, and the bolt is inserted. The perpetrator then causes the inner sleeve to expand into place. If placed correctly into sound rock, a bolt can hold thousands of pounds in any direction. Discussing their appropriate use is an excellent way to start an argument.

Boulder, Colorado, USA-a town full of dirty, dangerous hippies and some really good coffee shops.

Cams/Camming Devises-an expensive spring-loaded device that actually stays in place most of the time you climb past it. Two expanding lobes rotate outward as downward pressure is exerted.

Conservatives-people who spend too much money on the military and keep the rest for themselves.

Direct Aid-climbing using ladders and slings to hold body weight and ascend upward. In the 1950s and early 1960s, this was the main technique on harder climbs as the goal, according to Layton Kor, was speed: "You have to get off the big faces in the Alps before a storm comes in and freezes the team to the wall." Still employed frequently on **Big Walls**, especially in Yosemite, it is in some ways more a craft like fixing the roof than a sport. The antithesis of **Free Climbing**.

Free Climbing-using only the available holds and natural features of the rock to rest or ascend upward. Here rock climbing becomes a sport close to gymnastics, as opposed to **Direct Aid** climbing where the climber is more of a craftsman, like a plumber or tree cutter. Not to be confused with **Free Soloing**, which you would be if you fell. The antithesis of **Direct Aid** climbing.

Free Soloing-the purest, most natural, and most dangerous way to climb a rock: without ropes or safety equipment. Soloing holds a place in climbing history to be respected for its boldness and daring or despised as foolishness if one falls.

Mantra-repetition of sacred words designed to bring about a trance-like state.

Nut-1). a piece of metal often called by the trade names of Stopper, Rock, Hexcentric, etc., that is wedged into a crack in the rock to provide protection for the climber. Placement can be tricky as only downward force is helpful. 2). a person involved in activities described in this book.

Pranayama-a yoga breathing technique that focuses on the flow of breath.

Sport Climbing-ascending a climb or route equipped with expansion bolts.

Traditional or "Trad" Climbing-ascending a climb or route placing mostly nuts and cams into cracks to protect the climber in the event of a fall. Occasionally one may clip a fixed piton or bolt, but if the majority of anchors are removable it is considered a traditional lead.

WORKS CITED

Ayres, Alex, Ed. *The Wit and Wisdom of Mark Twain from A to Z.* Meridian, 1989.

Ellerbe, Helen. *The Dark Side of Christian History.* Orlando, Florida: Morningstar and Lark, 1995.

Godfrey, Robert and Chelton, Dudley. *CLIMB!* Boulder, Colorado: Westview Press, 1977.

Jung, Carl G. *Man and His Symbols.* New York: Doubleday and Company, 1964.

Keroac, Jack. *On the Road.* New York: Penguin Group USA, 1976. (Originally published by Viking Compass Edition 1959)

Kor, Layton. *Beyond the Vertical.* Boulder, Colorado: Alpine Press, 1983.

Randall, Glenn. *Vertigo Games Sioux City,* Iowa: W.R. Publications, 1983.

Sabini, Meredith, Ed. *The Earth Has a Soul: The Nature Writings of C.G. Jung.* Berekely, California: North Atlantic Books, 2002.

LYRICS CITED OR MENTIONED

Jagger, Mick, and Keith Richards. "Play With Fire." *The Rolling Stones Hot Rocks 1964-1971*. London Records, 1971.

Pink Floyd. *Animals*. Harvest / EMI Records, 1977.

Pink Floyd. *Dark Side of the Moon*. Harvest / Capital Records, 1973.

Pink Floyd. *The Wall*. Harvest / EMI Records, 1979.

The Doors. "The End." *The Doors*. Elektra Records, 1966.

Dylan, Bob "Visions of Johanna." *Blonde on Blonde*. Columbia Records, 1966.

Miller, Steve. "The Joker." *The Joker*. Capital Records 1973

Waters, Roger "The Bravery of Being out of Range." *Amused to Death*. Columbia 1992

www.ingramcontent.com/pod-product-compliance
Lightning Source LLC
LaVergne TN
LVHW011216080426
835509LV00005B/152